Welcome

THE OFFICE

Where we are:
Dennis Publishing Ltd, Bedford Technology Park
Thurleigh, Bedford, MK44 2YP
Email: editorial@lrm.co.uk

The editorial team:
Magbook Editor Dave Phillips
Technical Editor Ed Evans
Art Editor Dean Lettice

Regular contributors:
Richard Hall, Trevor Cuthbert,
Dave Barker, Patrick Cruywagen, Alisdair Cusick

Advertising:
Advertising Manager Steve Miller
+44 (0)203 890 3775, stevemiller@lrm.co.uk

Advertising and Promotions:
Managing Director of Advertising
Julian Lloyd-Evans
Group Advertising Director
Liz Jazayeri
Senior Production Executive
Michael Hills
Newstrade Director
David Barker
Head of Direct Marketing
Anna Marley
Syndication Manager
Ryan Chambers

Dennis Automotive:
Managing Director of Dennis Automotive
James Burnay
james_burnay@dennis.co.uk
Publishing Manager
Amrit Gill
Office Manager Jane Townsend-Emms

Dennis Publishing Ltd:
Company Founder Felix Dennis
CFO/COO Brett Reynolds
CEO James Tye

Accounts Administration:
Dennis Publishing ltd, 31-32 Alfred Place, London,
WC1E 7DP. Tel: 020 3890 3890

Land Rover Monthly is published every four weeks by Dennis Publishing UK. All rights in the licensed material belong to Felix Dennis or Dennis Publishing and may not be reproduced, whether in whole or in part, without their prior written consent.Dennis Publishing (UK) Ltd uses a layered Privacy Notice giving you brief details about how we would like to use your personal information. For full details please visit our website www.dennis.co.uk/privacy/ or call us on 0844 844 0053. If you have any questions please ask, as submitting your details indicates your consent, until you choose otherwise, that we and our partners may contact you about products and services that will be of relevance to you via direct mail, phone, email and SMA. You can opt-out at any time via www.subsinfo.co.uk or by emailing privacy@dennis.co.uk or calling 0844 844 0053. Full terms and conditions can be found at http://www.dennis.co.uk/comp/terms/

Printed by Wyndeham Bicester

WELCOME

WE ALL know that Defender is the car of the moment. Once the world learned that production of the iconic model was ending, it suddenly became fashionable. It's all got very silly. Happily, there are plenty of us who see Defender not as a must-have fashion accessory but as the world's most versatile vehicle. And this magbook is for you.

A magbook is a bit like a Defender. A Defender isn't really a car, nor is it a van, nor is it a tractor. But it can do the job of all three. A magbook is in magazine format, but bigger, and it's printed on heavier, glossier paper – just like a book.

It's built to last – just like a Defender. And that's important, because the practical information in this publication is something you will want to keep on your garage shelf for many years to come. Inside we have gathered some of the best workshop articles published in LRM in recent years, accompanied by exciting, all-new features – all aimed at the Defender owner who likes to work on his own vehicle.

Those of us who love Defenders know that the most satisfying thing about Defender ownership is the simplicity and accessibility of the vehicle. It's a cliche that the Defender is like a giant Meccano set, but it's true all the same. There isn't another vehicle that allows the amateur spannerman such deep involvement in its inner workings.

Better still, no other car lends itself better to modifications. You can literally tailor your Defender to your own tastes. For example, if you want to turn your hard top into a convertible for the summer you can. Inside this issue we show you how.

I hope you enjoy your LRM Defender Workshop. Have fun!

MAGBOOK EDITOR
DAVE PHILLIPS

inside...

Page 6
How Foleys make good Defenders even better

Page 54
Convert your pick-up or hard top to soft top

Page 60
How to create the perfect Defender workshop

Page 176
Engine transplant to transform your Defender

3

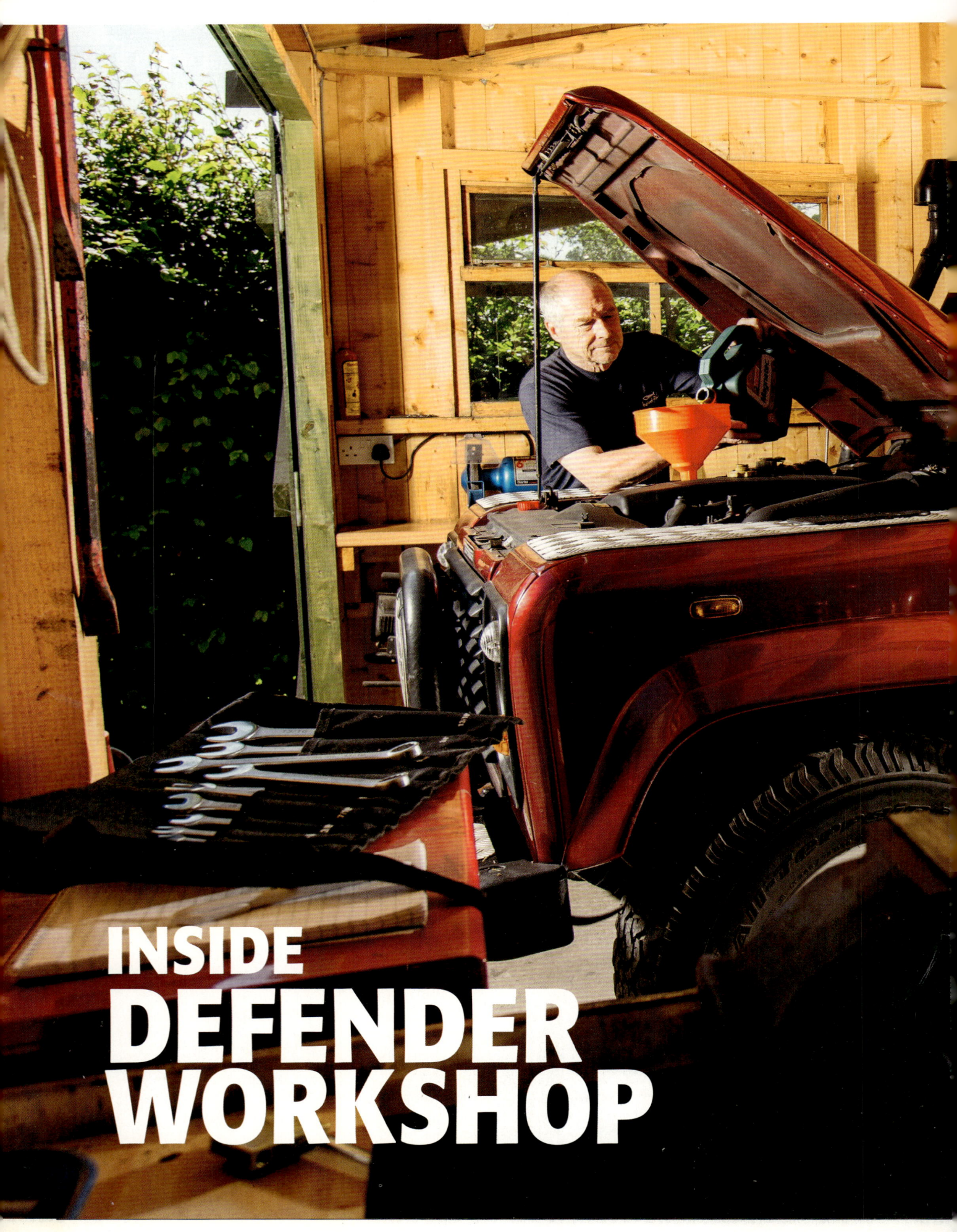

Contents

INSIDE
DEFENDER
WORKSHOP

IN ASSOCIATION WITH

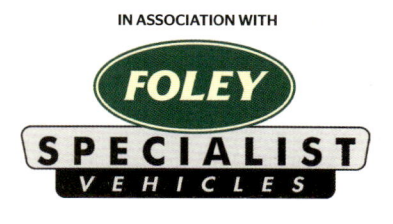

FOLEY SPECIALIST VEHICLES

Contents

006 FOLEYS DEFENDER PHILOSOPHY
Meet the company that makes good Defenders even better

014 FARM TRUCK TO COUNTY STATION WAGON
How to turn an abused workhorse into a luxury estate

042 DEFENDER PRODUCTS
From workshop essentials to bolt-on extras

046 TD5 SERVICE GUIDE
We share the tips of the trade

054 SOFT TOP CONVERSION
How to go convertible for the summer

060 PERFECT LAND ROVER WORKSHOP
How to create your dream spannering space

070 HOW TO CURE WATER LEAKS
Defeating the bane of all Defender owners

088 SUSPENSION UPGRADES
Replacing your springs and shocks

096 REPLACING REAR CROSSMEMBER
How to renew rusty rear chassis

108 SWIVELS OVERHAUL
Rejuvenate tired steering with this project

114 NEW FUEL TANK
Fuel tanks rust but are easily replaced

120 CHASSIS SWAP
Replacing the chassis on your Defender

138 FUEL TANK GUARD
Protect your vulnerable fuel tank

142 REAR AXLE REBUILD
Transform your ride with this weekend project

152 DOOR LATCH FIX
It's an open and shut case...

156 DISC BRAKES RECONDITIONED
Upgrade to enhance your stopping power

160 FIT NEW CAPPINGS
Galvanised trim adds the finishing touch

164 BIG PICTURE
Capturing the workshop mood

166 CRUISE CONTROL
How to fit it yourself

172 TDCI SERVICE
How to keep your Puma engine in fine fettle

176 SECONDHAND TD5
How to find and fit a good one

182 SEAT BELT MOUNTS
Replacing corroded ones

186 BATTERY BOX REPAIR
It's exposed to the elements – and rusts

190 TRANSMISSION
Complete overhaul and rebuild

204 ROCKER COVER GASKET
Simple workshop job for all owners

208 DEFENDER BUYING GUIDE
How to find, buy and live with your ideal Defender

Stuart Foley Interview

THE DEFENDER HUNTER

Foleys Specialist Vehicles Ltd have built up a global reputation as Defender restorers and rebuilders of the highest order. We caught up with Stuart Foley to talk – about Defenders of course…

Interview: Patrick Cruywagen Pictures: Patrick Cruywagen, Adam Swords and Craig Dutton

IN ASSOCIATION WITH

FOLEY SPECIALIST VEHICLES

LET'S REWIND to 1966. How did the Foleys SV story begin?
My dad Peter Foley bought a Series I in 1966 when living in Tottenham, North London. He couldn't sell it and so he broke it into parts and tripled his money. He then bought another one and did the same. Things just sort of grew from there, he also had a shop selling Land Rover spares in Enfield.

He later went on to bigger things and larger contracts, such as supplying 20 Land Rovers to Shell. He called them the good old days, as there were only three or four people in the country doing the same sort of thing at that time.

Today just about every town in the UK has a Land Rover garage though there aren't too many people like us, who only deal with Defenders. Yesterday I turned down a £20,000 rebuild on a Series III. Why? The passion is not there, plus I don't have the parts for it. That is like bringing me a Toyota to work on. I won't do it.

Are you worried about new Defender?
The new Defender is not here yet. Despite this people are still buying new-ish Defenders and bolting on bits. Those Defenders will get old and that top end of the market will diminish. Despite this, every other day I get a phone call from someone who wants to restore their Defender. I then give them a cost spreadsheet and we take it from there.

The days of restoring Pumas are still five years away. Whatever the new one looks like, and when it does eventually come out, it will be more Discovery or Range Rover-like, it won't be a Defender like we know it.

But will you work on it?
I don't work on Range Rovers, Discoverys or Freelanders because

Stuart Foley Interview

Stuart Foley: "I make Defenders that satisfy the exact needs of the customer."

our core business is all about keeping Defenders on the road. My staff and I have the skills and facilities to do just that. I've got a body shop and fabricator who utilise these Defender-specific skills and there is a market for it. You can buy a pair of shoes from a shoe shop or you can get someone to make a pair of shoes to fit your feet.

I make Defenders that satisfy the exact needs of the customer. They want me to work on their Defenders, bring them back to life and restore them. We listen to the customers and give them what they want. That is the key to what we do.

Remember, all customers are different. I get customers shipping me their vehicles from New York, Hong Kong, Australia and Africa, I restore them and send them back. Shipping these days is cheap, plus there are no import costs.

What happens if a customer in Canada is not happy with something?
If one or two things need tweaking, they get that done locally and we just cover it. It could be something small like a wiper motor making some noise. The big things like axles, engines and gearboxes are thoroughly checked and tested here before the vehicles leave us. Most of my clients are looking for an original or traditional Land Rover with a modern twist, such as heated seats or Bluetooth radio. They are not trying to turn it into a showpiece car or say: "Look what I have bolted on". Remember, less is more. That for us is the future and what we are trying to keep going. That is what we have always done.

Are you worried about running out of Defenders to work on?
There are enough Defenders out there for me to work on for now. Who knows how long this will last? If it is 15 years then I will take that. I have five years of work lined up, some of these include jobs that are in storage.

I am blessed in that we don't have quiet times here. We have either very busy times, or less busy times.

We are passionate about Defenders and once we knew their end was nigh we began stockpiling spares, including bonnets, bulkheads, doors and roofs.

They will always be producing mechanical parts for Defenders, genuine and pattern. It's the body parts and panels that are the worry. Once they've gone then they will only make pattern parts, which the purists won't really want.

I have customers in Africa who will only use Genuine parts as they can't afford a breakdown in the middle of nowhere. Manufacturing parts is not cheap and this all adds to the cost of rebuilding one.

Defender prices have just gone crazy. Your thoughts on this?
Yes they have gone up and up but I do think that they have hit a plateau for now and in the last six months they have fallen off the edge. Everyone is asking top money for them so if you want one, they are still out there, though I think that everyone who wanted one now has one. So you need to be really careful if buying

An expedition-ready Defender prepared by Foleys looks like it's ready to tackle anything. That's because it is.

> "Defender prices have gone up and up but they have reached a plateau for now"

one now, by making sure that you get the right one.

The Land Rover market is a changing market and you have to go with it it when it does. I reckon every three years or so one market ends and then it grows into something else.

People get attached to their Defenders, then 15 years down the line when it owes them nothing then they decide to spend £25,000 on it to get their new, original Defender back.

That is where we come in...

Do some of your customers want you to take their Defenders back to original?
If people buy a Defender with stuff on that they don't want they will come in and ask us to take it off. Some say please take the chequerplate off the wings and fill in the holes. They don't care about a little bit of invisible filler in the hole.

They might not want big wheels, but side-steps are useful so they keep those. Steering guards and snorkels are also taken off. They want a crisp and clean Defender.

If I have a Land Rover with loads bolted on then I cannot sell it because no-one wants other people's bits. I have so much stuff that I have taken off other people's vehicles.

Often people put on bits only for the look. I try and tell people to keep it simple and not get carried away.

You are known for building Defenders that will last and do the job. What is your secret?
Keep it mud-free, clean and Waxoyl it regularly. That should take care of the rust. The other thing is to try and tackle issues before it is too late.

You can repair something like a bulkhead but if it goes too far then it needs to be replaced.

The same can be said of the doors. If you repair the holes at the bottom of your doors and waxoyl them then you should get another 10 years out of them. You need to keep on top of things.

Stuart Foley Interview

What should someone like myself do, who has just imported a Defender from a place with a hot, dry climate?
Towards the end of summer clean it the best you can, then clear Waxoyl it. Waxoyling in winter is a waste of time as you are just sealing in moisture. A Land Rover is more enjoyable in the summer than the winter because it is not a car for everyday winter use, as it leaks, mists up and never gets warm enough, although Pumas are a little different as they have more of the mod cons.

You never see a classic car out of its shed in the winter. There is a very good reason for that. If you have a very early Defender, then you have something that is becoming increasingly rare. I've got one V8 One Ten CSW with 56,000 miles on it which I just won't sell.

You know the Tickford Series I? My father cut three of them up because no-one wanted that body on a Series I, they wanted a pick-up truck of course. That is what people did back then and that is what made them rare. In ten years time we will be saying the same about original One Ten V8s.

Are we running out of good Defenders for under £10,000?
There are still good ones out there - the trouble is the market means you have to literally hunt them down. I'm like a Defender hunter and I look at hundreds every day, but out every 50 there is maybe one that I want to buy relative to the cost that they want for it.

Auctions are overpriced and while previously you only had a few bidders, now there are 20 people bidding for Defenders. Any old car dealer can sell a newer Land Rover, but they cannot do what I do which is buy one that I know needs a door or something else doing to it, so I put it in the workshop and get the job done. They just buy it and sell it with a dent or split door rubber seal, I would never do that. You can't believe the levels we go to. No car leaves here with split mats, rusty bolts, door trim hanging off.

Foleys SV
Thinking of doing a rebuild or restoration on your Defender? Or do you need help sourcing a decent Defender? You need to speak to Foleys Stuart Foley at Foleys Specialist Vehicles Ltd, the Defender specialists. For more details see foleysv.com or tel (+44) 01279 793500.

"Waxoyling in winter just seals in the moisture"

www.foleysv.com
FOLEY
LAND ROVER SPECIALIST
email: sales@foleysv.com
7157
F

Stuart Foley Interview

only way you compete in this market is to care or else you are just another person selling a Land Rover.

There are loads of overpriced Defenders out there…
The more you spend the better Defender you will get, but you need to know what to look out for. An American said to me once the problem with Land Rovers is that they are pigs wearing lipstick. They are just painted and look great in the pictures but when you look closely they are just dogs done up. Anyone can do that.

I warn clients to be careful about who they buy a Defender from. I know people who have bought a 300Tdi Defender for £12,000 and then they bring it to me and I show them the 20 patches on the chassis. I then tell them it needs replacing and will cost £5000 plus VAT if done properly, as you will need to also replace the turrets, springs and bushes.

So is the Defender now a classic?
Yes, because they are over 25 years old. They are iconic and precious vehicles and you can't afford to leave them outside during the winter and not use them. Then in March or April people don't understand why they have rotted away.

We do a lot of chassis changes and we powder coat them as it protects the galvanising. If you are going to be spending a lot of money on your Land Rover then you might as well look after it properly. Preventive maintenance is the way to go. You can't just let it break and then attempt to fix it.

Simple things help like taking off the door trim, rubbing down the rust and then painting it. This will stop the rust. It's all about putting back some life into metal that has been damp forever. We do invisible repairs to bulkheads and then Waxoyl it inside; this saves it for another ten years.

"Be careful who you buy a Defender from…"

Foleys SV built this armoured Defender for CNN. After a life of abuse it was saved from a swamp and today it can be seen in the Imperial War Museum in Duxford.

RIMMER BROS

The Classic Parts Service

LAND ROVER

Range Rover
All models inc Evoque
Discovery
Freelander
Defender

All the parts and accessories you will ever need

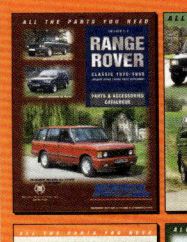

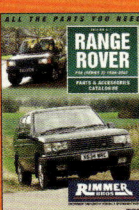

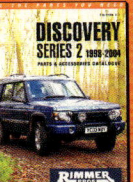

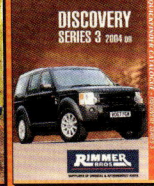

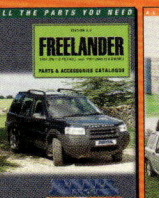

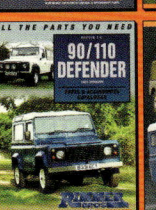

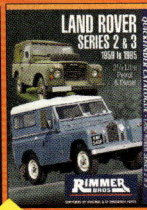

Free Catalogues

Visit our website for prices and availability:
www.rimmerbros.co.uk

tel: 01522 568000
fax: 01522 567600
email: sales@rimmerbros.co.uk

FOLLOW US

Parts service for Triumph, MG Rover and Jaguar also available

JAGUAR *from 1998 to 2011*

Triumph House, Sleaford Road, Bracebridge Heath, Lincoln, LN4 2NA. England

Farm truck to CSW

PART 1
RAISING THE ROOF

Can a battered and abused truck be turned into a stylish County Station Wagon? Yes, of course it can. Ed Evans reports

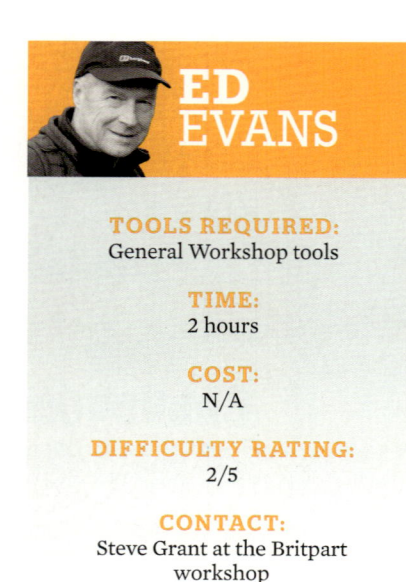

ED EVANS

TOOLS REQUIRED:
General Workshop tools

TIME:
2 hours

COST:
N/A

DIFFICULTY RATING:
2/5

CONTACT:
Steve Grant at the Britpart workshop

A 61-PLATE 2.2-litre TDCi Defender should be in reasonable fettle, given that it's only four years old and has covered lower than average miles. But life on the farm has been hard for this truck cab 90. It's freshly retired from its job as a farm truck, and comes with a mud-loaded chassis, a well-worn interior, and beaten up front panels. Mechanically, it has survived the ordeal but, in it's present state as a battered workhorse, it's still on the road to decline. Only a transformation into a special vehicle is likely to change this Defender's life expectancy, and that's exactly what's going to happen.

Britpart MD, Paul Myers, has bought the truck, and it's now in the workshop where Paul, Steve Grant and myself will be working on the transformation. Naturally, before turning the truck into a station wagon the truck cab roof will have to come off, and that's it for this first installment. In Part 2 you'll see why we first did this job.

Farm fresh

1 Both front wings are buckled and the wheelarch eyebrow on this side has been wiped off.

2 The rear crossmember hasn't rusted away yet, but it's ready to have a go. Drop-down tailgate is long gone.

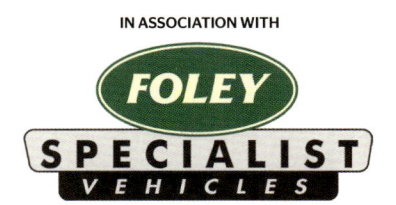

Off with the lid

IN ASSOCIATION WITH FOLEY SPECIALIST VEHICLES

1 First job is to remove the interior furniture from the roof, starting with the sun visors. The mirror is simply twisted free of its mount.

2 The mirror mount is removed after releasing three screws. The lamp unit is unscrewed and the security sensor unclipped and wires disconnected.

3 The door seals, which are damaged and in need of replacing anyway, are pulled off to gain access to the headlining's fir-tree clips.

4 Pry bar is used to push on the clip release tool, loosening the clips here behind the door seal roof lip without damaging the headlining.

65 There are more clips on rear of headlining. They grip tightly, so a forked trim removal tool is needed to pull these thin flimsy heads.

6 The plastic interior trims are removed from each A-post at the side of the windscreen – simple cross-head screws.

7 We remove the seat assemblies for better interior access for detaching the roof. They need to be out anyway, for next month's job.

8 Seat belt fixings (17 mm AF) are unbolted from the B-posts as a precursor to removing the B-post trim to access the roof-to-body mountings.

9 Here's the trim fastener removal tool at work on the trim. It's just a thin forked plate, but it needs to be hardened steel – cheap to buy.

Farm truck to CSW

10 With side trims off, Steve eases the headlining down and gently works it out of the doorway. It will be used, with roof, on another Defender.

11 With the trim removed from below the rear window, the mountings holding the roof to the rear bulkhead and the sides of the rear tub are unbolted.

12 Up front, six 10 mm AF bolts holding the roof to the screen are removed. Their captive nut plates are retrieved through the rectangular holes above.

WORK SAFELY:
We advise wearing gloves to protect against exposed body panel edges and other surfaces.

Wear eye protection when working overhead and when releasing clips and fittings.

Take care when lifting and ensure sufficient helpers are available to take the weight.

13 At each side of the windscreen frame header rail, a cross-head screw locating the side front corner of the roof to the rail is removed.

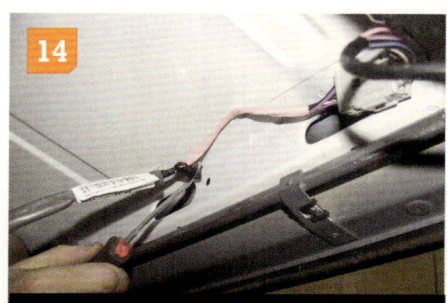

14 The wiring harness is unclipped from the roof header and, for now at least, it is left to hang down out of the way.

15 The roof/screen joint has a seal, but is also bonded with black mastic which has to be cut through, straight across and over the A-posts.

16 We lift the rear just enough to break the seal. Then, with a gentle thump, up comes the front and, hey presto, it's ready to lift off.

17 After a washdown, the roofless farm truck looks good from a distance; but it won't by the time we've finished with it in Part 2.

16

Go off-road at a moment's notice.

New Goodyear Wrangler® All-Terrain Adventure

The versatile All-Terrain tyre with Kevlar® Toughness.

GOODYEAR

MADE TO FEEL GOOD.

Kevlar® is a trademark or registered trademark of E.I Du Pont de Nemours and Company.

Farm truck to CSW

PART 2

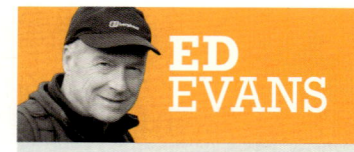

RAISING THE ROOF

Interior space and legroom is restricted by the bulkhead behind the seats, but there's a kit to change all that...

ED EVANS

TOOLS REQUIRED:
General workshop tools, thin cutting discs for the angle grinder, spot weld drill bit.

TIME:
3 hours

COST:
£138

DIFFICULTY RATING:
3/5

CONTACT:
Steve Grant at the Britpart workshop

THERE ARE THREE big advantages to fitting a Bulkhead Removal Kit: it increases the interior space, allows great access rearward between the two front seats, and also allows the front seats to move further back to increase the front seat legroom.

Removing the roof is a precursor to installing this kit, allowing the necessary access for us to cut out the bulkhead from behind the front seats and to then replace the strength in the body by fitting the tubular frame. This isn't a job to be taken lightly, and not only because the roof needs to be removed. The act of cutting out the bulkhead is a one-way affair – there's no going back if you get things wrong, and the structure of the vehicle is dependent on getting it right. That said, it is fairly straightforward.

Given patience and care, with a bit of forward thinking, this job is a DIY prospect and the kit is supplied with full instructions. This is a well-proven alteration to a Defender 90, first introduced by Land Rover itself to increase rear access and storage space. So, despite cutting a yawning hole in the rear body structure, there need be no concern about preserving the vehicle's rigidity and safety, if the job's done properly.

Britpart sells these kits, so the company's development mechanic, Steve Grant, knows the process by heart, and demonstrates the job for us here. In theory, the work could be done without removing the roof, but the roof would still need to be partially lifted in order to drill into the top face of the rear body sides. Having the equipment, or helpers to lift the roof off will make the job much easier.

THE JOB SO FAR:
This 61-plate 2.2-litre TDCi Defender has endured a tough life as a farm truck. Now we're transforming it into a special vehicle, a station wagon with plenty of extras. We have already removed the battered truck cab roof which will be replaced by a station wagon top but, while the roof is out of the way, there's a major space-saving job to be done.

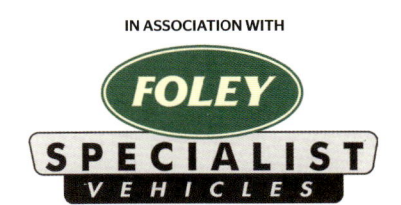

The brave cut

1. Before removing this rear bulkhead, the front seats are removed for working access, and seat belts are removed to avoid damage.

2. All the rivet heads along the bulkhead's top capping rail are drilled off, plus these two inner rivets from the side capping.

3. The bulkhead's capping rail is also riveted from both the front and rear edges, so these rivets are also drilled out, right across.

4. If the drilling has been clean, the capping rail can now be lifted off and discarded. Take care with the sharp flange edge now exposed.

5. These strengthening brackets also need to be collected from underneath the rail at each end on the front side of the bulkhead.

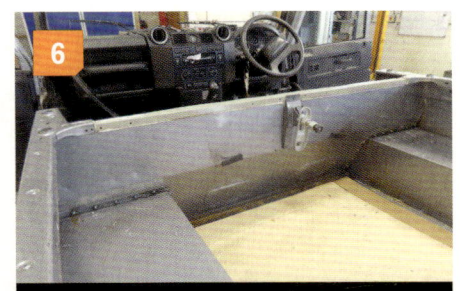

6. We're now ready to cut the bulkhead out from the front, but we need to avoid cutting into the wheelbox flanges riveted behind the bulkhead.

7. The distance from the flange rivets to the outer edge of the flanges is measured, and the measurement transferred to the front of the

8. The flange positions are marked on the front of the bulkhead. Note the vertical cut line up to the inner edge of the side rail bracket.

9. Before cutting the bulkhead, and to ensure a neat corner, Steve drills a 12mm hole on each side, inboard of the marked lines.

10. From the front, we cut between the holes along the bottom of the bulkhead. Note the floor is slightly lower at the back, seen here.

11. The next cuts are made along the vertical lines (clear of the wheelbox flanges) and connecting in with the hole drilled at the bottom.

12. The cutter is then turned 90 degrees, moving from the top of the vertical cut across to the marked line which runs up to the side rail bracket.

IN ASSOCIATION WITH
FOLEY SPECIALIST VEHICLES

Farm truck to CSW

13 The final cuts run (each side) up from the wheelbox flange to the edge of the body side bracket on the top of the bulkhead.

14 These last cuts culminate in slicing through the bulkhead's top flange, then the cuts are checked to see they link up cleanly.

15 Wearing protective gloves against the sharp cut edges, the bulkhead can be manoeuvred free and out of the vehicle.

Trimming the metalwork

1 We're now bulkhead-free but, before installing the kit, there's some remaining metalwork to remove and some to trim into shape.

2 The top of the body side rail on each side is marked for cutting, giving a good profile and leaving maximum strength in the top rail.

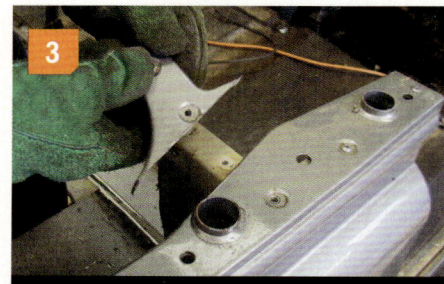

3 A careful slice through with the cutting disc leaves a neat shape to the top of the side rail, before removing the bulkhead ends, below.

4 The remaining ends are removed by drilling these three spot welds (one above) from inside without drilling out through the body sides.

5 The end pieces still need to be cut along the bottom, just clear of the wheelbox flange. Here, Steve uses an air-powered hacksaw.

6 The end pieces are pulled out with only their curved section being held to the wing by sealant, which is trimmed from the wing with a knife.

7 The sharp corners on the remaining bulkhead material in front of the wheelboxes need to be radiused about 2 inches (50mm).

8 The radii are cut using the angle grinder with cutting disc. Then all edges, including this leading edge of the loadbay floor are buffed smooth.

9 We now have a spacious and neatly finished interior. The next stage of the job is to restore the body strength by fitting the tubular frame.

Restoring the strength

1 The Bulkhead Removal Kit, Britpart number DA1810, comprises the main structural bar, two side uprights, plates, fasteners and instructions.

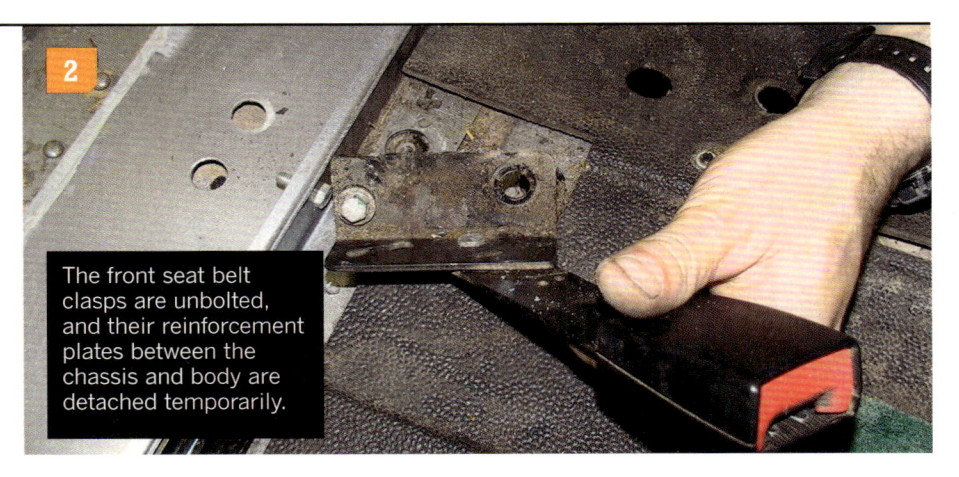

2 The front seat belt clasps are unbolted, and their reinforcement plates between the chassis and body are detached temporarily.

3 The two centre brackets on the main bar will be secured to the studs on two of these mounting plates, pushed up from under the floor.

4 The studs on the mounting plates pass up through the four existing holes (arrowed) in the floor. Grommets (left) need to be removed.

5 The mounting plates are positioned, with their studs through the floor holes and held with a nut until the seatbelt clasps are refitted.

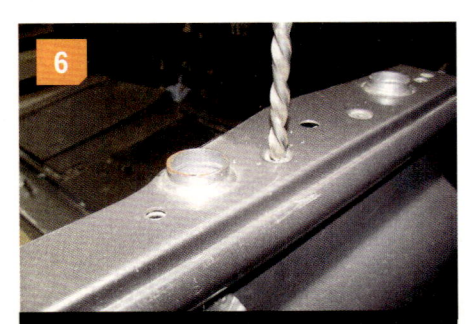

6 The tubular side struts are bolted under this body top rail and onto the wheelbox endplate. We start by drilling this existing hole out to 10.5mm.

7 Each strut is inverted on its opposite rail to mark the bolt pattern. With the nut (right) aligned with hole, the other two are marked on.

8 After drilling the two further holes, each correct side strut is bolted into position to the rail, while its bottom flange is left free for now.

Farm truck to CSW

9. The main tubular frame can now be tried in place, connecting it to each side strut. Our wheelbox corners needed trimming to clear the frame.

10. The ends of the tubular frame engage in the clamps on the side struts. All nuts and bolts are fitted finger tight for now.

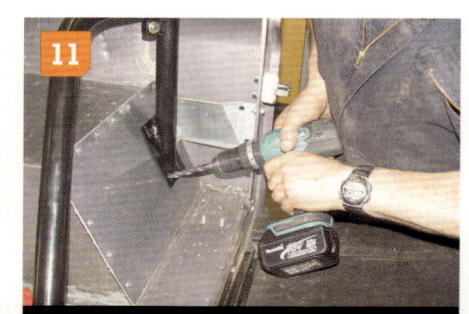

11. With the side struts now held against the wheelbox endplates, we can drill the bolt holes through using the struts' bracket holes as a guide.

12. The bolts are screwed into a backing plate with three captive nuts, inside the wheelbox. All of the bolts can now be finally tightened.

13. Tubular structures are more rigid than flat sheet used in the original bulkhead, and the new frame imparts plenty of structural strength.

Coming up…

IF YOU were simply making this bulkhead removal modification to a 90, the next job would be to refit the seats, seat belts and, of course, the roof. In our case, it's more complicated because next we'll be fitting a secondhand hard top roof from scratch, complete with new seals, and we'll also be cutting the side panels of the hardtop to fit side windows. It's all part of the ongoing plan to produce a bespoke County Station Wagon, and there are great plans for the seats and interior to follow in Part 3.

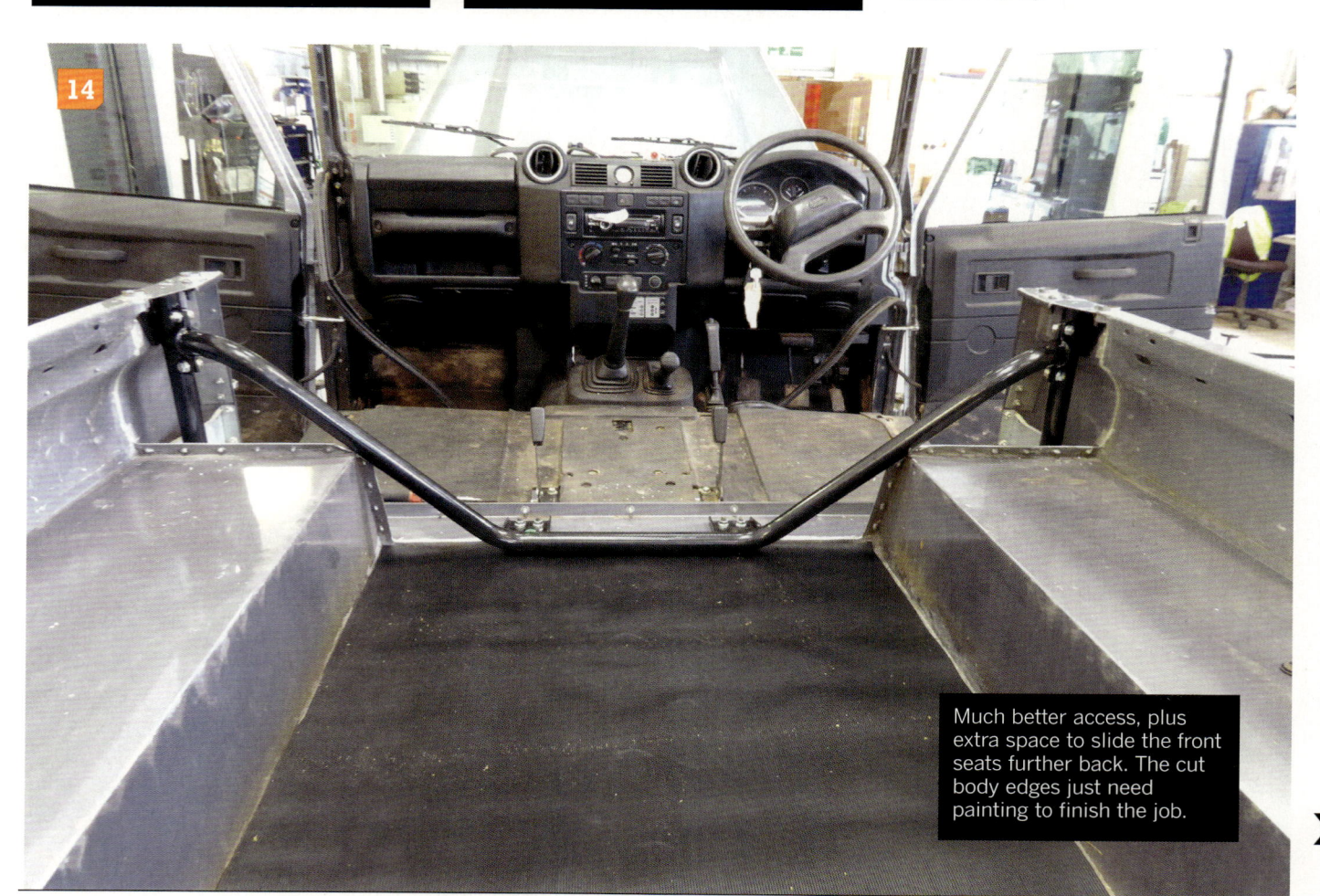

14. Much better access, plus extra space to slide the front seats further back. The cut body edges just need painting to finish the job.

WWW.YRMIT.CO.UK

YRM
METAL SOLUTIONS
• ESTD 2008 •

Ravensford Farm House | Hamsterley
County Durham | DL13 3NH
01388 488150

We know you love your Land Rover, so YRM it

Astwood 4x4 Ltd
The Land Rover Specialists

We are a business that cares about your Landy and about the customers needs, a company who understands what the Landy is all about.

We specialise in restoring, rebuilding Land Rover Defenders, galvanised chassis changes, engine upgrade and all types of mechanical & body work.

We export Land Rovers worldwide supplying not only refurbished but also used Land Rovers.

Astwood 4x4 Ltd - Land Rover SpecialistsRefurbishment/Restoration Specialist, Landrover Servicing, MOT's, Mechanical, Diagnostics, SKYTAG Agent, Galvanised Chassis,Body Repair/Paint Shop Works

Astwood Bank, Astwood Business Park, Astwood Lane, Redditch. B96 6HH

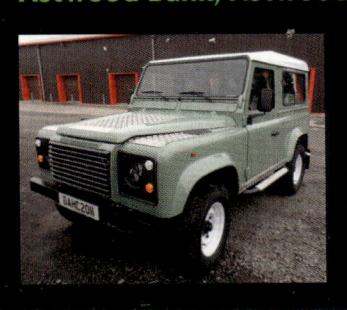

Tel: +44(0)1527 892 377

Mobile: +44(0)7974075932

www.facebook.com/Astwood4x4

www.twitter.com/Astwood4x4   www.astwood4x4.co.uk

Email: astwood4x4@gmail.com

Farm truck to CSW

PART 3
BUILDING THE HARD TOP

Successfully building a hard top roof onto a Defender while adding side windows is a matter of keeping to an exact fitting sequence, as Ed Evans explains

ED EVANS

TOOLS REQUIRED:
General workshop tools, pop-riveter, sealant applicator

TIME:
4 hours

COST:
Auction Prices

DIFFICULTY RATING:
3/5

CONTACT:
Steve Grant at the Britpart workshop

WORK SAFELY:
We advise wearing gloves to protect against exposed and cut body panel edges and other surfaces.

Take care with body posture when lifting weighty body sections, and seek assistance.

OUR FARM TRUCK conversion into a bespoke County Station Wagon begins to take on a new appearance now with the addition of a secondhand full-length black hard top which has been sourced from an internet sale. The roof side panels have already been resprayed to match the Defender's original body colour, but the roof panel will be left in its original and contrasting black livery.
Other damaged body panels have been repainted, together with new rear panel gusset plates and even the new rivet heads have been painted – an important detail that will leave the converted vehicle looking original.

The secondhand roof assembly is free from damage and the original paintwork is good, too. When buying a used roof assembly it's important to confirm the whole structure is straight.

Any slight twist in aluminium panels will mean the relatively soft aluminium has stretched, making it impossible to remove slight deformations during assembly.

The result, even when repainted, could mean an annoying deflection in the paint reflection, which will be permanent. It's also important to obtain all the bolts and fittings that hold the hardtop assembly to the screen rail and rear body tub, though these can be bought new.

We're fitting the new roof in the Britpart workshop with Steve Grant and the vehicle's owner, Paul Myers, who is also sorting front wing damage and front end accessories which we'll see in Part 4.

Assemling the hardtop side panels

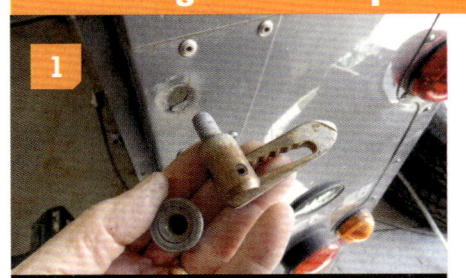

1 Because the original truck cab-style drop-down tailboard will be replaced with a full height door, these tailboard latches can be unbolted.

2 The two tailboard cable retaining brackets are unbolted from the wheelboxes. There are captive nuts on the underside of the wheelboxes.

3 Reinforcement plates, for the tailboard latch bolts, will be swapped for the hardtop type without latch hole. Rivet heads are drilled off.

4 New, pre-painted blank plates and rivets are fitted into the same position. Masking tape, slid over the rivet ends before riveting, protects the paint.

5 Screw and nut each side of tailboard aperture is removed, the tailboard seal removed, and this flange top is straightened to accept new door seal.

6 Securing studs with nylon locators are fitted to the rear corner of the body tub. They will hold the sides and rear quarter panels.

7 The side/rear panels of the secondhand roof assembly have been resprayed in body colour, prior to having the sides cut out to fit window.

8 Side panel-to-roof seals are pressed into the top edge, starting at the rear corners and working across the back, then forward up the side.

9 The thick foam lower seal (side to body) is self-adhesive. We're using the early one-piece seal, though a two-piece is normal for TDCi Defender.

10 Brackets locate each side to the body tub. This at the B-post, another next to the tailgate, and a plate bracket giving mid-length stiffness.

11 Steve tries the first side panel to check the alignment of brackets and body fittings. The hole for the left rear stud needed filing out.

Farm truck to CSW

12. Both side panels now sit correctly. Before bolting down, the roof needs to be fitted to provide weight to compress the lower foam seals.

13. The roof has polished up well, and only needs old sealant cleaning from the front edge/screen joint and the door frame top flanges before fitting.

14. Before attaching the fitting brackets, Steve cleans the underside surfaces of the roof with thinners and attaches self-adhesive soundproofing panels.

15. A new seal, between the roof edge and the windscreen frame, is fitted into position, complete with adhesive rubber finishing pads at each end.

16. The roof is not so much of a heavy lift, but the size needs a few hands to position it, and also the side panels, before lowering.

17. With the roof placed on top, we check the alignment and find just one rear corner out of position, but a toggle bar soon aligns the bolt holes.

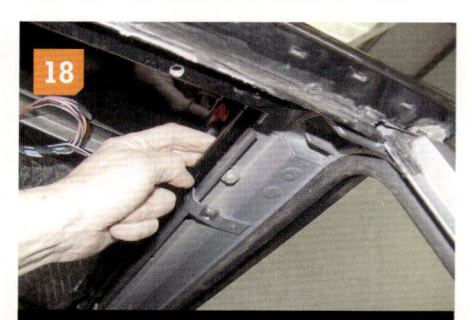

18. With the roof now aligned with the screen frame, body tub and door frames, the leading edge is lightly bolted to the captive nuts in the screen

19 This large self-tapping screw (one at each side) passes through the screen frame corner casting to secure the roof's front corners to the frame.

20 The side panel to roof bolts are fitted loosely into Rivnuts along the sides, and into L-shaped brackets with captive nuts at each rear corner.

21 At each side, Steve bolts in the seat belt upper mounting plates which brace the roof to the B-post sections of the side panels.

22 All the roof bolts are now tightened, working back from the B-posts and across the rear side corners and, lastly, the front bolts across the screen.

23 The roof/sides assembly now sits correctly, but we can't tighten it to the body because the sides are weak due to the window cut-out.

24 If these brackets at mid-point on the sides are tightened, the sides' lower sections just twist, so we need to fit the windows first, to give rigidity.

Fitting the windows

SIDE WINDOWS are easily fitted to a van-bodied Defender. The most exacting part is accurately marking the area to be cut out, and also making a clean cut all around. The frames are riveted to the edge of the panel and the rivet holes are drilled to accept countersunk rivet heads, though small head plain rivets can be used providing they leave clearance for the finishing trim to be fitted over them.

In this case, converting the vehicle to County standard, internal trim panels will also be fitted, hiding the cut edges from the interior.

1 We're fitting a Britpart window kit, with the right side glass and frame seen here still wrapped in its protective covering until it is installed.

2 Our window openings have already been cut, but it's still necessary to test-fit the window to confirm it fits easily without distorting the body side.

3 The windows are fully assembled and frames pre-drilled for riveting. Here, a frame is held by tape while the rivet positions are marked.

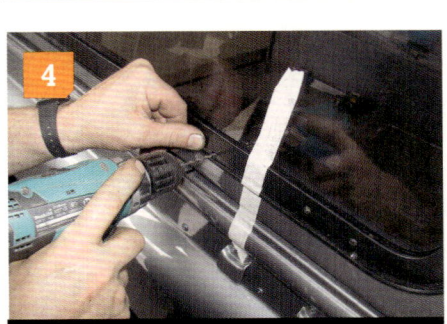

4 Rivet holes are drilled 3mm into the panels. The frame accepts countersunk rivets, but small-headed plain rivets can be used.

5 After drilling the rivet holes in the side panels and clearing the swarf away, a bead of Tiger Seal adhesive sealant is applied around each frame.

Farm truck to CSW

6 When the frames have been pop-riveted into the side panels, excess sealant oozing out of the joint needs to be cleaned off before it sets.

7 Rubber finishing strips are pressed into the frame, starting at the bottom centre, to hide and seal the rivet

8 The end result is a professional-looking window installation with the sliding glass fully sealed and ready to use.

Completing the pull-down

1 With the side window frames now providing rigidity, the assembled hardtop sides can be tightened to the body, starting at the B-posts.

2 The rear corners are then hardened down, checking the seal between body tub and sides is compressed equally along its length.

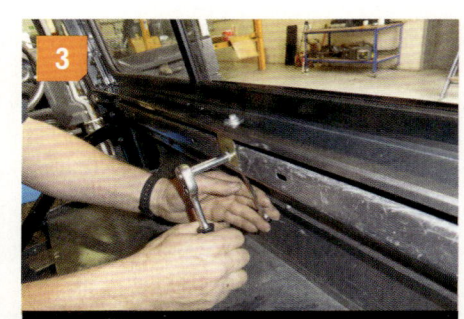

3 Finally, the mid-point brackets on each side panel are positioned and tightened, before re-checking the alignment and the seal compression.

4 Steve completes the job by wiping freshly oozed sealant from the window frames. Meanwhile, the front bodywork has been stripped off for repair.

UPGRADE YOUR LANDY
WITH WORLD CLASS ADVENTURE GEAR FROM FRONT RUNNER

45L WATER TANK
- FOOD GRADE & BPA FREE
- INCLUDES RACK MOUNT BRACKETS

GAS / PROPANE BOTTLE HOLDER
- ADJUSTABLE & LOCKABLE
- BOLTS ON

GULLWING BOX
- EASY ACCESS STORAGE
- WOODEN BACK PANEL
- ADJUSTABLE SHELVES

GULLWING WINDOW
- AVAILABLE IN GLASS / ALUMINUM
- LOCKABLE

PRO CAMP TABLE KIT
- DURABLE STAINLESS STEEL TOP
- STORES FLAT UNDER RACK
- EASY OPEN LEGS

SPARE TIRE MOUNT BBQ GRATE
- LASER CUT STAINLESS STEEL
- STORES OVER SPARE TIRE

DRAWER
- EASY ACCESS STORAGE
- LOCKABLE
- VEHICLE SPECIFIC DESIGN

CONSOLE SAFE
- VEHICLE SPECIFIC DESIGN
- TAMPER PROOF LOCK
- HIDDEN

36L WATER TANK
- FOOD GRADE & BPA FREE
- EASILY MOUNTABLE

DOUBLE JERRY CAN HOLDER
- ADJUSTABLE CLASP
- ALL STEEL CONSTRUCTION
- RATTLE FREE

10" LED FLOOD LIGHT
- 120° FLOOD BEAM PATTERN
- EXPECTED 30,000 HOUR LIFE SPAN
- OFF-ROAD TOUGH ROCK GUARD

WOLF PACK BOX & UNIVERSAL MOUNTING BRACKETS
- ALL WEATHER PROTECTION
- BRACKETS ADJUST TO ANY SIZE

FRONT RUNNER ROOF TOP TENT
- QUICK OPEN AND CLOSE
- SLEEPS 2+
- INCLUDES MATTRESS
- WATERPROOF

SPADE / SHOVEL BRACKET
- FITS ALL SIZES

SLIMLINE II ROOF RACK
- STRONG
- LOW PROFILE
- LIGHTWEIGHT
- DURABLE
- MODULAR
- VERSATILE

SUMP GUARD
- HEAVY DUTY STEEL BRACKETS
- ALUMINUM PLATE

NOT PICTURED:
EVEN MORE COOL FRONT RUNNER STUFF FOR CAMPING, STORAGE, AND SAFELY HAULING TOYS AND GEAR TO THE MOST REMOTE ENDS OF THE EARTH.

ADVENTURE PROVEN ROOF RACKS AND ACCESSORIES FOR LAND ROVERS AND MORE. **FrontRunnerOutfitters.com**

FRONT RUNNER

Farm truck to CSW

PART 4
TAIL DOOR AND DOOR SEALS

Replacing a rear door is a common job on the Defender, but it needs a lot of skill to get the job right

ED EVANS

TOOLS REQUIRED:
General Workshop tools

TIME:
4 hours

COST:
N/A

DIFFICULTY RATING:
3/5

CONTACT:
Steve Grant at the Britpart workshop

THE PLAN FOR this stage of the project is to fit the rear tail door, which involved more alterations to the original truck cab type rear body tub, as well as all the extra door fitting jobs that a conversion from pick-up truck to station wagon entails.

The new tail door has already been sprayed black to match the roof panel, and the new hinges are bolted to it.

Now we're ready to drill the body to accept the door hinges and begin the assembly. When the door is hung, we'll add the latch and striker, the central locking mechanism, rear wiper motor, the new window glass and its seal, and a new gas strut in place of the standard door stay.

When all of that is done, we'll fit the new door frame seal before moving forward to fit the front door seals and ensure they stay watertight.

There are a few tricks in getting all this just right. For instance, the positioning of the door hinges is partly dictated by the amount of compression of the seals between the body side panels and rear tub, fitted last month. To get around that, we bolted the top hinge first and set the door centrally in the frame before marking the holes for the lower hinges.

We're in the Britpart workshop where mechanic Steve Grant is leading the conversion into a bespoke 90 County Station Wagon.

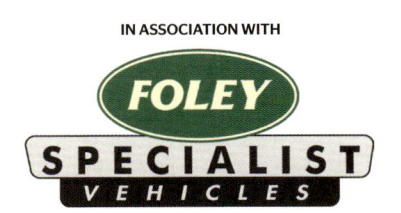

Hanging the tail door

1 To convert this Defender from a truck cab with drop-down tailgate, these tailgate hinges are removed before fitting the station wagon one-piece

2 Steve marks the hinge bolt position (measured from another Defender). Masking tape gives a base for the pencil, and protects the paint when

3 Our hardtop is already drilled for the door's upper hinge, so we bolted it here to check the positions we'd marked for the lower hinges.

4 Our measurements (from another Defender) were well out. So instead, we just marked through the hinge holes.

5 The bottom and mid-height hinge bolt holes were drilled through. Middle hinge holes are drilled through the plate gusset we replaced last month.

6 With the masking tape off, we saw the lower left rivet in the gusset plate prevented the middle hinge sitting flat, so the rivet was drilled out.

7 So far, so good – the assembled door has an equal gap all around the frame. Now we need to fit the handle and latch.

Farm truck to CSW

Fitting the latch and striker

1 Circular lock-barrel finisher is fitted into the hole before fitting latch and lever assembly from the inside the door.

2 Inside, the latch securing nuts are fitted and the handle checked for operation, before the remote linkage is fitted and connected to the latch.

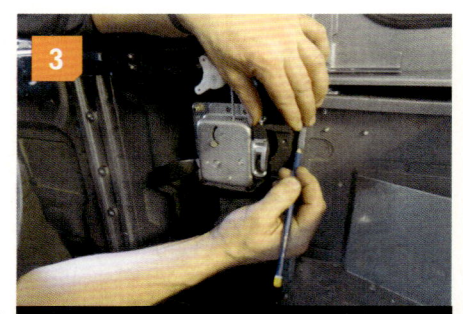

3 With the door closed, the striker plate is held in place from inside, while its position is marked on the flange of the body tub.

4 With the door opened, the striker plate is positioned in line with the earlier marks and the bolt hole positions drawn onto the body shut face.

5 The two bolt holes for the striker are drilled and the striker bolted into place, then the door is test closed to check the alignment.

6 Our striker did not project sufficiently to meet the latch mechanism. So, Steve made this spacer plate to fit between the latch and body.

7 After re-bolting the latch into position with the spacer, the assembly was now correctly aligned and the door latched and opened easily.

8 To finish, this courtesy lamp switch bracket (which also supports wiring harness) was fitted inside the door (switch fits in hole on the left).

Installing the screen and fittings

1 The seal is fitted to the glass with the fitting cord inserted around the recess that locates the body edge, before brushing lubricant on.

2 The screen with seal is located into the aperture with the cord hanging inside the vehicle, then it's pushed into position from outside.

3 Paul presses from outside while Steve, inside, pulls the cord progressively out of the seal, engaging the seal lip over the panel edge. Job done.

4 More fittings are yet to be attached, including the windscreen wiper motor assembly and wiper arm, plus routing of the wiring harness to the motor.

5 The central locking actuator is bolted on and connected to the harness and the rod linkages and quadrant which connect it with the latch.

6 The spare wheel carrier is bolted on with the nuts fitted from inside over large washers to spread the load over the door's internal frame.

Door stay conversion kit

THE STANDARD Defender's early tail door stay rarely break and will remain serviceable for years. But they don't always hold the door open against wind, nor when the vehicle is tilted on a slope.

The door stay kit that we're fitting here includes a gas strut that not only holds the door securely open, but also assists the effort needed to open the door, which can be a tad heavy considering the bulky spare wheel is bolted to it, and especially when the vehicle is parked and leaning on sloping ground.

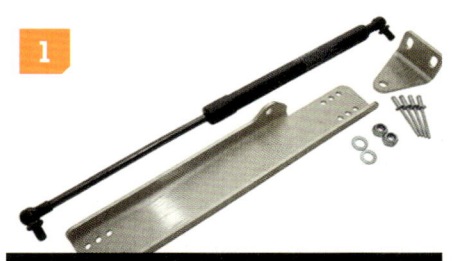

1 The door stay kit includes: gas strut, frame, anchor bracket, rivets, nuts and instructions. It's a straightforward job after removing the interior panel.

2 The rear tub wheelbox is drilled for the anchor bracket. Again, masking tape is good for marking on, and protects the paint when drilling.

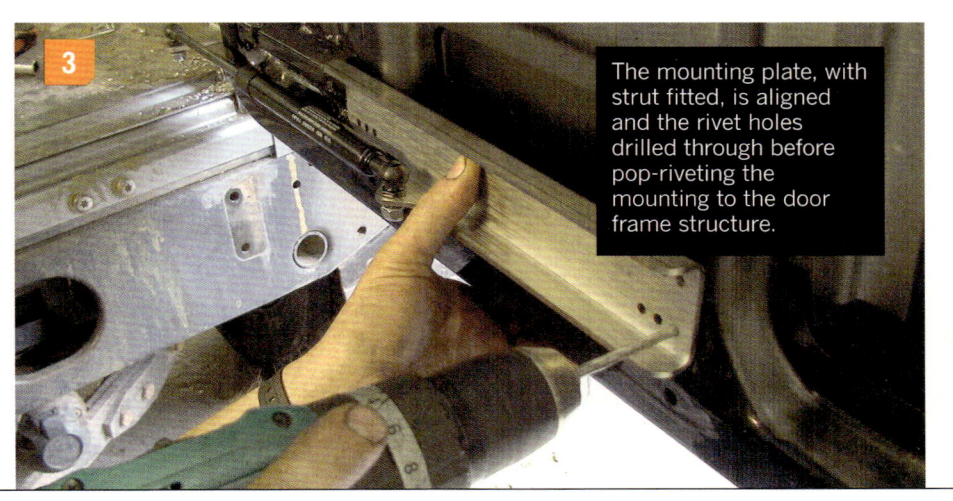

3 The mounting plate, with strut fitted, is aligned and the rivet holes drilled through before pop-riveting the mounting to the door frame structure.

4 The gas strut is held in place by a single nut at each end – to the body bracket, and to its frame mounted on the door.

Farm truck to CSW

5

When the new tail door interior panel is fitted, it hides the new gas strut, leaving a strong and neat installation.

Fitting door seals

WE'VE FITTED new seals to the two front side doors as well as the new tail door. It's always worth fitting new seals when replacing the doors or when working through a rebuild such as this one.

Even if the original seals do not show physical damage such as cuts or tears, on most well used vehicles they will have become flattened and distorted, so they will no longer be draught, noise and rain proof.

Fitting the seals onto the frame flanges is simple enough. It's best to start in a top corner where the seal is preformed in an angle to suit the angle of the door frame. This is the most difficult area, so starting here means you're not trying to stretch the seal to get it fully into the corners.

As you work from corner to corner across the top, and then down each side, push the seal onto the flange with the palm of your hand.

If it's too tight to push fully on, check that the frame lip and the metal insert inside the seal are both straight, then gently tap it on using a mallet and a protective wood block to avoid damaging the rubber.

1 We need to seal the door frame joint where the roof panel meets the lower body. There is always a gap here which the door seal won't cover.

2 Bridge the gap with adhesive seal strips (part LR 028972). Right-angled pieces (part LR 028971) fit the corners of the door frame flanges.

3 Fit a pad at the back of the flange, fill the recess with mastic, and stick another over the front face. Use right-angled pads at roof to body/

4 When the mastic/sealant is set, press the door seals gently into place over the pads, ensuring the pads are not pushed out of place or shape.

34

Off-roading

Protecting

Carrying

Towing

Enhancing

Repairing

Diagnosing

Improving

Winching

Lighting

Servicing

Upgrading

Restoring

BRITPART

The quality parts for Land Rovers

For over 35 years, servicing and repairing Land Rovers has been made easy with Britpart.

As the leading independent wholesaler, we've a wide range of accessories, service and repair parts for the entire Land Rover marque.

We can supply body components right down to replacement nuts and bolts and everything else in between and with our range of accessories you can make your Land Rover as unique as you.

To find your nearest stockist - www.britpart.com/distributors

Series / Defender / Discovery / Freelander / Range Rover / Range Rover Sport / Range Rover Evoque

Farm truck to CSW

ED EVANS

TOOLS REQUIRED:
General Workshop tools

TIME:
10 hours

COST:
See panel

DIFFICULTY RATING:
3/5

CONTACT:
Steve Grant at the Britpart workshop

PART 5
TRANSFORMED!

IT'S THE WAY DEFENDERS are built. They're so easy to take apart, to add things on to, and to personalise with extra equipment that it's relatively simple to transform the most battered example into an outstanding and unique vehicle.

Of course, a wad of money comes into the plan. But for the sake of two or three grand's worth of accessories and upgraded components (excluding this vehicle's Corbeau seats), plus the cost of a respray, a very average Defender can be moved towards the realms of new vehicles, and its value dragged up there accordingly.

Build up a vehicle like this, and you're likely to get your money back – that is, if you can ever bear to part with the result.

At the end of the last installment we left our ex-farm hack in the workshop with a few front body panels missing, yet looking like a half-reasonable TDCi Defender. Now, it's time to complete transformation.

Ed Evans concludes the story of how this one-time battered and abused farm truck has been turned into a bespoke County Station Wagon

WORK SAFELY:
We advise wearing protective gloves when fitting components

Wear eye protection when drilling

Support the vehicle securely on stands with brake and gear engaged when changing wheels

IN ASSOCIATION WITH
FOLEY SPECIALIST VEHICLES

Completing the front end

1 The front wing is removed for repair, and the front panel is off to fit a CoolAir Logan air conditioning kit (condenser, fan and pipework seen

2 The radiator has been removed to give access to install the aircon compressor (top left) and the associated drive pulleys and the new drive belt.

3 Britpart MD, Paul Myers, assembles a new pre-painted outer wing to the existing wing top and front panel assembly.

4 Indus Silver front grille and lamp panels are installed with LED side and indicator lamps, all contrasting with the black bonnet shut panel and lower grille.

Wheel arch eyebrows

1 A set of wheel arch eyebrows need to be added, and this new set, sprayed in black to match the roof, should contrast nicely with the body paint.

2 Each eyebrow is fitted by starting at the centre of the wheel arch and working out toward each end, securing it with plastic rivet plugs.

3 The plugs are turned as they are inserted into the body. Then the pin is tapped in with a hammer to expand and lock the plug.

37

Farm truck to CSW

4 The front eyebrows are clipped to holes in both the outer and inner wheel arches, fixing to the outer arch first, then the inner.

Setting the bonnet

THE BONNET latching and locking sequence needs to be set accurately so the bonnet can be closed gently by hand until it latches, and then to press it down with a hand at each corner (to avoid denting it) to fully lock it.

We adjusted the central catch to the correct height for it to engage the latch, but it needed the force of dropping to make it fully lock.

So we screwed the rubber stops (on the underside of the bonnet) in slightly to allow the bonnet to go further down, and it could then be push-locked easily by hand.

1 The bonnet, painted in black to match the roof and front body panel, was carefully lifted onto the bulkhead hinges and propped up.

2 Initial adjustment of the height of the centre catch allowed the bonnet to lock onto the front panel, but wouldn't fully latch by pressing it down by hand.

3 Raising these rubber stops on the underside of the bonnet front edge allowed it to sit lower on the shut panel, and be locked by hand pressure.

4 The Defender is looking good now with its coded colour scheme, but something is obviously wrong. Can you spot what?

38

Getting some grip

1 We were desperate to get those rusty old steel wheels and hacked tyres off the Defender, to see how it looked with a set of black alloys.

2 The saw-tooth alloy wheels shod in Atturo Trail Blade AT rubber, instantly transformed the vehicle into a business-like machine.

3 There is now a fair weight of rubber hanging on the tail door. Door structure needs to be in good condition. Gas strut will assist opening.

Practical embellishments

1 Extra lighting is provided by this LED lamp block subtly fixed below the front bumper.

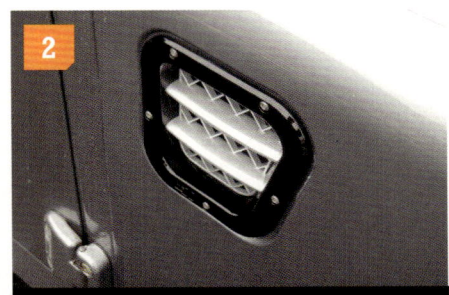

2 KBX intake grille adds a distinctive touch of technicality to the outward appearance.

3 Change of mind – grille is swapped for black version, plus matching black Defender lettering.

4 The centre switch console was removed, stripped down, and sprayed to match the silver of the external bodywork.

PARTS AND PRICES:
From Britpart suppliers, unless no number given:
- Indus Silver Front Grille and Headlamps Surround set (DA1257), from £180
- Black front grille and headlamp surrounds (DA1357), £210
- Wheel arch eyebrow kit (DA1059), £229 unpainted
- Plastic rivets for eyebrows (MWC9918PMA), 86p each
- Front Bumper, First Four (SKU PM701), from £194
- Corbeau seats (DA7312), £2950 pair
- Glove box conversion kit (DA2603CF), £97.50
- Grille (on front wing) KBX, around £53
- Sawtooth wheels (LR 025862), £135 each
- LED lamp cluster (DA1192), £129.50

Farm truck to CSW

5 A passenger side glove box conversion adds much-needed interior storage space.

6 These expensive bespoke Corbeau seats are a special design, only recently available.

7 The colour coding works superbly with the black roof, bonnet and taildoor complemented by the black sawtooth wheels.

8 The combination of black grille and front panel, with Indus Silver lamp panels contrasting with the main body colour, produces a busy, but balanced, beast.

INTRODUCING THE LAND ROVER DEFENDER 07-16 DIESEL MANUAL

MAINTENANCE • SERVICING • REPAIRS

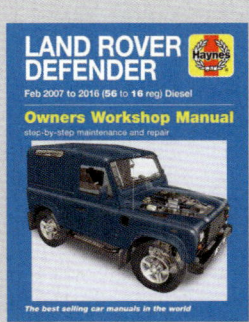

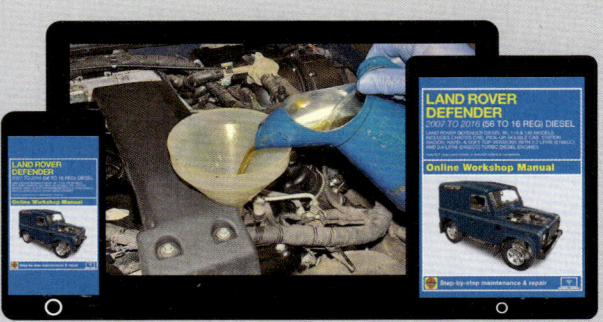

NEW!

Haynes shows you how

AVAILABLE IN PRINT AND ON YOUR DEVICE

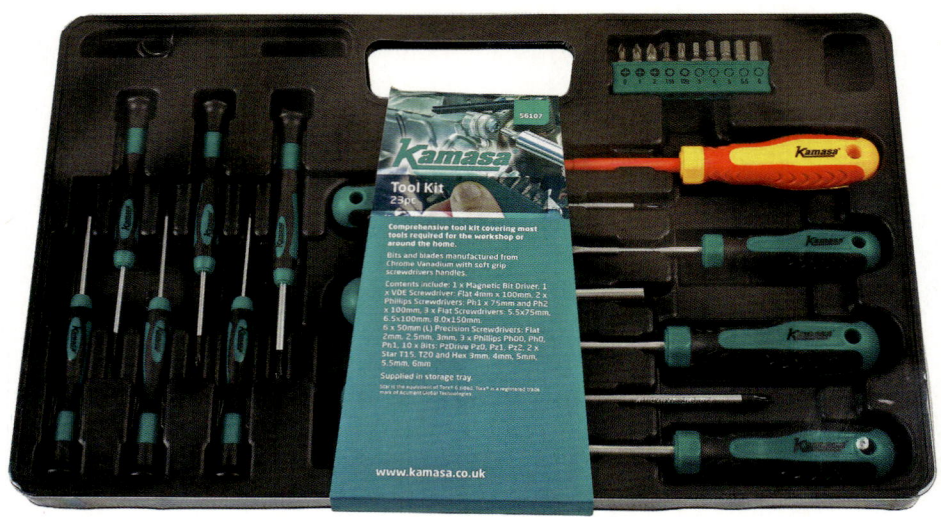

Products

PRICE: £23.84
SCREWDRIVER SET

This quality 23-piece set from Kamasa includes three flat screwdrivers (2 mm x 50 mm, 2.5 mm x 50 mm and 8 mm x 150 mm); two Phillips head screwdrivers (Ph1 x 75 mm and Ph2 x 100 mm); one magnetic bit driver plus ten assorted bits (PzDrive Pz0, Pz1, Pz2, 2 x Star T15, T20 and Hex 3 mm, 4 mm, 5 mm, 5.5 mm, 6 mm); plus an insulated VDE screwdriver for electrical work. Also included is a set of six 50 mm long precision screwdrivers for intricate work. We liked the soft grip handles and the virtually unbreakable chrome vanadium steel shafts and bits.
kamasa.co.uk

PRICE: £1285
REAR BUMPER

The GOBI-X HD Rear Bumper with wheel carrier option (one or two) is the mother of all Defender rear bumpers. Made from double powder-coated 3mm steel and internally braced for extra strength, it includes two recovery points, two Hi Lift jacking points and replacement vehicle lights. It also has a gas strut for ease of operation even if carrying a big wheel.
tuff-trek.com

PRICE: £195
DEFENDER SECURITY

The Defender Defender security system is one of the most comprehensive Defender security systems available on the market today. Designed to stop the criminals before they have the chance to drive your precious Defender away. You can monitor your Defender 24/7 by making use of the system's mobile app, too. Even if you don't see the alarms via your phone, the remote isolator switch kicks into action.
defenderdefender.co.uk

PRICE: £289.99
SPECTRE FAUX BEADLOCK

Everyone loved the wheels on the Defender used in the Bond Spectre movie. The only problem with them is that they are not street legal in the UK. Fortunately Weller Wheels now offer a road legal version of this popular wheel. Note that the beadlock is welded onto the outer rim and serves no actual practical purpose. Unlike a traditional steel wheel this semi-gloss black wheel has five large hand-welded steel tubes. The faux beadlock with its 24 hexagonal bolts protect the outer rim.
wellerwheels.com

IN ASSOCIATION WITH

FOLEY SPECIALIST VEHICLES

FROM: £319.95

BUCKET SEATS

Heavy-duty leather bucket seats with dual reclining mechanism. These comfortable seats have a width of 54 cm across the base and backrest while standing nearly a metre tall. Suitable for all Defender models except County and pick-up.
bbclassics.co.uk

PRODUCTS

There's no shortage of must-have Defender goodies to choose from. Here are just a few of our favourites...

PRICE: £24

PUMA SWITCH MOUNT

While new vehicle designers prefer the minimalist no switches look, Defender owners are constantly installing new switches. This Puma switch mount will provide a neat solution for those looking to add additional switches in their Defenders. You can add up to six Carling Technologies switches onto the mount.
mudstuff.co.uk

PRICE: £32.95

DEFENDER MEMORY STICK

If you are a sucker for all things Defender then this diecast metal Defender model memory stick is for you. It has 16 GB of memory and unlike your Defender it operates at high speeds.
britpart.com

Products

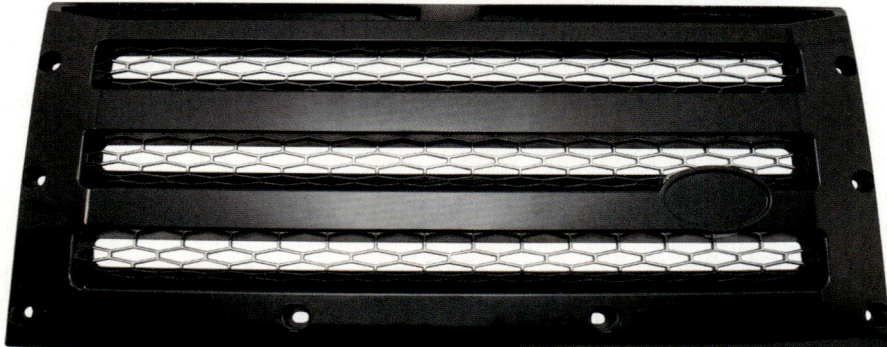

PRICE: £210

XS FRONT GRILLE AND HEADLAMP SURROUND

Improve the look of your Defender with these XS front grille and headlamp surrounds from Britpart. Only suitable for non-air con Defenders. Available in black with silver mesh and silver with black mesh.
www.britpart.com

PRICE: £115

TOMB RAIDER SIDE STEPS

Made from good quality steel and with a polished black finish, this chequer plate top gives your Defender 90 that cool Tomb Raider look and will protect it when off-roading. Comes with a 24-month guarantee.
getoffroad.com

PRICE: FROM £30

SECURITY KITS

Defender Door Security Kits are now available for pre-order. The 90 cost £30 and the 110 £45. They fit inside your doors, so if the hinge bolts are removed the door cannot be pulled off. They're easy to install, and made for front and middle doors. They fit all Defender models and years. Each kit consists of two stainless steel plates which fit inside each hinge point.
tmdtuning.com

FROM: £115

JUMP START

Winter is that wonderful time of the year when flat batteries and struggling starts are pretty common. Sealey have a whole range of Batteryless Electrostart Power Starters. Thanks to innovative technology, the E/START requires just five volts to jump start a vehicle. All you have to do is connect it to the discharged battery and the unit will fully energise within a matter of minutes.
www.sealey.co.uk

FROM: £1350
GALVANISED CHASSIS
Thanks to Land Rover producing poor quality chassis, Richards Chassis can now make a healthy living from producing replacement chassis. This particular one will fit a Defender 100 from 2007 onwards. That means the factory standard chassis did not even see out a decade of service.
www.richardschassis.co.uk

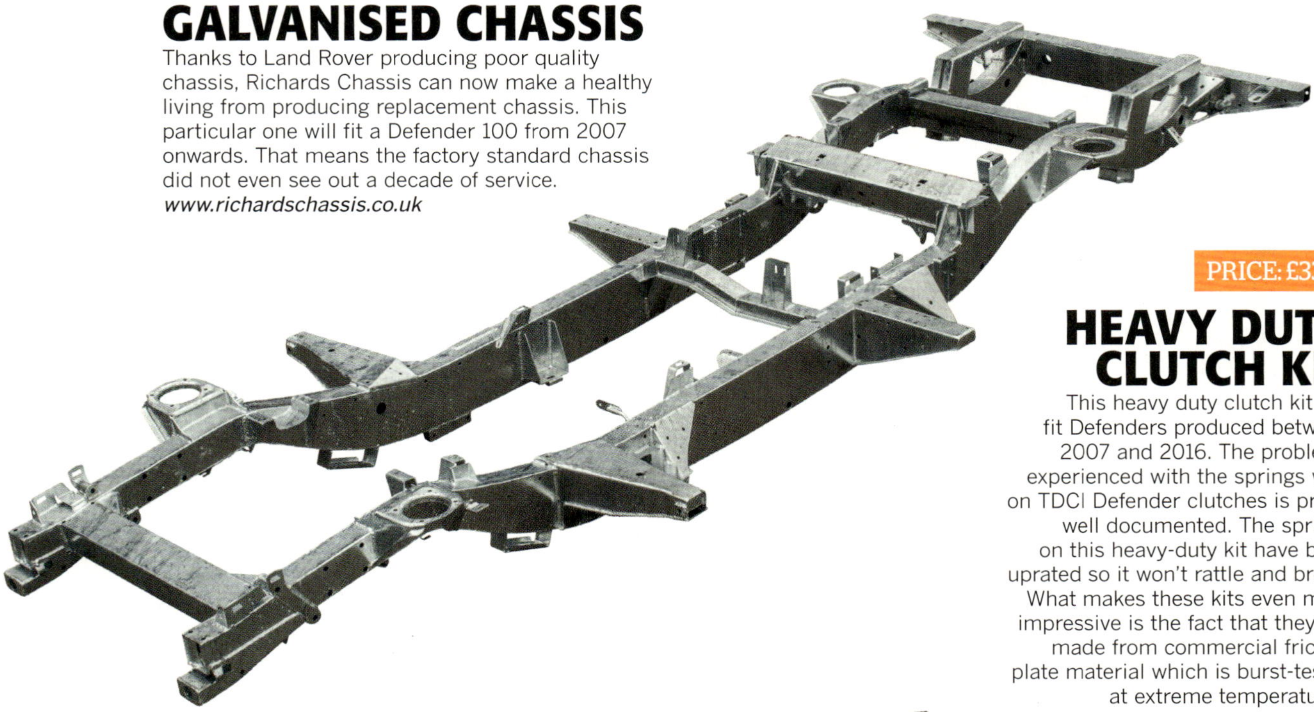

PRICE: £330
HEAVY DUTY CLUTCH KIT
This heavy duty clutch kit will fit Defenders produced between 2007 and 2016. The problems experienced with the springs with on TDCI Defender clutches is pretty well documented. The springs on this heavy-duty kit have been uprated so it won't rattle and break. What makes these kits even more impressive is the fact that they are made from commercial friction plate material which is burst-tested at extreme temperatures.
www.tmdtuning.com

PRICE: £39.50
XS AIR INTAKE GRILLE
Upgrade the air intake grille on your Defender with the XS air intake grille from Britpart. Available in black with silver mesh and silver with black mesh.
www.britpart.com

PRICE: VARY
REBUILT GEARBOX
Is your gearbox getting notchy? Has the synchromesh seen better days? A remanufactured box from Derventio Autocentre could be the answer. All Defender gearboxes are available off the shelf, along with transfer boxes, steering boxes and diffs. Engines reconditioned to order.
www.derventio-autocentre.co.uk

Td5 service

DEFENDER TD5 SERVICE

Standard servicing is simple, but the best service involves knowing the extra tricks and checks that guarantee future reliability. Ed Evans reveals the tricks of the trade

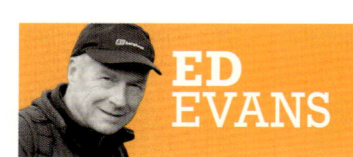

ED EVANS

TOOLS REQUIRED:
Socket spanners, rings and open-enders. Oil filter wrench. Trolley jack, axle stands, wheel chocks.

TIME:
Allow half a day

COST:
£100 for fluids, filters and consumables

DIFFICULTY RATING:
2/5

DEFENDER IS one of the easiest Land Rovers to service, and all models are a practical DIY proposition, given a reasonable tool kit and safe lifting and support facilities.

Before starting a DIY service, it's worth buying the Land Rover official workshop manual which details the procedures, items to be checked, and the lubricant and fluid specifications.

The manual is written for trained and experienced mechanics, so our feature guide tells you the information that isn't in the manual – the trade tips and tricks gained from experience and intimate knowledge of the vehicles.

Armed with this information, you'll be able to produce a better than standard service and, at the same time, gain an intimate knowledge of the condition of your own vehicle and know it's durability and future needs.

For this feature I visited independent Land Rover specialist James French 4x4 in Standlake, near Oxford to join mechanic Andrew Langford as he serviced a 2004 Td5 Defender 130.

To properly service a vehicle with an eye to future reliability and cost savings, we need to be on the look out for signs of impending failure, such as wear, corrosion, and deteriorating pipes and wiring. While working underneath and in the engine bay, it's the ideal time to make a close check of the whole vehicle, in particular looking for parts that might fail the next MoT test.

Many of these servicing tips apply to other Land Rovers, especially other Defender models.

IN ASSOCIATION WITH
FOLEY SPECIALIST VEHICLES

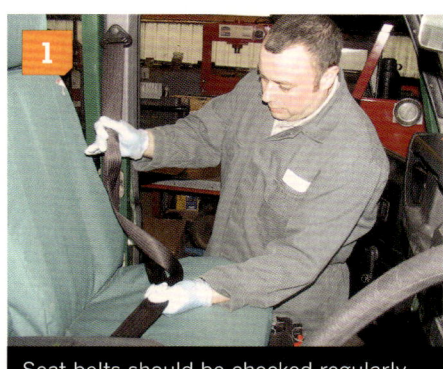

1
Seat belts should be checked regularly on all seats, not only at service and MoT intervals.

2
Aim the washer jets slightly high to account for wind pressure at high speed.

ROAD TEST
Andrew road tested the vehicle first, though not all garages will be so diligent. But it's important to know how the vehicle drives, and to listen for unusual sounds and to notice any handling and braking problems so that these can be investigated more fully during the service. When servicing our own vehicles we'll already have a good idea of their road-going condition, but it's still beneficial to make a critical assessment prior to the service. Obviously, symptoms such as worn gear selectors, clutch release bearing or a noisy Td5 flywheel spigot bearing are jobs that won't be tackled during a service, but they need to go on the list of upcoming repairs. It's worth keeping a list of extra jobs highlighted during the service so they won't be forgotten, and can be planned in when convenient. Before starting the test drive, check that all the dashboard warning lamps illuminate when the ignition is switched on, and that they extinguish after a few seconds when the automatic system checks have completed – the ABS lamp (where fitted) may stay on until you drive away. Before the full road test, check that the transfer box low ratio gears and diff-lock (with dashboard lamp) will engage. You may need to reverse slightly to disengage diff-lock.

INTERIOR AND EXTERIOR CHECKS
It make sense to do the interior checks first, while your hands are clean. Inspect the seat belt webbing for cuts, edge fraying or damage from door shuts. The belts should unroll easily and lock when jerked outward. The buckle should latch easily, and should spring apart on pressing the release button. Finally, confirm the seats are secure on their frames.

Under the left seat, clean any corrosion from the battery terminals and protect them with battery grease or petroleum jelly. Top up the battery electrolyte with distilled water or, if it's a sealed battery, confirm the condition indicator is the correct colour. Confirm the battery retaining clamp is secure.

Check the steering wheel's radial free play, and feel for column bush movement. If the steering has a tight spot, check the column joints in the engine compartment, otherwise the steering box may be over-adjusted and can be corrected by a garage.

Operate the screen washers to confirm both jets are correctly aimed. If not, adjust the nozzles by levering with a pin inserted. Replace wiper blades if they are damaged along the working edge or are split. Lift the arms to feel there is

Underside Jobs

good spring pressure to push the blades against the screen.

Oils
Check the complete underside for signs of oil leaks. If significant leakage is noticed, try to follow the stains to identify the source of the leak and make a note for repairs to be made. If the leak source cannot be found, clean the whole area and re-check gasket joints, pipes and connections for fresh seepage. The leak might only occur when the vehicle is being driven; if so, inspect again after a short drive.

Fuel leakage dripping down onto the starter motor will be from the fuel pressure regulator on the rear right of the cylinder head (see how to replace this in LRM June issue).

Before draining oil or checking the levels, clean dirt away from around the oil filler and level plugs to prevent it entering when the plug is unscrewed. After topping up and refitting the plugs, clean the casing so that any fresh leakage from the plugs can be easily spotted and dealt with. Check transmission and axle oil levels every 12,000 miles, and renew at 24,000.

When draining the sump oil, check the condition of the initial oil flow. On early Td5 engines, a thin grey oil may be the

1
Oil leaking down the right side of the bellhousing on a Td5 is usually from a hardened half-moon seal in the rear of the cam cover gasket.

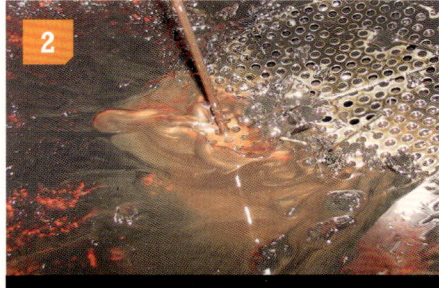

2
Streaks in the oil drained from the gearbox is typical of normal wear. If all of the oil is grey, there may be internal problems or water ingress.

3
Fine particles collected on the gearbox's magnetic drain plug here is normal – it's the magnet's job to extract this debris. Clean it off and refit the plug.

4
Transfer box filler/level plug is up on the rear face of the unit, sandwiched between the casing and the transmission brake. A half-inch ratchet head fits.

47

Td5 service

5 Oil leaks under the transfer box are likely to originate from the intermediate shaft seal (white arrow) or the input shaft seal (yellow arrow).

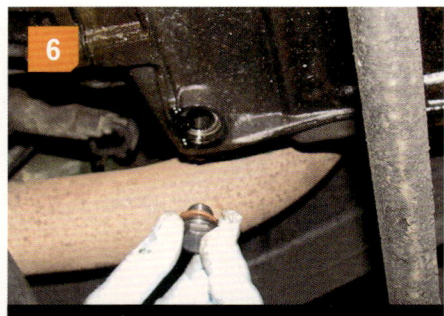

6 Always refit the engine sump plug with a new sealing washer to avoid leaks. Renew the plug if the spanner flats or thread are damaged.

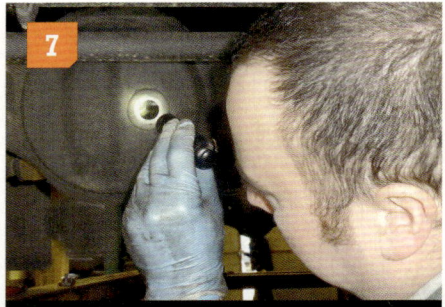

7 With the wheels free, and using a strong light through the front diff filler hole, rotate the prop to visually check the diff components.

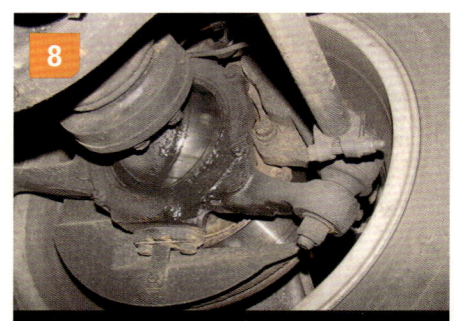

8 There is usually slight seepage from the swivel housing seal. The amount seen here would not be expected to fail an MoT, but it's on the list of jobs

9 Check this fuel cooler hose at right of engine which can chafe on the engine mounting bracket. Secure it with cable ties to hold it away.

result of fuel getting into the sump from a crack in the cylinder head which allows diesel in the fuel galleries to pass through to the combustion chamber or oil galleries.

Differentials
When the oils are drained, Andrew inspects the differential components through the filler plug opening, using a strong light. With the wheels free to rotate, and turning the propshaft, it's possible to check the condition of roll pins, depending on the diff type, and to spot broken or loose crownwheel bolts.

Grey axle oil suggests water ingress. A dark green tinge from the front axle suggests swivel grease contamination via

10 Check play in A-frame joint and bushes with pry bar. A very loose joint can let diff dip at the nose. Rubber boot is MoT fail, if split.

a defective axle seal.

Swivel housings
Leaking swivel seals can fail the MoT test, and they can let water into the swivel housings, leading to bearing and axle damage. It's worth replacing defective seals during the service because, as Andrew explains, the seal can be quickly changed by releasing the steering track rod and drag link joints and unbolting the inner swivel from the axle. The complete assembly with the half shaft can then be withdrawn. Stand it upright (in an old steel wheel for stability) to change the seal.

Checking the fixings
By fixings, we mean all of the underside nuts and bolts that hold the driveline, suspension and brake components. Each one should be checked by applying a spanner to ensure it isn't working loose or been insufficiently tightened during previous maintenance. There's no need to put additional pressure on them, it's just a matter of checking that nothing is loose. Include the tie bar on the bottom of the steering box. If the bolts holding the steering box to the chassis are not tight, you may hear a squeak on full lock. Everything can be checked using just 21, 24 and 30mm AF socket spanners.

While checking the fixings, wire brush the exposed screw threads and bolt and nut heads, then apply protective grease to help ensure they release easily when needed for maintenance. Doing this can save big money on future garage labour bills, or save your own DIY time and frustration.

Check the security of the towing equipment which is now an MoT inspection item, and add a squirt of WD40 into the tow hitch's electrical socket to keep the contacts clean.

Bushes and joints
In general, joints should have no movement, and bushes should have some flexibility without being loose. Most can be checked by inserting a pry bar and levering gently between the two connected components while watching or feeling for movement in the joint or bush. There are exceptions, such as the steering drop arm joint, which has intentional vertical sprung movement.

Steering
Examine the steering damper for leaks, and its right hand bush for wear. Slight fluid leakage from underneath the steering box can often be cured by replacing the lower seal, though this seems more successful on Discovery 2 than Defender Td5 where the best option is a new steering box. Significant leakage will fail the MoT test. Sight upwards from underneath to check for fluid leaks from the power steering hoses, pump and

48

11 At the chassis end of the radius arm, check the mounting bushes by pulling up and down. Loose rear radius arm bushes can affect steering.

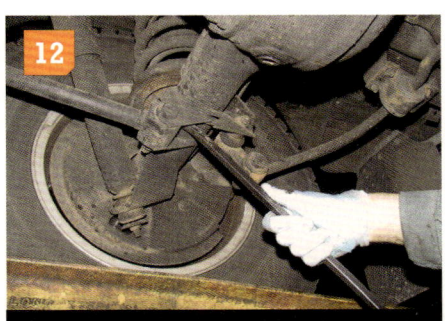

12 Insert pry bar between the radius arm and axle to show any looseness in the bushes. Check for crack where bracket is welded to axle.

13 Pull on rear anti-roll bar and all dampers to see/feel play in bushes, and in roll bar joint. Check condition of rubber boot on joint.

14 Test transmission and engine mountings with the pry bar. Look for rubber separation from the steel brackets, and softening from oil.

15 Check earth connections are tight and clean: secondary earth from ECU on right of trans box (shown), battery earth to trans box, body earth to chassis.

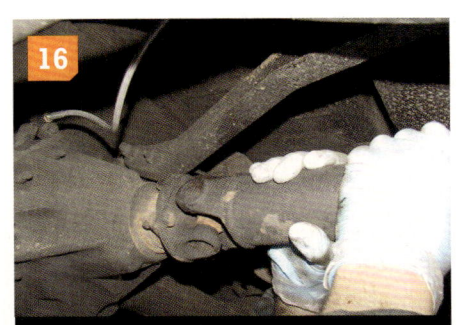

16 Significant wear in the propshaft universal joints can be detected by rocking the shaft while watching and feeling the joint.

steering box.
Check the drop arm (not the joint, which is mentioned in the picture captions) for play. If the steering box vertical shaft allows up and down movement here, the play can be adjusted out, but it is not a DIY job and needs an experienced mechanic.

Chassis
Paint protection on the Td5 chassis is improved over earlier models, but the usual rust areas still need to be checked during the service. In particular the rear crossmember and the forward outriggers, and the upper structure ahead of the rear axle on long wheelbase models. Check the sections are sound at the tow bracket attachments.

Exhaust
Exhausts are long lasting, but all systems need a close check for signs of soot escaping from developing cracks and joint leaks. Check the steel hangers for off-road damage, and confirm the rubber loops are all present and fully engaged. The rubbers should allow controlled movement of the system without allowing it to touch other components. Check the flexible section in the downpipe from the manifold which can break up and allow gas to blow. Look for heavily corroded bolts and nuts at the pipe flanges, and replace any that might fall apart after an off-road knock.

Pipes and cables
Here, we're checking to confirm no pipes or cables are stretched, loose or hanging free. Look for perished rubber fuel pipes and corroded metal pipes. Pipes, cables and hoses need to be secured away from sharp edges that could cut through them as the vehicle vibrates.

Slight surface corrosion (not pitting) on brake pipes can be cleaned off using emery cloth and the surface greased to protect them. Obviously, any brake fluid leakage needs immediate repair, but also check the clutch fluid pipe and slave cylinder – spotting a slight weep here could avoid a breakdown later.

Propshafts
Grasp the popshaft near the U/J and push-pull it in each plane, looking and feeling for looseness in the joint. If not lubricated regularly, joints can become partly seized. If this is suspected, check by unbolting the flange, and slowly working the joint through all positions while feeling for resistance.

Lubricate the joints using a grease gun on the nipple until grease begins to seep out of the joint – if the joint is full, water is less likely to get in. While working on the rear prop, check its flange nuts at the brake drum are tight.

17 Steering drop-arm ball joint is sprung inside. It should have vertical springy movement, but no looseness, vertically or horizontally.

18 Chassis corrosion protection is improved on Td5 models, but remove collected dirt and mud, and repair damaged paintwork.

49

Td5 service

Wheel arch work

Hubs and swivels
Before unbolting the front wheels, raise each wheel off the ground to test for bearing and joint play. Try to rock the wheel, gripping the tyre at 3- and 9-o-clock to test for play in the track rod and drag link joints. Grip the tyre at top and bottom and lift to reveal play in the upper or lower swivel bearings. If any movement disappears while a helper holds the footbrake on during these tests, the play will be in the hub bearings. Spin the wheel to listen for roughness or rumble from the hub bearings.

With the road wheel removed, prise off the hub cap to inspect the condition of the axle-to-drive flange splines. Rock the hub rotationally to check the play here. Slight movement is acceptable, otherwise examine the splines carefully: they should be squared off at the tips, but if they are worn to a knife-edge they may soon strip, losing the drive.

On ABS-equipped vehicles, check the wheel speed sensors are secure and sat down squarely. If not fully seated, they can be tapped gently on the shoulder to help ensure the correct air gap (fronts are through the swivel top plate, rears are behind the brake backplate).

Wheels and tyres
Inspect the inner and outer rims for impact damage. Tyre wear should be even across the tread, otherwise suspect tracking or worn rear radius arm bushes.

Brakes
Renew brake pads on both sides if any are down to 3mm thickness. Clean dust and rust from the pad seats and check the pins and springs for corrosion. The discs should be worn evenly across the front and back faces and be free from scoring. Surface rust, after standing for a day or so, is normal and harmless, but rust blotches usually lead to pitting.

Look for signs of fluid leakage from the piston seals in the caliper and around the hose and brake pipe connections. Clean light rust from pipes and fittings and protect with grease. Inspect brake hoses for cracks and bulges by sliding the protective coil clear and flexing the hose to expose surface splits.

Brake fluid is scheduled for replacement every 24,000 miles, though in practice a moisture meter test can confirm whether the fluid is suitable for further use. Land Rover recommends replacing all fluid seals, hoses and the servo filter at 48,000 miles, though the components regularly last much longer.

Suspension
Look for rust around the damper turrets' sides and lower flange. Clean and grease the turret nuts if they are corroded.

Examine the coil springs for cracks, especially at the top inboard side where breaks are difficult to spot. If the external coating is damaged or the coils are rusted, then it's time for renewal to avoid breakage and ensure good performance. Clean the exposed threads of the springs' lower seat retaining bolts and protect with grease.

Before refitting alloy wheels, lightly smear the inside of the wheel centre with copper grease to prevent it corroding and seizing on to the hub spigot.

Fuel filter
At the 24,000 miles service, replace the fuel filter on the chassis, forward of the right rear wheel. The steel cover over the filter has a quick-release latch which allows it to fold back and disengage from its bracket.

After a filter replacement, the fuel line needs to be primed to remove entrapped air. Carry out the sequence explained in the pictures, and you will hear the fuel pump running in the tank – when it stops running, the system is ready.

While you're still in the area, check the fuel tank filler and vent pipe connections are tight and that no pipes are abrading on metalwork.

IN ASSOCIATION WITH

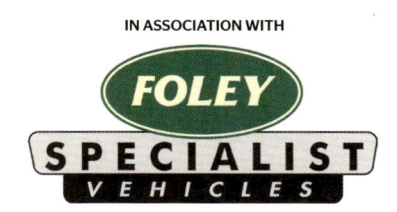

FOLEY SPECIALIST VEHICLES

1 Andrew checks for vertical movement of the front wheel which would indicate possible wear in the upper or lower swivel bearings.

2 With wheel off, look through the swivel top filler plug to confirm that sufficient one-shot grease is being picked up on the rotating CV joint.

3 Prise off the hub cap to check for swivel grease leaking through from a defective stub axle seal. Check the spline condition (see text)

4 Use grips to squeeze the brake pads back to confirm the pistons are not seized and that the pads are free to move on their locating pins.

6 With the old filter removed, carefully wipe the thread and the sealing face of the fuel housing with a clean cloth.

5 Td5 fuel filter is on the chassis. Remove the cover plate and unscrew the filter, having placed a receptacle to catch spilt fuel.

7 Apply a smear of clean fuel to the rubber seal on top of the new filter to help it seal, then screw the new cartridge on hand tight.

8 With the ignition on, but the with engine off, press the accelerator pedal six times to start the in-tank fuel pump to prime the system.

9 Before refitting the wheels, check for tread condition and embedded objects which might cause a puncture. Inspect both sidewalls for cuts or bulges.

Td5 service

WORK SAFELY:
When working underneath, try to do the maximum number of jobs while the vehicle is on its wheels. Engage gear and handbrake, and use wheel chocks.

Work on one wheelarch at a time so that when the wheel is off, the vehicle stands on the remaining three. Support the corner being worked on with an axle stand, and place a secondary, fail-safe support underneath.

If working with a helper to check steering joints, ensure you can hear each other clearly to avoid actions that might trap fingers.

Beware of hot oils when draining, and allow the cooling system to fully cool before opening or draining.

Dispose of old oils at a recognised recycling facility.

Wear eye protection when working with fluids and under the vehicle, and protect skin from contamination with oils.

Avoid inhaling brake dust – use brake cleaning fluid, and wear a particle mask.

Engine compartment

Engine filters
The Td5 has two oil filters. The centrifugal filter removes fine carbon particles and needs to be changed every 12,000 miles or 12 months with the engine oil, otherwise it will fill up with particles and stop cleaning the lubricant. Because the centrifugal filter removes so much fine deposit, the conventional full flow oil filter cartridge needs to be renewed only every 36,000 miles. The full flow filter is an awkward reach under the turbo. Use a filter band wrench to unscrew it, and fit the new one hand-tight.

When changing the air filter element (24,000 miles), check and clean the ambient air pressure sensor on the side of the air box.

Antifreeze
The correct anti-freeze solution will always protect the engine from freezing, but the effects of mechanical pumping deplete its corrosion protection properties which are vital for aluminium components including the cylinder head. It is best renewed every 36,000 miles.

Visual checks
The Td5 engine is fairly accessible in the Defender installation. From the left side, check the clutch fluid hose and the metal pipe above for swelling, leakage and contact with other parts. Check for oil leakage from the supply and return pipes at the turbocharger – leakage from the latter usually needs only a flange gasket replacement. Confirm the exhaust downpipe to turbo connection is tight and that the downpipe flexible section is in good order. Higher up on the engine, look for soot marks along the top of the exhaust manifold at the cylinder head which would indicate gas leakage from a warped manifold. If that's the case, some manifold studs might be broken or loose, and will need replacing before the situation worsens. This can be caused by prolonged high-load driving, and has been associated with electronic engine tuning.

Check the heat exchangers at the front panel for signs of leakage due to corrosion or splits on the matrices. A distorted or bowed intercooler is usually the result of a turbo boost pressure problem, such as a seized wastegate. Behind these, check the viscous fan is free to rotate when the engine is cold and stopped, and feel for excess play in the fan hub. Confirm the ancillary drive belt is in good condition, correctly aligned and has correct tension.

1 When renewing the air filter, remove the bonnet to confirm the filter casing's rear clips are fully fastened, otherwise water can enter.

2 Check air pipe to filter is securely connected and not deformed leaving gap. Check flap valve on bottom of air pipe is free – important if wading.

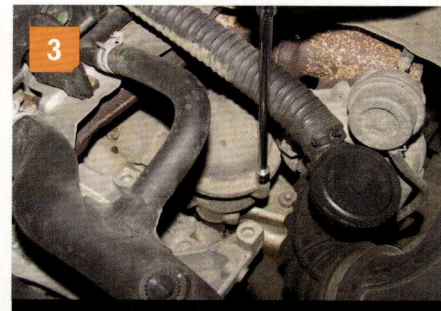

3 The centrifugal oil filter is under this domed cover on the left side of the engine. Use socket and extension to remove the two 10mm AF bolts.

4 The filter is a lift-out canister. This replacement has been fitted after cleaning the bowl and seal face. Spin new filter to confirm correctly seated.

5 Refit the filter cover using a new seal (supplied with filter) lubricated with fresh engine oil. Tighten the bolts gradually and evenly.

6 Underbonnet visual checks at the left-hand side include: the hydraulic clutch system, exhaust down pipe, turbo oil supply and exhaust manifold studs.

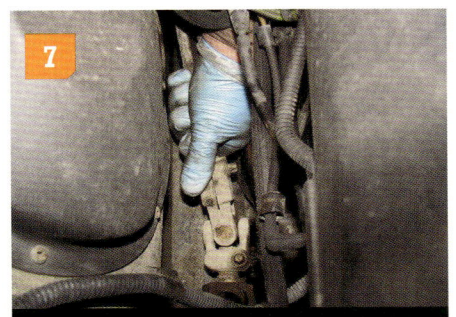

7 The steering shaft can be reached to test for play in the joints. A reliable helper can rock the steering wheel slightly, but take care with fingers.

LONG TERM TIPS:
Suspension dampers have no replacement schedule, but generally they perform well for around 60,000 miles after which, a new set should be considered.
Fuel injectors are usually good for 100,000 miles, but much depends on the vehicle's use, and Td5 injectors can last far longer than this.
If your vehicle endures a particularly tough life, such as regular heavy towing, frequent off-roading, wading or dusty conditions, consider reducing the service intervals.

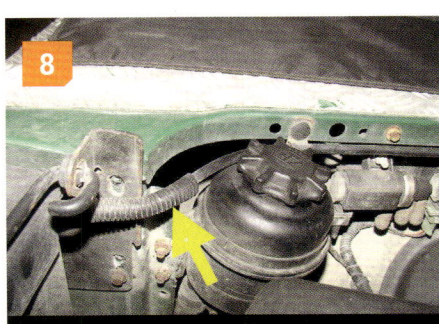

8 Check the condition of all coolant hoses. This overflow pipe can become brittle. Sheath protects from sharp edges. Later vehicles have armoured pipe.

9 Check all heat exchangers on both the front and rear faces for leakage, damage or blockage due to leaves or mud accumulation.

53

Soft top conversion

TREVOR CUTHBERT

TOOLS REQUIRED:
Spanners, socket wrenches, hole saw, drill, hacksaw, rivet gun

TIME:
1 day

COST:
From 700+ Costs: Canvas hood £250, Seat belt bar £300, Header rail £96, Hoop set and hardware £350

DIFFICULTY RATING:
2/5

CONTACT:
All Wheel Trim: Tel: 01993 776800
www.allwheeltrim.co.uk

HOW TO GO TOPLESS FOR THE SUMMER

It's simple to turn a hard top Defender into a canvas convertible – and just as easy to refit the hard top again for winter. Trevor Cuthbert shows how…

MY FRIEND Steve Wright's Ninety pick-up wasn't right for his needs. Passenger carrying capacity was the issue, but a hard top or Station Wagon conversion was not the answer. So we looked at the cost of a full soft top conversion, to which rear seats could be added. I contacted Kim Johnson at All Wheel Trim to see what parts we would need.

Although I had some of the components in my store from an old 110 soft top, I knew that All Wheel Trim could supply good-quality canvas with side windows, as well as all the other missing parts. A well-packed box duly arrived and we were ready to start work on the Ninety.
The job should take about a day. It takes around the same time to convert a hardtop, where the main difference is dealing with the rear safari door.

WORK SAFELY
Take care when cutting the screen's rubber seals. Wear protective gloves and cut away from yourself with your free hand well clear of the blade.

The upper body and roof assembly is cumbersome and heavy, and requires at least two people to lift it clear.

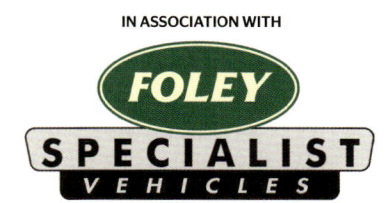

Remove the lid

STEVE WAS keen to be able to reinstate the truck-cab if he decided that a soft top wasn't always for him, so the cab would be stored. For this reason, and because I had a windscreen and frame already fitted with the top rail and clamps needed, we opted to remove the cab with windscreen still attached.

Without a soft-top screen frame, it's necessary to fit a new rail and clamps to the existing screen frame, as we'll see later on. The truck cab is removed by releasing eight M6 bolts along the top of the rear bulkhead, which can be got at behind the seats after removing the trim. The bolts are in pairs, holding four brackets from the cab to the bulkhead.

At either side by the door catch, two M8 nuts need to be loosened and removed (13mm AF). This will allow the stud attached to the cab to be lifted clear. The seat belts' top mounts need to be released from the cab.

If the windscreen is to remain with the Land Rover, the roof panel needs to be unbolted from the top of the screen frame by dropping the headlining in this area (held by the sun visors and interior light) to access to the M6 bolts.

These are fixed to captive nut plates within the windscreen frame (10mm spanner or socket). Two large self-tapping screws have to be removed on either side of the screen. Finally, to separate the roof panel from the screen frame, the bond between the two needs to be cut with a sharp craft knife.

However, on this Ninety, the screen was being removed *with* the cab, which only requires the removal of two M10 screws into the top of the hinged windscreen frame mount, concealed behind the windscreen frame clamp.

The top of the mount is then levered out of the way from the outside. On later models, the windscreen mount is not hinged and must be completely removed – top and bottom – by removal of three M8 bolts or cap bolts.

A hardtop model will not have the row of eight M6 bolts to deal with. Instead, there are two M8 nuts at the rear corners and two on either side of the tail door.

There is also a bracket to be removed between the sides of the hardtop and the rear body capping, half way along.

There may also be a rear screen washer; the hose from this to the engine bay will also need to be removed at the washer bottle, and the pump exit neatly sealed off. The door frame seals are pulled clear of the cab section on each side and the cab is now ready to lift off.

The windscreen wipers also need to be propped away from the screen to prevent fouling.

1 Our Land Rover Ninety is a Turbo Diesel pick-up model. The job is very similar on a hard top Land Rover with only a few key differences.

2 Using a trim tool, the interior trim around the lower part of the cab is removed to access the brackets holding the cab to the rear body tub.

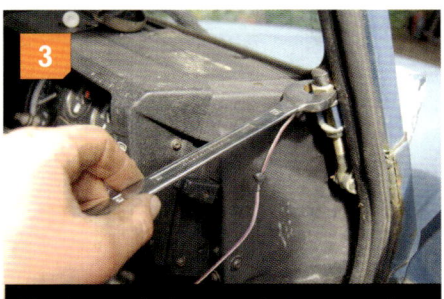

3 The inner windscreen clamp on each side is loosened (19mm AF), so the clamp can be swung down to access the outer mount screw.

If the mounting screw (Pozidriv No.3 head) is tight, use a spanner on the screwdriver shank for leverage. When removed, lever the hinged mount clear.

4

5 An M8 nut needs to be removed from each side of the cab beside the door jamb, using a 13mm spanner. These are the last points of cab attachment.

6 Upper seatbelt mounts are loosened from the truck cab using a 17mm socket wrench. This bolt may have an 18mm head on some Land Rovers.

7 The truck cab, with windscreen still attached, is lifted off the Land Rover as one assembly and set aside. It will be stored for future use.

Soft top conversion

Soft-top screen rail

WE HAVE converted this truck cab by removing the windscreen frame and replacing it with a spare frame from an old soft-top model. Normally, the existing screen frame would be retained and a soft-top header rail purchased and fitted on to hold the leading edge of the canvas. The standard windscreen frame on a hard top or pick-up model is drilled along the top of the frame for six fixing points, where it is bolted to the roof. The screen rail shown here from All Wheel Trim is drilled for four clamp fixing points, and has two slotted holes for attaching the clips from the canvas tensioning straps.

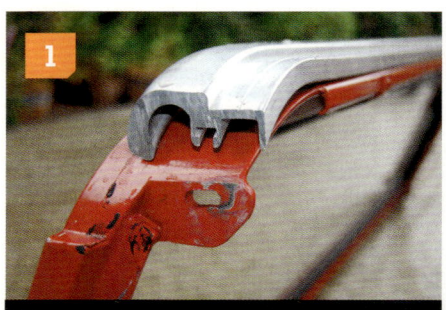

1 The standard hardtop type screen frame needs this All Wheel Trim rail fixed across the top of the frame to hold the front of the new canvas roof.

2 M8 bolts fitted in two slotted holes in the rail (coinciding with existing holes in frame), hold the rail in the correct location for drilling.

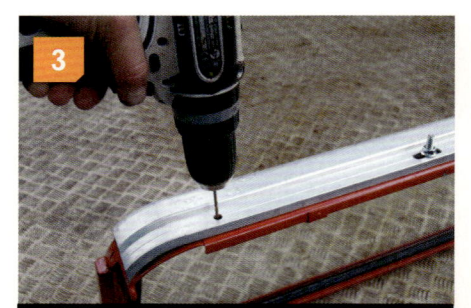

3 A small pilot hole of 3mm is drilled in the frame at the centre of each of the holes in the screen rail, before the rail is unbolted and removed.

4 At the pilot hole locations, an 8.5mm bolt hole is drilled for the 8mm clamp spindles. Extra 0.5mm allows spindle room movement when clamping.

5 The screen rail has a centre groove into which the seal is pulled through. The seal will stop the weather getting past the clamped hood.

6 Four special clamps are fitted across the screen rail. Two on each side of the vehicle, with the clamping handles pointing together when closed.

7 The clamp spindle is fitted through the frame from below...

8 ...with the spring between the frame and the rail, secured by a 6mm Nyloc nut and washer.

9 The windscreen frame is ready for use on a soft top Land Rover. The new screen rail could be painted, but it will be hidden by the hood.

Installing the hood frame

ON OUR VEHICLE, the replacement soft-top windscreen frame is fitted in place on the two hinged screen mounts, with a new gasket between the top of the mount and the frame to prevent any water getting in.

The frame is loosely clamped to prevent it from toppling forward. The front hoop is slotted into the tubes within the capping, near to the rear edge of the door and clamped down.

It has a panel attached that the door seal fits on to, and a recess for the hood side to be tucked into. An over-door panel is fitted to each side, secured with a pair of M6 bolts.

A standard Ninety or Defender 90 frame-set simply has a rear hoop, with side bars attached between the front and rear hoops and a middle top support between the two side bars. However on Steve's Land Rover we wanted to fit a roll bar incorporating seat belt mounts. All Wheel Trim call this a "seat belt bar" as it has not been officially tested as a roll bar, though it offers more protection than the standard hoop.

Once the seat belt bar is fitted in place, the side bar has to be adapted to suit the new arrangement. All Wheel Trim can supply the correct side rail sections, that do not need modification, but we had ordered the wrong parts on this occasion (our seat belt bar was a later addition). The modification was pretty straightforward and a hammer can be used to crush the ends of the rails, if a press is not available.

On a hard top model, at this stage the rear tail door would need to be removed and a drop-down tailgate fitted instead. Alternatively, the tail door can be cut and adapted to make a side-hinged rear tailgate, removing any wiring to the heated rear window and wiper motor.

1 As we are fitting a seat belt bar, this hole in the tub needs to be enlarged. This wooden plug allows the hole-saw to follow a pilot hole.

2 The hole-saw is used on the cordless drill to make a larger 40mm hole in the rear body tub capping, to allow the seat belt bar to be fitted.

3 The larger hole will be completely concealed by the seat belt bracket but it is good practice to clean off the remaining rough edges with a file.

4 The seat belt bar is fitted in position through the capping on each side and four 8mm holes are drilled to accommodate the fixing bolts.

5 In order to access one of the bolt holes on each side, for the seat belt bar stay, a discrete hole is made in the capping using a smaller 25mm hole-saw.

6 To get the seat belt bar stay bolted, it's easier to insert an M8 captive nut plate through the apertures, rather than trying to get a nut on.

7 The stay is fixed to the seat belt bar using an M10 cap bolt, which is fed through the bar on an Allen key and into the thread hole in the stay.

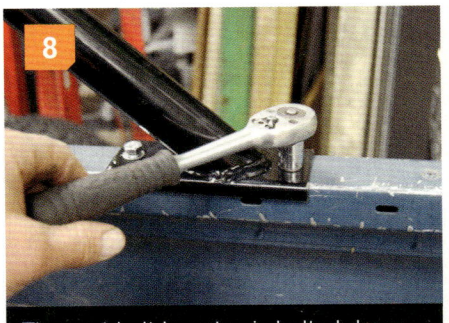

8 The seat belt bar stay is bolted down to the capping using M8 set screws into the captive nut plates. Spring washers prevent loosening.

9 The top mount for the seat belt is re-fitted to the new bracket on the seat belt bar, using the original UNF bolt, driven by a 17mm socket.

Soft top conversion

10 The rear hoop simply slots down into the existing tubes within the tub cappings on each side. No drilling is required – it's a perfect snug fit.

11 The hood hoops – front and rear – are fixed in place using these C clamps, bolted to the capping using an M8 bolt and nylock nut.

12 Since we have fitted the seat belt bar, our standard hood frame side bars need to be shortened, and the cut ends flattened again and drilled 6mm dia.

13 This is how the adapted side bars will look when fitted to the finished soft top conversion. Here the canvas hood is fitted with the sides rolled up.

14 The seat belt bar is supplied with load-spreading brackets which are riveted to the body sides, floor and rear bulkhead, using 5mm blind rivets.

Fitting the canvas

WITH THE hood frame installed, the canvas hood can be placed over it. The buckles, belts and fasteners are self-explanatory, but there are some additional small pieces to rivet in place to the rear body tub for anchoring and tying off the ropes.

Because the hood canvas is a natural fibre, the fitted hood will take up to three months to settle and be stretched into the right shape for the Land Rover, necessitating some tweaking of the ropes and buckles. Since this conversion was completed, Steve has been out enjoying his Ninety much more often.

1 The front edge of the canvas hood, with rubber piping sewn in, is slotted underneath the windscreen rail and carefully centred.

2 We're getting there... Now the screen rail is clamped on to the hood by handles across the width of the frame, behind the visors.

3 With the canvas hood clamped to the windscreen frame at the front, it is carefully pulled back over the frame on the Land Rover.

4 The canvas hood is loosely in place and the process of attaching and tightening the straps can begin, with some small hardware to be fitted too.

5 Two main straps stretch and tension the hood to the back of the Ninety, pulling against the windscreen clamp. These staples are fitted for each strap.

6 A horseshoe cleat is riveted to the corner of the rear body tub on each side of the Land Rover. Two ropes will be tied off on each of these.

7 At the front of the rear body tub on each side, a handed cleat is riveted in place as an anchor point for the side ropes to attach to.

8 The fitted hood will take up to three months to settle and be stretched into the right shape for the vehicle before final adjustment.

Perfect Defender Workshop

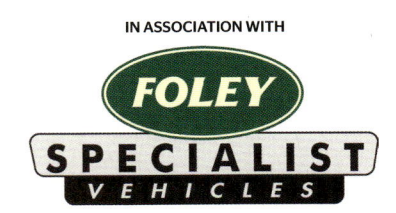

IN ASSOCIATION WITH
FOLEY SPECIALIST VEHICLES

YOUR IDEAL DEFENDER WORKSHOP

You and your Defender deserve a special work station. No matter what size your garage or shed, Ed Evans shows how to create the optimum service bay

DEFENDERS ARE amazingly DIY-friendly and, with a good workshop manual and reasonable facilities, most maintenance and all service jobs can be carried out in a home garage or workshop. Even if you entrust this work to a professional garage, your Defender still needs to be housed, and we always need tinkering space. All jobs, from tinkering to transmission removal, are so much more enjoyable in a practical workspace where tools can be easily found and stored and floor space and workbenches are uncluttered. Good use of space, and general organisation of tools and facilities goes a long way to making your workshop or garage a safe place to be, and that's especially important in a home workshop where family members might wander in to see how you're getting on.

The thrust of this feature is making the best of the real life facilities that most of us have – that might be a shed and a driveway, a garage attached to the house, or a purpose built Land Rover workshop. The home workshop featured here is designed specifically for Land Rovers, and while it's little more than the size of a double garage, it houses a 110 with room alongside to fully dismantle a 90. It's all achieved by using the correct storage systems, a few useful gadgets, roof modifications and strict organisation.

If you're building a new garage or workshop, or fitting out an existing facility, the tips and ideas here will help make the most of the space available, and that applies even if there's space only for a small shed with a bench inside. Tailoring the place for your Defender's needs means that fixing and modifying can be just as much fun as driving.

›

Perfect Defender Workshop

A kick stool makes an ideal seat for those jobs at half height. You can kick it out of the way because its on wheels, but sit or stand on it and it locks firmly to the floor. Ideal for safely reaching high shelves or leaning into the high engine bay.

THE FLEXIBLE LAYOUT
A lot of careful thought is needed in deciding where to locate the large essential items around the workshop. Ideally, we need a hefty bench, a strong storage cupboard and a large tool chest as a minimum. The larger these items are, the more efficiently we can work. More tool storage means space to organise the tools so they are easily located when needed, a bigger storage cupboard means parts can be stored neatly and found quickly, and fitting the largest bench means more space and organisation for a bench-top stripdown of components.

These units need to be strategically positioned with respect to the number and size of vehicles you intend to have in the workshop, and what sort of work you intend doing. For example, if the bench is fixed in position at the top end of the workshop, you'll need to be able to park the vehicle with the bonnet near the bench when working in the engine bay, or to reverse it up to the bench when working on the rear end. Placing the bench at the side is ideal for working on both ends of the vehicle, but that may not leave room to open the Defender's doors and squeeze past, or to get a second vehicle in.

There are tricks to help this situation, which we'll come to. But the best solution is to have the workbench, tool chest, storage cupboard and any other bulky items mounted on lockable castor wheels. That means whenever you're doing a lengthy job such as removing an axle, working with the side or tail door open, or even lifting an engine out, the Defender can be placed in the best working position and the wheeled bench, tool chest and other bulky items can be re-positioned around the workspace to suit.

DEFAULT WORK STATION
The garage needs a default work base – the place you naturally gravitate to when fixing parts, sorting stubborn threads, reading the workshop manual, opening packages of new components, and a safe place for your coffee mug. All your regular gadgets and consumables are here. It's the main bench with the vice, and anything might happen there from delicately soldering a cracked ECU connector to applying heat and heavy blows to some seized part held in the vice. So a built-in bench needs to be solidly built and fixed. This default bench needs to be kept clean and uncluttered if possible, which means storing all the

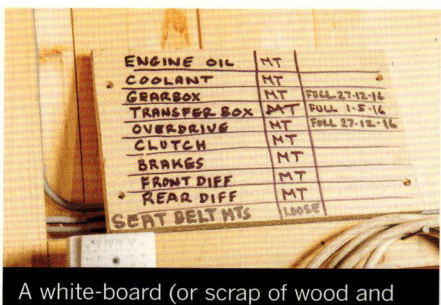

A white-board (or scrap of wood and marker pen) will help remind you of jobs, lists and part numbers.

A work lamp can be adjusted over and around the vice for fitting small screws and springs and checking gasket faces.

Moveable benches and toolboxes on castors means silver 90 can be maneuvered in and over to one side.

frequently used cleaners, lubricants, small tools, gloves and safety specs on shelves above or nearby where they are handy, but not affected by vibration from bench work.

MAXIMISING SPACE
In a small garage or workshop, access to a fixed bench may be difficult when the vehicle is inside, or perhaps there's no space for a permanent bench. In this case, a couple of drop-down work tops fitted along each side can provide a handy place for tools and parts as, and where, needed. Simply keep the worktops folded down for maximum space, and lift into position whichever one is nearest to where you are working.

CARING FOR THE FLOOR
A strong and level concrete floor is essential if the vehicle is to be safely raised and supported on stands. But when concrete is swept clean, dust will rise and settle all over the benches and the vehicle. Covering it with a wash of concrete sealing fluid is a cheap and quick way to prevent this and help it resist oil stains, but it will wear off after a few years. The best protection is a coat of workshop floor paint (light grey will

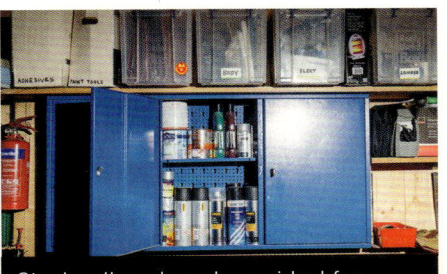

Steel wall cupboards are ideal for storing paints and other inflammable materials away from grinding sparks.

Workbench on lockable wheels means tools and parts a can be positioned close to where you are working.

A tool chest cholds far more tools than a series of wall racks, and the wheeled chest can be easily moved around.

"When space is tight, there are tricks to help this situation"

Useful space-saving fold down worktops can be made from kitchen worktop, hinged to the wall with a simple wood prop underneath.

Perfect Defender Workshop

WORKSHOP ESSENTIALS

- HEAVY-DUTY STORAGE CUPBOARD
- ENGINE CRANE
- WELDING SET
- MOVEABLE WORK BENCH
- TROLLEY JACK
- CAR CREEPER
- HEAVY-DUTY AXLE STANDS
- LEVEL CONCRETE FLOOR

STORAGE BOXES FOR LIGHTWEIGHT ITEMS ON HIGH SHELVES
WINDOW VENTILATION
SLIMLINE STEEL WALL CUPBOARDS FOR PAINTS AND CONSUMABLES
WORK LAMP OVER FIXED BENCH
FIRE EXTINGUISHER & FIRST AID KIT
WHEELED TOOL CHEST

Perfect Defender Workshop

"Before ordering your garage measure height of your vehicle"

spread light around) or interlocking floor tiles which are more comfortable to walk and stand on, though may be prohibitively expensive.

BUILDING A NEW WORKSHOP OR GARAGE
Standard domestic garages and workshops may not have the height above the entrance door to allow a Defender through with a roof rack, high profile or oversize tyres or a suspension lift. Before ordering, physically measure the vehicle's actual height. Also consider whether there is sufficient headroom in the workshop to jack the vehicle, or to lift an engine out, bearing in mind that even with a high roof, the roof trusses may need to be spaced to suit your lifting requirements.

Lifting an engine is a difficult and dangerous job without the correct equipment. A lifting girder can be incorporated into a new brick or blockwork garage, but you'll need an engineer to calculate the size needed, and the structure supporting the beam. Otherwise, and for all timber buildings, the best option is a folding engine crane, but confirm the capacity with the manufacturer, bearing in mind it may need to lift the combined weight of the engine and transmission during a rebuild, though these can always be moved individually.

In small garages it may be necessary to work with the vehicle only half in the garage to allow space around, say, the engine compartment, so ensure the main doorway is wide enough for you to walk in and out while the vehicle is part way in.

> The height of the entrance door must allow for larger tyre size and roof rack/tent, if fitted. Roof shape and position of trusses needs to facilitate the vehicle being lifted.

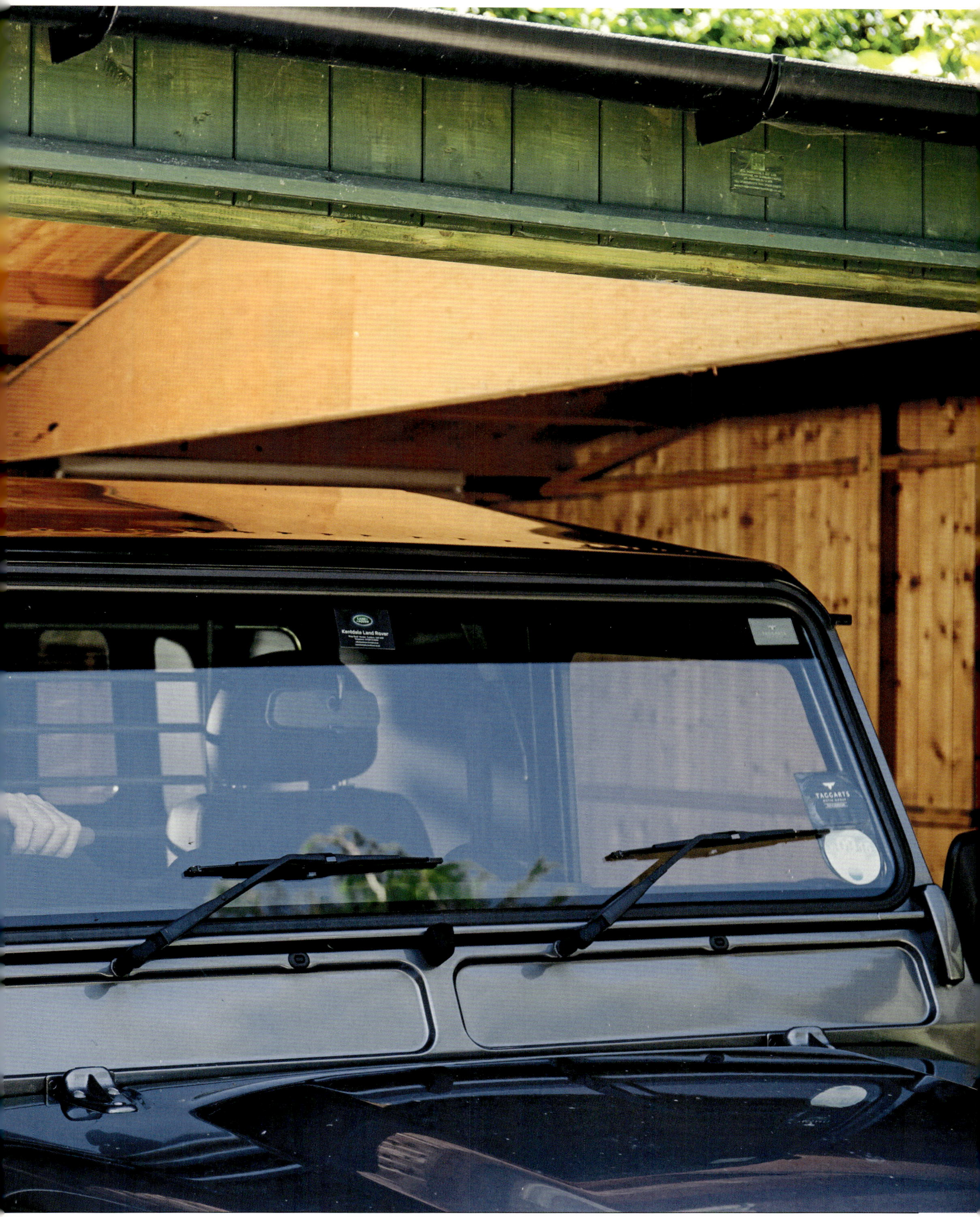
Kentdale Land Rover
TAGGARTS

Perfect Defender Workshop

You need these. Clockwise from top left: fire extinguisher, grinding and welding masks, barrier cream, ear defenders, first aid kit, safety specs, RCD, mobile phone, particle mask, welding gloves, lightweight gloves, cap for underneath.

A bench electric grinder is useful for sharpening tools and many other duties. Keep thick gloves and eye protection to hand, plus water for quenching hot items.

KEEPING EVERYONE SAFE
Safety is not just for the person doing the work. In a home workshop any member of the family, or the dog or cat, might call in to see how your work is progressing.

They might not share our familiarity of the dangers of tripping over electrical leads, slipping in an oil spillage or looking at a welding spark.

While adults can be told of the risks, kids and pets may not listen but there's an easy way to protect them.

Simply fit a latch high up on the door where kids can't reach, so they have to knock to get in. Never lock the door from inside because, if you have an accident, you might need someone to get inside quickly.

SAFETY ESSENTIALS
- Keep a mobile phone in the top pocket of your overalls where it won't be damaged. Then, if you injure yourself, you can call for help.
- Wear quality overalls that protect from oils and sparks.
- Don't even pick up an angle grinder without first donning heavy gloves and a full face visor.
- Wear all recommended safety equipment for welding and painting, and ensure adequate ventilation.
- Where dust might arise (brakes, body repairs) wear a particle mask.
- Keep safety glasses handy and wear them whenever sparks or small objects such as springs might fly, or when fluids may be released.
- NEVER work under a vehicle supported by a jack. Jack it up and place axle stands and ramps under, chock the wheels and check the stability before even reaching under. As a fail safe, put a spare wheel or ramp under the chassis, too.
- When working on tight bolts underneath your Land Riover, take care not to dislodge the vehicle from its supports when heaving.
- Wear steel-capped work shoes at all times when working on your Land Rover.
- Plugging electrical tools in via a circuit breaker helps protect from the potential risk of electrocution if a defect arises.
- Keep electrical mains leads clear of jacks, axle stands and heavy parts – anything that might cut into them.

"Always keep a mobile phone in the top pocket of your overalls"

KBX UPGRADES

Designed & Manufactured in the UK

Evolve & Enhance with KBX

www.kbxupgrades.co.uk

- Grille & Lamp Surrounds
- Lower Splitter Grilles
- Hi-Force Wing Top Air Intakes
- Sport Side Air Intakes
- Lamp guards
- NAS Lamp Mounts (Dual & Triple)

AB Parts can supply Genuine, OEM & Aftermarket parts & Accessories for any Defender-World Wide
Phone or Fax 01388 812777

Water leaks cured

PART 1
HOW TO CURE LEAKS

DEFENDER BODYWORK is renowned for suffering water ingress. It need not be like that though, and it is possible to get them dry inside without a lot of expense, once you've found out where the water is coming in.

Utility Land Rovers suffer leaks because of the way they are designed and built, and partly due to the way they're used. On Series Land Rovers, little attention was paid to the passage of water over the body, and the modern Defender suffers from this design aspect that it inherited.

Any of the metal roofs can leak, and it is ironic that a soft top in good condition is usually the driest type of Defender to own. The Meccano-type onstruction is one of Defender's strengths in that the basic design is readily adaptable and can go from hard top to truck cab and canvas tilt with relative ease. The downside is the leak potential at the joints.

Most ordinary cars find their way to the breaker's yard after ten years' use. The door seals and window rubbers are fine for this life, but the 110 was launched over 30 years ago and most still have their original rubber seals that are well past their best. This is exacerbated by off-road use which flexes the shells, and carrying heavy loads on roof racks can damage old hardened sealant.

Defenders leak in different ways according to whether they are stationary

Some folk accept water leaking into their Defenders as inevitable. But it doesn't have to be that way as we explain in this special feature...

TOOLS REQUIRED:
Water hose and variable nozzle, torch, trim removal tools

TIME:
1-3 hours

COST:
Time only

DIFFICULTY RATING:
1/5

or driving. The causes and the mechanisms of the water ingress are different, though some of the former are only noticed with the latter.

We'll deal with stationary leaks first.

Leak test
Identifying the leak is not always easy because water travels, and a leak at the back might manifest itself as a wet front seat. A garden hose outside and a torch inside are useful diagnostic aids, spraying water onto the problem areas and watching for water coming in.

Use a rain-type of pattern, falling as if to mimic rain – a direct jet will push water through places that will not leak in even heavy rain. You probably won't find massive gaps. In fact, small gaps can move more water because capillary action comes into play as well as gravity. Be careful not to confuse condensation with leaks, because even a dry interior will form condensation overnight on bare metal parts such as the roof.

Land Rover recommended using Dum Dum putty to seal leaks, but this is a throwback to the fifties, and production was discontinued in 2011. Modern alternatives are available, but brushable seam sealer or PU adhesive sealer such as Tiger Seal work much better. We will cover their application later.

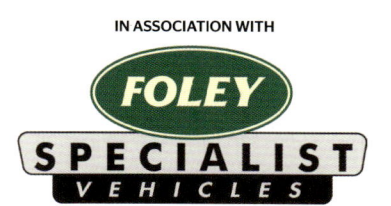

How the water gets in

1 This split in the upper front corner of the door seal, together with missing sealant, will let the rain water pour into the inside of the vehicle.

2 If the door's window frame is not tight on the seal, it will leak past the seal where shown, about half way down the window.

Doors and windows

Starting at the front, the most common cause is through the door seal. Water from the roof usually runs into the vehicle about half way down the screen pillar. It can be cured with a new seal or adjustment of the door frame to compress the seal a bit more. The seal will also leak if it is damaged or incorrectly fitted. They only cost around £50 for all the three seals on a three-door and about £75 for a five-door station wagon, and this is money well spent.

Water also comes in a bit higher, where the screen lip joins the roof lip to carry the rubber seal. The factory used Dum Dum putty with black tape to cover the joint and stop water going over the top of the seal. If the vehicle has been taken apart or the seal has been pulled off, the tape will often come away and not be replaced, and so the joint leaks.

The doors can leak into the vehicle if the plastic diaphragm behind the door card is damaged or not sealed properly, or if the drainage holes in the door bottom are blocked. This also applies to the second row of doors on five-door models. The rear side windows leak on these as well. The drain slot in the bottom gets blocked, so they flood. The rubber sealing strips get damaged and leak between the frame and body side, especially at the top. It is not unknown for these to have been refitted upside down, in which case water pours in.

The early type of screen hinges don't tend to leak, but from 1992 onward the one-piece bracket types can channel water straight into the vehicle. It comes through the bulkhead through the lower fixing bolt tube if their sealing gaskets are damaged in any way. (The tube is made oversize to accommodate production dimension variations and it's worth filling

3 Despite the condition of this screen seal, the windscreen might not leak whilst stationary, but the roof joint above will because the sealer is missing.

4 This condensation barrier helps keep leaked water out of the door casing, but only if it is undamaged and is sealed all round.

5 This bracket on the bulkhead has a damaged gasket, so it channels water into the interior past the bulkhead fixing bolt.

| Water leaks cured

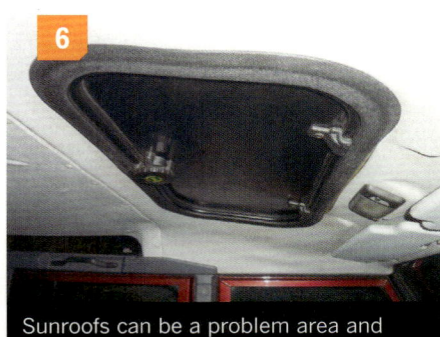

6 Sunroofs can be a problem area and usually leak past the seal between the frame and the glass, due to deterioration or poor adjustment.

7 Alpine window seals become hard and brittle with age. Replacing them with new seals is the best solution, rather than trying to patch them with sealant.

8 All the roof seams can leak. This front crosswise seam with its lap joint is a favourite, though the front-to-back seams are also prone.

9 On this roof panel seam, a long strip of sealant is missing. Water pours through this joint when the vehicle is standing, due to capillary action.

10 These rear vents were a terrible source of water ingress. Water flowed forward on the cant rail, dropping down about six inches back from the windscreen.

11 This later clinched-style of roof (looking down into the gutter) is better than the old riveted one, but it still leaks if the sealer is cracked or missing.

12 The split rubber seals along the bottom of this side window, and debris blocking the drain slots, means water floods into the station wagon rear body.

13 Water can also enter the body interior through a rivet hole, especially if the rivet is not the sealed type, or if it has become loose.

The mastic and the joint tape behind the seal are missing on this station wagon rear body-to-hardtop joint. It's not surprising that water pours in here. **14**

We can see daylight through this rear body tub-to-hardtop joint because of slight damage to the hardtop flange. Water runs down the side and pours straight in. **15**

the void with mastic, even if they don't leak yet.) New gaskets and/or just slackening them off and applying sealer before tightening, will cure the leaks though. The gaskets cost around £5 per set. Also check the bolts for corrosion.

Roof leaks
A leaking sunroof can sometimes be fixed with a new seal or by adjustment to the hinges and locking mechanism. A desperate measure is to seal it permanently shut with mastic, which is crude but effective. They rarely leak from the joint where they are fitted to the roof skin, but it is possible.

The Alpine window rubbers age with UV degradation. You can reseal them if you remove the locking strip and introduce screen sealant or mastic to the glass side and the metal side before refitting the locking strip. But if they are hard and brittle, it is best to renew them at around £30 a pair. A supple new rubber should not need any sealant. They also leak on the joint, especially if they have been cut short and shrunk back a little.

The roof can leak where the top meets the gutter. The revised design from the early nineties onwards is less prone than the earlier type, but not immune. There is a bead of sealant along the outer edge which will leak if damaged or cracked with age and, because the whole roof is draining down this part, it ships in a lot of water. It drops into the inner cant rail, and the only escape for it is at the front.

It drops down near the windscreen if the vehicle is facing downhill, or it gushes over when the brakes are first used and ends up on the driver's knee.

Water may also leak down where the two plastic studs hold the headlining up to the cant rail, especially if they are damaged or missing.

They can also leak where the flat panels are joined together, and are especially prone where the front sloping section of the roof meets the flat rear section.

The scrolled lip at the front also leaks if the sealant is old or damaged. With all these issues, it's a matter of finding the problem and applying mastic to the inside when dry.

Using a roof rack will make the roof more prone to leaking because it will flex more, and the gutter fixing damages the sealer here. The legs hold water in the gutter, giving it more opportunity to find its way inside.

The most serious roof leak is through the ventilators fitted on some models to the back of the roof above the tail door. These pour into the vehicle and the water sits on the inside of the cant rail, making its way forwards and pouring through the headlining fixing holes over the driver's or front passenger's knee. They were fitted for a period from the mid 1980s to the early 1990s, though they can show up on a vehicle of any age that has had its original configuration changed. The only fix is to seal them totally from the inside. Glassfibre mat and resin is a good solution, as is PU sealant. Silicone does not tend to last for long.

Body sides
The body sides can leak at the rubber waist seal and also where the side meets the top. These are best sealed with PU sealant. The seals are technically easy to replace, but it is a long job and not guaranteed to work if the body is distorted.

The rear door seals can leak where the hard top meets the body tub. A bit of mastic in the gap and some tape over it before refitting the seal sorts these out.

The pop rivets in the body sides leak, too. Sometimes they are loose, and replacing them sorts it out. Use a sealed-type pop rivet. Otherwise a bit of mastic on the inside works wonders.

Take some time to explore and identify the water entry points and leak paths, then turn the page and learn how to fix them for good...

16 *Despite the damage at the joint, sealing it from the inside is still possible and is quicker and easier than fitting a new seal.*

17 *These are the best products to seal the gaps. The PU sealant comes in black, grey or white, but can be painted over if your roof is another colour.*

18 *An assistant using a hose set like this to mimic falling rain is the best way to find the leaks. Direct pressure is no help as it will force its way past good seals.*

Water leaks cured

PART 2

HOW TO KEEP THE WATER OUT

Preventing rain water from getting into your Defender is a quick and simple job if you follow LRM's step-by-step guide

WET INTERIORS are often regarded as normal with Defender bodywork. It need not be so however, and great improvements can be made for relatively little expenditure of money and time. I can't guarantee a perfectly dry interior, but we can have a good go at achieving one. There are two types of leaks: those coming in when the vehicle is stationary and those on the move. We are dealing with curing the stationary leaks here.

In wet weather a 110 may have to shed more than 400 litres of water per day from its outer roof skin and, if just one per cent enters the vehicle, that's four litres a day. As most Defenders are not that wet inside, we're only dealing with small quantities of water in relation to the amount they shed. But that small amount permeates the seats and carpets, producing an unpleasant damp interior and misted windows.

There are two methods of entry for water and we need to understand the mechanics of them. The main one is simply leaking through an air gap. The main area of concern is the front screen pillar because, if the vehicle is on a slight side slope, most of that daily 400 litres runs over one of the screen pillar-to-door areas, and usually some leaks in. The other method is by capillary action through small gaps where flat panels are joined together. The roof top is made up of seams that can leak in this way. The water is drawn into the joint by surface tension and drops down inside. This does not bring in much volume, but any that can be stopped is worthwhile, especially if it prevents it falling on your head.

TOOLS REQUIRED:
PU adhesive/sealant tube and applicator gun. Black, grey or white, as appropriate, Duct (Gaffer) tape, Door seals as required specific to your Land Rover's VIN, White spirit, scraper, craft knife, Small hammer and simple hand tools, Hot air gun/hair dryer

TIME:
Up to 2 hours

COST:
From £40

DIFFICULTY RATING:
2/5

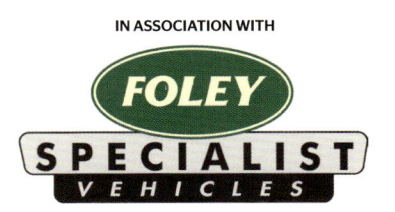

Tackling the roof seams and gutters

THE ROOF needs inspecting along all the seams to identify areas where the sealant is cracked or broken, but don't disturb good areas. Use a sharp tool to scrape out the old sealant from the joints; this will probably open the joint slightly. Use a hot air gun to drive moisture from the joint and to pre-warm the panel by carefully using a paint-stripping gun on low heat, or a hair dryer. Do not use a naked flame blowlamp because the sealants are inflammable.

The replacement sealant is polyurethane panel adhesive and sealer. It is made by several companies, and Tiger Seal is a well-known brand. Choose black, grey or white, to suit the roof colour. You can paint over it when dry, so a small touch-up brush can disguise the repair. One tube is sufficient to seal most roofs.

Work the sealant into the joint with the end of the nozzle and push it with a vinyl-gloved finger to avoid skin contact.

Now gently tap the roof skin back into place with a light hammer or mallet. Remember it is soft metal. I use a light panel hammer which has a large surface area. Sealant will exude into, and out of, the joint.

Leave it for about 45 minutes and then wipe away the excess with a rag liberally soaked in white spirit.

In the roof gutters, rake out any loose sealant and blow-dry the area with the hot air gun. Trim the nozzle back on the sealant tube so it will leave a bead about 10mm wide. Wipe it into the gutter using your index finger in a glove. Wipe it carefully as you don't want to draw the sealant out of the gap where it needs to be. You will not be cleaning this joint afterwards as it is out of sight, so do it as neatly as you can.

That is all that is needed to have the roof seams and gutter water-tight.

1 This is the main roof joint that leaks. It's the cross vehicle seam at the point where the flat roof angles down to the front.

2 Gently prising the joint open will allow the scraper to get inside and remove more of the failed sealant from between the panels.

3 Using a fine nozzle, force as much sealant as possible into the gap between the panels, and keep working it to force it in further.

4 Your finger is the best tool in the box to push more of the sealant into the gap. Vinyl gloves are thin, yet will protect your skin from chemicals.

5 On the gutter, remove only the damaged sealant. It is usually caused by carrying a roof rack at some point in the past.

6 Gently tap the layers of metal closer, forcing sealant in, and out. After 45 minutes max, remove excess with rag and white spirit before it sets.

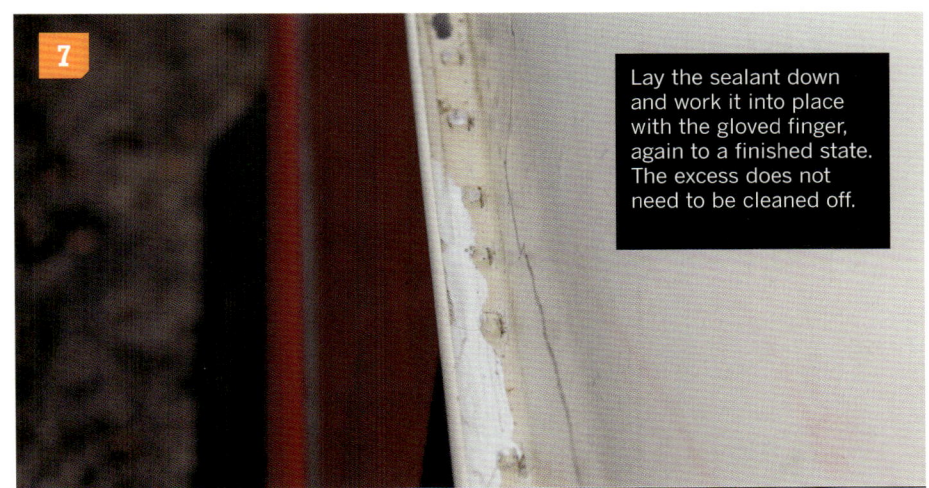

7 Lay the sealant down and work it into place with the gloved finger, again to a finished state. The excess does not need to be cleaned off.

Water leaks cured

Door seals

DOOR FRAME and bottom seals are available from Britpart stockists, quoting your VIN or chassis number. The main sections of the front seals simply pull off, revealing the flanged edge. There are four body joints on this flange which need sealing before the new seal is fitted. But first, get the new seal out of its bag and lay it out on the bonnet so the rubber relaxes a little and its proper shape is regained. The four joints are: where the tub meets the body side panel; the body side panel to roof; the roof to screen; and the screen to bulkhead.

The edges need to line up, and the body side panel can be moved on its mount slightly by removing the fixing nut and replacing it when the side is in the correct place. Note the washer with the offset hole that is fitted to allow you to align properly. If this is not enough, then gentle bending of the flange is required, as is the case for the other three joints.

With the flange lined up, the rubber seal will fit over them but it leaves a gap at the back, and water will come straight through. The answer developed by Rover, and still used by Land Rover, is to tape the joint and use mastic to bulk up the tape in the gap. The tape needs to be fabric-reinforced, such as duct or gaffer tape. The original mastic was Eldro's Dum Dum putty, no longer available. A similar alternative is Strip Caulk made by 3M, but Tiger Seal is just as effective as a semi-flexible bulking agent for the tape.

First dry the joint to ensure the tape sticks. Cut a strip of tape about 60mm long with scissors from the roll. Don't tear it, as it distorts the tape and it may not fit inside the rubber. Place it on the back side of the joint and press down hard. The tape adhesive is pressure-sensitive and needs to be pressed hard to stick. Squirt enough mastic to fill the gap onto the tape and then fold the rest of the tape over to cover it and stick to the outside of the flange and the face of the body. Repeat on the other seams.

Fit the door seal by pushing it well into one of the top corners, then the other corner and the top section in between. Push on by hand, and gently tap it into place if it is a bit reluctant. Use a hammer shaft but do NOT use the metal end as it will distort the seal. Run down the rear edge next, feeding it into place as you go, and then fit the front. Take care to follow the rounded section below the waist.

The door's lower strip is now replaced by simply drilling out the securing rivets and riveting the new strip on with 3/16th [three-sixteenths] inch pop rivets.

Shutting the door reveals how well it fits. The lock striker may need adjusting to get the outer door skin fitting flush with the rear tub or B-post. Once this is right, check the front of the door. I use a piece of polythene cut from the seal packaging. Trap it in the door when you shut it, and pull. If it is difficult to pull out, then the pressure is fine. But if it slips out easily, it will not fully seal.

There is no inward adjustment available, but you can shim the door-end of the hinges with extra gaskets to put pressure on the seal if needed. The critical area is the part adjacent to the screen pillar, and here it is a matter of gently twisting the door frame to tighten it up. Go easy – it is better to bend it in increments than having to unbend it.

Jam the middle with a piece of wood and support the bottom with your knee and leg, and gently push on the top. You will probably not feel it move but it will have done so, so keep checking it before you go too far. The critical area is about a third of the way down the screen from the top. Concentrate on getting this right and the rest will probably then be okay.

> "Wet interiors are regarded as normal. It need not be so"

1 Worn out door seal needs replacing, but the four body joints (arrowed) need sealing first, or your effort and expense is wasted.

2 The old seal was hard and split, and had broken at the corner joints, so was well past the point at which it should have been changed.

3 New Britpart seal is more supple, but needs a few minutes out of its packet to relax and regain shape. Save the bag, as you will need it.

4 The seal flange needs to be aligned perfectly before fitting seal. This one can be adjusted by loosening the roof side and moving it over ...

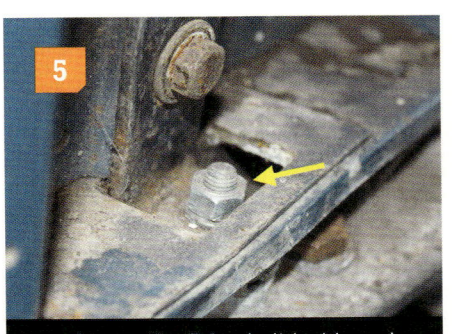

5 ... so loosen the fixing bolt inside and remove it with its washer. Push the top over and refit the washer, split washer and nut ...

6 ... noting the special washer has a shaped hole in it so that it will fit comfortably over the pin in many positions.

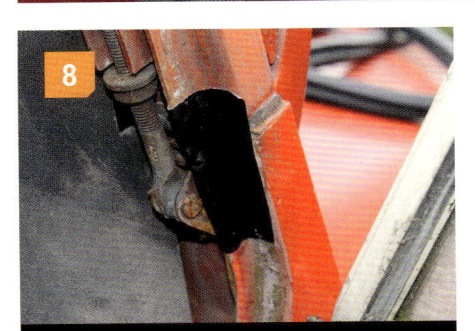

7 If you cannot move the panel all the way, bend the flange slightly to line it up using a tool like this panel hammer, or simple pliers.

8 Dry the area and stick a 60mm length of tape to the back of the flanged edge. Run some sealant into the gap as required.

8 Fold the tape over and gently work the sealant to evenly fill the void. Use pressure on the areas in contact with metal to make the tape stick well.

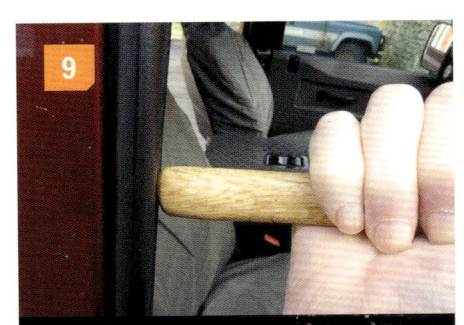

9 Push the seal into place and tap it home with the hammer shaft. Don't be tempted to use the metal end or you will ruin the seal.

10 The lower (door bottom) seal is simply drilled off and refitted with rivets. There is a metal section within it pre-drilled at the appropriate spacing.

77

Water leaks cured

11 Shut the door on a piece cut from the packaging. It should be quite difficult to pull out if sealed at the lower end of the screen.

12 The top pulls out easily and offers no resistance here, so the door needs tweaking to make it fit better, as this is the critical area.

13 Jam a piece of wood against the bulkhead and the door just below window level in such a way that it holds the door bottom ...

14 then push gently on the top of the frame. It takes less effort to bend than you'd imagine, so go easy and don't go too far.

15 This time it passes the tug test and is tight enough on the seal. It might loosen as the seal acclimatises, needing further adjustment.

16 A well-fitting door with panels in alignment – don't look for perfection. If you want knife-edge gaps buy a Freelander or Discovery 3.

17 A bucket of water thrown on to the roof shows why this part is leak-prone – it all runs down over the door seal by the windscreen.

Tail door

THE TAIL DOOR'S main seal is fairly standard but the bottom seal varies, so order it quoting your VIN. Unscrew the lower plate to renew this bottom seal. Remove the main seal by starting in one lower corner and working around the aperture. The seal is refitted after taping the four gaps and reshaping the flange, which is prone to damage when loading cargo. There is little adjustment available on the door, other than to move the lock striker inwards slightly to align the door skin with the rear of the tub. If the hinge side is proud, fit washers under the hinge bolts to push the door into the aperture, making it tighter on the seal.

1 The rear lower seal is renewed by unscrewing the fixing strip along the floor and pulling it up to reveal the old seal.

2 The rear seal flange is usually damaged and needs to be bent back into shape before you begin fitting the replacement seal.

3 The four tail door joints are sealed and taped as before. The big gap to the side needs a plug of sealer when filling the tape.

4 Start fitting the new seal in the lower corner on the hinge side. This seal fits close to the bodywork with no gap, so should be waterproof.

Rear fittings

1 If you can see daylight (arrowed) through this side panel to tub joint, it will leak. A new seal might not work if there is body distortion.

2 It's quicker to squirt PU sealant into the gap from the inside and the result is guaranteed. The white sealant is not visible from outside.

REAR VENTS on early roofs need to be sealed too. Remove the headlining end piece from inside, then clean and blow-dry the vents. Run a bead of sealant around the outer edge and fill the vent slots with sealant, smoothing it with a gloved finger. The sealant will be hidden when the headlining is refitted.

> NEXT STEPS...

YOUR VEHICLE should now stay dry when standing in the heaviest rain.
But driving it on the road brings more opportunities for water ingress, which we'll tackle next...

3 If you have roof vents like this, they will leak. The water travels forward inside and comes down towards the front of the front doors.

4 This is the inside view of the vent, showing the tell-tale sign of water running down the rear panel and into the inside rail channel.

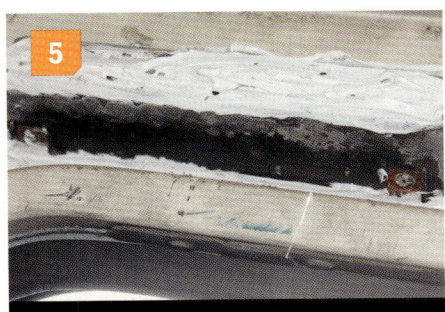

5 Run sealant around and fill the vents using a gloved finger to push it in. Interior trim will cover it, or use black with a smooth finish.

Water leaks cured

PART 3

WHY DO DEFENDERS LEAK?

The more we drive, the more rain and spray gets blasted inside. This is how it happens...

SO FAR IN this series, we've looked at how rain water gets inside a Defender while it's parked up, and how to cure those leaks. But the speed and energy that comes with driving the Defender introduces opportunities for even more leaks. Most of these leaks are localised to the bulkhead area and, unfortunately, most water ingress ends up joining the front seat occupants. But with a little bit of money, a few hours spent and some inexpensive tools, most of these leaks can be fixed.

Water usually gets in when underway in a horizontal direction. The falling rain will try to enter the structure, rather than make its way around it. The flat front of the body and windscreen does it no favours in this respect, and even a few degrees of curvature in the design, such as on a Discovery, would significantly reduce water ingress. In the case of Defenders, the water would rather go through your bulkhead than be forced to move tangentially and go around it. On the other hand, the airstream carries the water straight on down the side of the body while it gently falls downward, rather than forcing it through the side door and window seals.

The best diagnostic tool is an assistant with a garden hose. This time, use a powerful jet applied horizontally on to the bodywork from the front to mimic the vehicle at speed colliding with falling rain. A lot of force is needed because you are mimicking the effect of the water hitting the vehicle at speeds of up to 70 miles per hour.

Do not spray it on door seals from the side because they will probably leak under such an onslaught, whereas in operation they will not.

You don't want to be trying to fix things that are not a genuine problem. Spray from the front, down the sides at an angle to represent the actual path of water. A pen type torch is handy to look for the water ingress points on the inside.

TOOLS REQUIRED:
Water hose and variable nozzle, Torch

TIME:
Up to two hours

COST:
Time only

DIFFICULTY RATING:
1/5

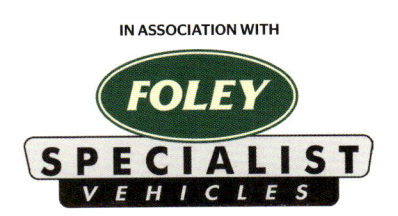

Roof and Screen

These splits around the curve of the screen seal, or sealant missing from the screen to roof joint, will let water in whilst driving.

THE TOP of the roof does not tend to leak when driving because little of it is presented to the wet airstream. But the top seam will leak where the roof angle changes just above the front seats.

The roof-to-screen frame joint will leak if damaged, as does the rubber screen seal if split in the corners. It's worth renewing the screen seal if split where the rubber bends. The water comes in on top of the headlining and makes it damp, but also flows down and drops off along the door opening.

You rneed to ascertain where water is coming from, as a leak at the front or at the back of the roof ends up showing at the same point as a leaking door seal. You obviously need to fix the one that is leaking, but you might have three sources of water showing at this point.

Replacing the seal is advisable as it is not expensive or difficult to do and will cure the leak as well as improve the vehicle's appearance

The roof seal is made up of two parts. There is a sponge rubber strip between the roof and windscreen which is held as it is bolted together, and the outside is finished with a mastic bead. This bead is often cracked or has chunks missing, and the inner seal cannot cope on its own. Whilst it is possible to replace the inner seal by unbolting and lifting the roof, just repairing the outer one will usually fix the leak problem with less effort.

As for the screen rubber, replacement is obviously the best solution as they are not expensive. The rubber is a one-piece component which makes the screen difficult to fit. If your glass has any damage whatsoever it will almost certainly crack when it is reinstalled or possibly even when removed, and so the job escalates and becomes expensive if the screen has to be renewed.

If this is the case, then raking out the debris in the cracks and filling neatly with black PU sealant is the best compromise.

Bulkhead

THE DOOR to screen seals tend not to leak whilst moving because the air flow carries the water past them and off down the sides, even if the seals are quite poor. The lower screen-to-bulkhead seals are another ingress point, but it is rare for them to leak here and any water getting in may be confused with leaks from the screen hinges or brackets, which leak whilst stationary or when driving.

The later fixed screen brackets are the worst offenders but can be fixed with inexpensive gaskets and PU sealant. The skinned sponge rubber seals on the vent flaps are usually mis-aligned, damaged or even totally missing, and water will pour through these when driving if not attended to. They cost about £20 for a pair, and replacing them is probably the biggest improvement you can make on a cost to benefit ratio.

Corrosion is common along this area, and any tiny gaps or poor repairs in the bulkhead will allow more water to enter the structure, speeding up the corrosion process before it exits on to the floor of the vehicle. If the footwells have been replaced or repaired at any time, they need to be sealed along the welds with brushed-on seam sealant, to prevent water entering.

There is a rubber seal between the bonnet's rear edge and the bulkhead which, if missing, lets water drop down on to the electrics, the pedals and the heater, all of which may let it through into the footwells – especially if the grommets for the wiring and speedometer cable are damaged or missing. The seal needs to be properly fitted so it forces the water to travel sideways and drop on to the top of the wing and then go off around the side of the body. They only cost around £10 to replace, making it very cost-effective.

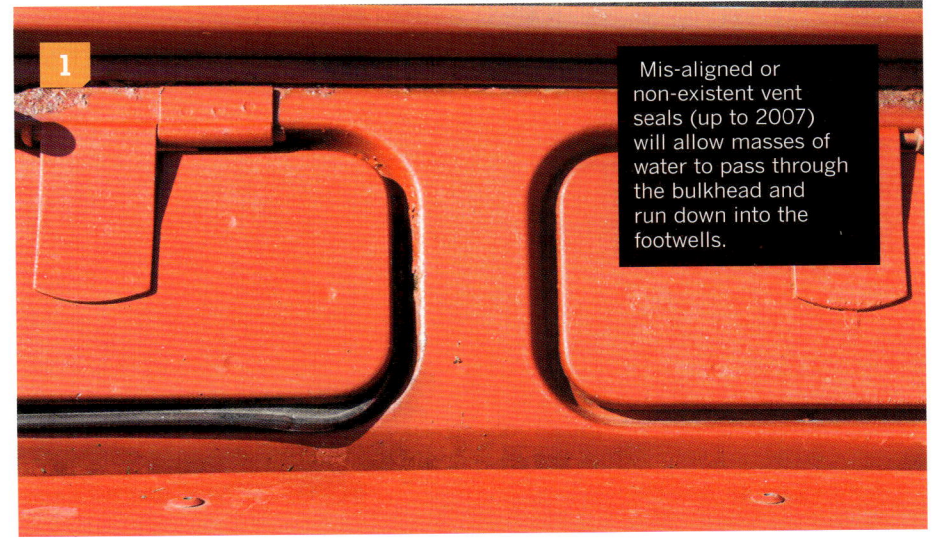

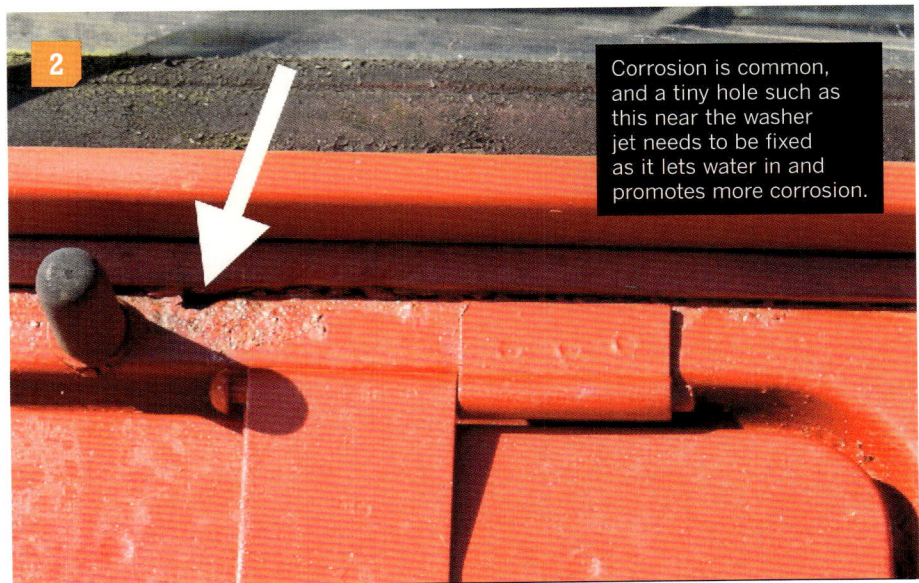

1 *Mis-aligned or non-existent vent seals (up to 2007) will allow masses of water to pass through the bulkhead and run down into the footwells.*

2 *Corrosion is common, and a tiny hole such as this near the washer jet needs to be fixed as it lets water in and promotes more corrosion.*

81

Water leaks cured

The pedal boxes have rubber seals underneath which are often damaged or missing. These seals are not expensive to buy, but are tedious to fit because you have to dismantle the hydraulic systems. External sealing is easier and possibly better for these.

The wiring loom, throttle and speedometer drive cable run through rubber grommets which are often missing, damaged or not fitted properly. They can be replaced but, as long as they are not missing, simply applying sealant is the best way forward, as with any other small holes in the bulkhead caused by corrosion or poor repairs.

Water will leak past the seal between the heater casing and the bulkhead, especially if the drain is blocked, so that water entering via the wing-mounted air intake vent can't escape.

Water entering the engine bay between the bonnet and wing top will also impinge on the heater box, and can pass down by the matrix if the sponge sealant strip is missing from here.

Leaked water tends to evaporate on the hot matrix and enter the vehicle as vapour, but condenses again when it is inside the colder vehicle structure.

The seal between the floor plates and bulkhead can leak when driving through splashes if not properly jointed. I don't necessarily mean river crossings, as splashes from puddles will do it just as easily. You really need to lift the floor plate and seal with mastic before bolting them down again, but brushing seam sealer on the outside works just as well and is less time consuming.

The handbrake and gear lever rubber seals will also let water pass in if they are not fitted properly, and they let a lot of mechanical noise in as well.

The engine cooling fan cowl needs to be in place, otherwise the engine fan will pick up water and throw it against the back of the bulkhead. The fan cowl is an important safety feature and also improves the fan's cooling effect.

3 The sponge seal between screen and bulkhead rarely leaks, but the hinge fixings do. They can easily pass a massive amount of water through the fixing holes.

4 The gaskets under these hinges are inexpensive and, if applied with sealant, will stop water coming in behind the speedo and wiper motor.

Other Bodywork

STATION WAGON rear side windows leak when moving. The culprit here is the vertical seal between the glass panes. Water travelling along the glass drops into a low pressure area and falls down into the bottom channel. If the seal is not touching, or missing, the water comes straight into the vehicle. It should drop down and out through the drain holes, but the muck and moss that usually is present here blocks them and so the water runs off onto the wheel box on the inside. Cleaning them and sorting the seal out usually fixes this. The opening sunroof on Station Wagons does not tend to leak whilst driving as the natural movement of water is at right angles to the point of entry, so it tends to pass it by. The rear end does not tend to leak when driving as it is a low pressure area, meaning water and air will be sucked out of the rear seals, rather than leak in.

So if you focus attention on the imaginary one metre wide slice from half way down the front wings to half way along the front doors, which includes the bulkhead, you will cure most of the leaks that occur when driving your Defender or Series Land Rover either in rain or through water.

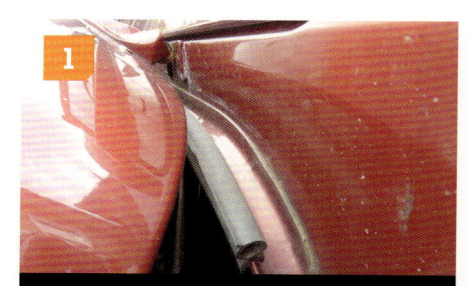

1 The rubber seal under the rear of the bonnet deflects water away from the front of the bulkhead, so it needs replacing if damaged or missing.

2 This tiny gap in the speedometer cable grommet, and the drilled hole to the right, will allow water to get into the bulkhead and the vehicle itself.

3 The rubber gasket from the bulkhead under the pedal boxes is obviously damaged. They're difficult to replace, but external sealant will work.

4 This tiny hole in the inner wing does not lead into the bulkhead structure, and so can be ignored as a potential route for water to get into the vehicle.

5 The throttle cable passes through the bulkhead and will allow water to pass down into the footwell if it is not sealed properly from the outside.

6 If the footwells have been replaced or patched, it's important to apply seam sealant to prevent water working through weld pinholes and causing corrosion.

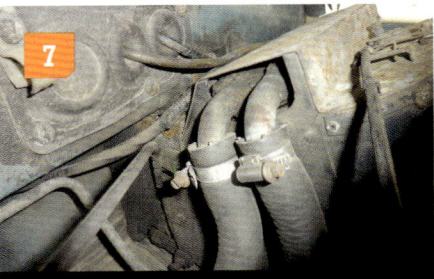

7 The sponge plug needs to be present on the heater box, otherwise water entering between wing and bonnet comes in here ending up inside as vapour.

8 A lot of water will enter through the heater intake, but is supposed to fall out through the drain system unless it is blocked by debris.

"The flat front of the body and windscreen does it no favours"

9 The engine cooling fan cowling stops the fan picking up water and flinging it at the bulkhead with considerable velocity, so needs to be fitted.

83

Water leaks cured

PART 4
HOW THE PROS CURE

We share the pros' secret fixes on how to stop rain and splash-water leaking into your Defender

TOOLS REQUIRED:
General workshop tools, Scrapers, sealant and applicator gun

TIME:
Up to 2 hours

COST:
up to £100

DIFFICULTY RATING:
1/5

WHILST GETTING INTO a damp Defender is one thing, having water pour on to you whilst driving is quite another. The distraction is probably dangerous and certainly unnecessary and quite easy to fix. Last month we looked at how water gets into the Defender while it's stationary. This month, we see how to prevent ingress under way. The bulkhead needs careful attention because it is the main vertical area that presents itself to falling water as the Land Rover is moving forward. A rain drop may be falling at 20mph, but the Defender is hitting it at three or four times that speed, and the combined energies mean that water droplets will penetrate even the smallest gap in the forward-facing part of the cab.

Sealing the Screen
THE JOINT between the screen and the roof is often not a perfect fit. Even though a sponge seal is fitted, it also needs a thin bead of Tiger Seal PU adhesive and sealant to prevent water coming straight through.

The windscreen rubber will leak mainly in the corners where it is cracked, and replacement is the answer at around £50 for a genuine part, or £10 aftermarket. Otherwise, a little black PU sealant injected into the cracks and smoothed over will stop it leaking. The technique is the same with all the sealing, in putting the sealer in place, and smoothing it down with a gloved finger. Leave it to partially cure for around 45 minutes and then wipe the excess away with a rag soaked in a solvent such as white spirit.

The rubber seal between the screen frame and bulkhead rarely leaks. It is time-consuming to replace. If damaged, unless a small repair can be executed, it will need the roof unbolting and the door seals removing to allow the roof to lift a few inches and the seal to be pulled out and replaced. It is not usually damaged as it has no movement on it and little sunlight to degrade it, and renewing it will usually introduce leaks elsewhere.

Being made of foam, it is possible to introduce a thin bead of sealant above and below it, and it's best trying this first. Water leaking through it drains out at the side of the bulkhead on the inside, adjacent to the hinge fixings and must not be confused with leaks at the hinge bolts.

To cure leakage from the windscreen hinges or brackets, unscrew the inside fixings and replace the gaskets after cleaning off the old ones. Water enters through the bolt tubes, so partially fill the tubes with sealant, then re-fit the bolts.

Often the fixing bolts have corroded to almost nothing, in which case they need to be replaced as they contribute to the vehicle's structure. Make certain the bracket is sitting flush and the gasket is fully held before you fully tighten the fixing bolts.

1 The joint between the roof and screen frame is missing a bead of sealant here, so a simple run pushed in with a gloved finger is sufficient.

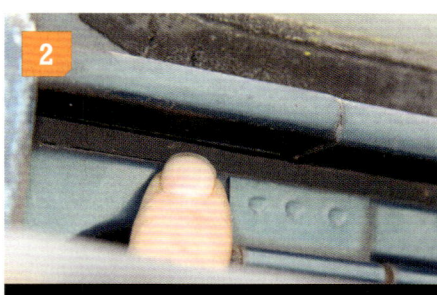

2 A gap on the top of the foam seal under the screen causes internal leaks and should not be confused with the hinge gaskets leaking.

3 The most effective remedy is a thin bead of black Tiger Seal introduced between the top of the seal and the screen frame to fill the void.

4 These new Britpart gaskets are being fitted between the bulkhead and the screen hinges. The earlier type are less leak-prone.

5 The later bulkhead/screen brackets are held on with three 13mm socket size bolts on the inside. They are often corroded and snap off easily.

Bulkhead vents

THE BULKHEAD vent seals are the most common point of entry for water. There are two types, with the change being in 1992. The earlier type (part MUC4299) sticks to the bulkhead and is the same as the 1958-onwards Series vehicles. The later type (part JAE000030) sticks to the vent flap. All cost around £18 a pair. Buy quality, as some non-Genuine seals are slightly small and pull out of place as the adhesive dries. To replace the seals, open the flap and remove the two bolts that fix the lever to the back of the flap. On more recent vehicles use an 8mm socket or combination spanner. Older vehicles need a 2BA socket, though an 11/32 AF socket is a loose fit and works if it is a six-sided type. The hinge pins on later vehicles are threaded rods with dome nuts. The earlier version is a bifurcated rivet needing the ends closing before pulling out. The seal can be pulled off the bulkhead before cleaning the area behind and applying adhesive. The original contact adhesive – applied to both parts and assembled as they dried – failed after a few years. As an alternative, the same PU adhesive sealer we have been using elsewhere works and lasts well. With the seal in place you can reassemble the flap but leave it for a while before you shut it, as the seal might dislodge. The post-1992 types are easier. Use an 8mm spanner to undo the hinge pin and the two bolts holding the vent to the mechanism, then lift off and clean the old seal from the vent. It helps to gently warm the outside of the panel with a hot air gun or hair dryer. Alternatively lay them on a flat surface and pour white spirit into the channel where they attach, and leave for an hour. They will then just lift off as the adhesive has been denatured. Replacement is easy. Just pull the backing strip off the adhesive as you place them on the flap.

1 As expected, the bulkhead vents are leaking on this vehicle. One seal is missing and the other is out of place. Buy good quality seals.

2 Remove the bolts, holding the closing mechanism to the rear of the flap, then pull the hinge pin out after closing its end.

3 Glue and debris that has accumulated over the years needs to be scraped out of the slot that carries the seal. A blunt screwdriver is perfect for the task.

Water leaks cured

4. Tiger Seal PU sealant and adhesive is perfect for sticking down the seal, and is better than the original contact adhesive used in manufacture.

5. A thin bead of sealant is all that is needed for this job. Don't put in too much as it squeezes out and makes a mess on the outside.

6. Carefully push the seal into place and ensure it is located in the channel properly. Leave 45 minutes to partially cure, then refit the flap.

7. These flaps have been refitted with perfectly-located seals. The excess sealant will now wipe away with a solvent rag whilst still soft.

8. The post-1992 flap is held on with threaded hinge pins with dome nuts on the ends. Stainless steel replacements cost about £18.

9. The post-1992 foam seal is stuck to the flap and comes with adhesive tape on it. Both types are interchangeable and the later type is best.

In the engine bay

1. The rubber seal on the bulkhead lip is most important as it directs water to the sides rather than on to the bulkhead itself, so it must be in place.

WATER ENTERING the heater when driving falls out of a rubber dump valve under the unit. But if this is blocked with debris, water can enter the vehicle, so check the valve is clear and working. Removing the heater risks damaging the foam seal between the heater box and the bulkhead so fit a new sponge seal as a matter of course, or to correct previous damage if you have a leak here.

The seal across the back of the bulkhead stops water reaching the engine bay by directing it outwards down the sides of the vehicle. If it is missing or damaged, it should be renewed, otherwise the water flows off the back of the bonnet and down on to the bulkhead where some will find its way into the cab area.

The bulkhead has many manufactured holes, and the cooling fan drives water back against it. Any damaged wiring grommet can let water pass and needs to be sealed. Likewise, the rubber gasket under the pedals, which is difficult to replace as the pipework has to be disturbed. It is easier just to loosen the six fixing bolts on each pedal and introduce sealant where the gasket is leaking, before retightening them. If you ever remove them for such as a cylinder

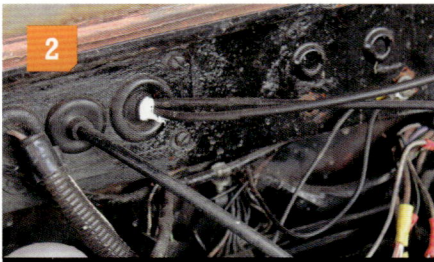

2. Water leaks through grommets, but a blob of black sealant in the void woarks well (white sealant shown here for clarity).

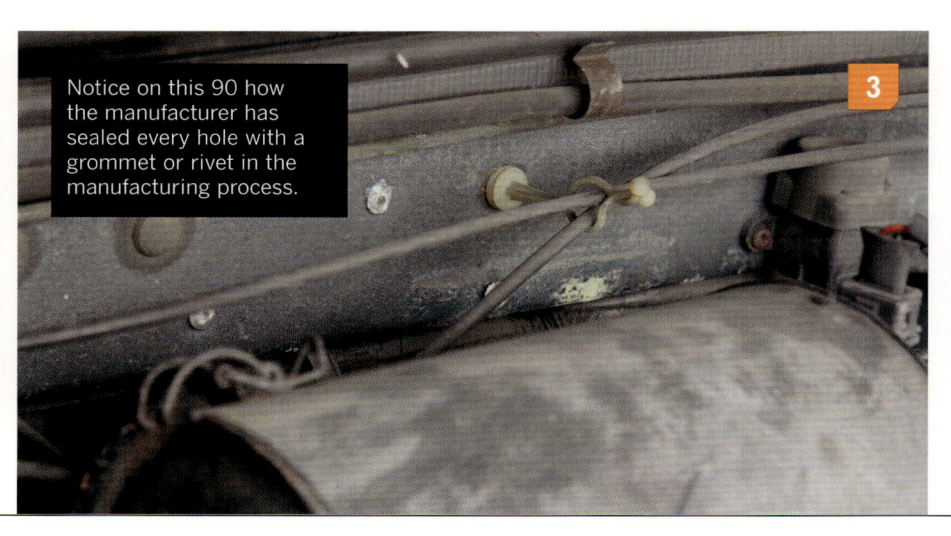

Notice on this 90 how the manufacturer has sealed every hole with a grommet or rivet in the manufacturing process.

3.

4 This throttle cable entry shows a telltale leak stain. The outside of the cable needs seam sealant smearing round it with a gloved finger.

5 The rubber seal on the pedal box here does not show any signs of leaking. That's good, because replacing it is a bit of a chore.

6 When driving, rain is blasted through the grille and the bonnet gaps, and blown against the bulkhead – it needs to be sealed.

7 When rust stains are visible at the top of the footwell, it's an obvious sign that water is entering the bulkhead.

replacement, then fit new gaskets with a bead of sealant.

The throttle cable lets water into the driver's side footwell. Sometimes the outer cable is not clipped in properly. Use brushing-type seam sealer here or a band of PU sealer pushed into place with a gloved finger or an old paint brush. Leave it for a few hours to cure before driving.

Staying Dry
These are all factory standard leaks, and any work done to the vehicle since then introduces a greater opportunity for more water ingress. Common problems are caused by not replacing seals, such as those under the pedal boxes, when parts are disturbed, and not seam-sealing any welded repairs to the bulkhead.

The One Ten shown here has cost about £120 to make it dry inside. As the vehicle is used and ages further, more leaks will appear which will need to be tackled.

WORK SAFELY
When using adhesives, wear protective gloves, ensure there is good ventilation and check the manufacturer's safety information. Wear eye protection when scraping dried adhesive and gasket material.

Suspension upgrades

SUSPENSION REPLACEMENT

TREVOR CUTHBERT

TOOLS REQUIRED:
17mm, 19mm, 24mm, 30mm Socket wrenches and/or spanners. Pry bar, axle stands with trolley jack (or ramp and transmission jack). Copper mallet, pliers, Stillson wrench

TIME:
Half day

COST:
From 70+ Costs: Bearmach +2" coil springs rear £70 pair Pro Comp ES9000 dampers rear £89 pair

DIFFICULTY RATING:
3/5

CONTACT:
Bearmach www.bearmach.com
Super Pro www.superpro.eu.com
BLRC
www.blrcvehiclespecialist.co.uk
Tel: 028 9751 1763

Trevor Cuthbert renews Defender suspension, and swaps the rear axle while the parts are off and it is more accessible

DEFENDER suspension comprises the usual coil spring and a damper (shock absorber) at each wheel.

At the front, the damper is mounted between the chassis and the axle, within the coil spring.

The rear damper is just forward of the spring and angled forward at the top.

A used Land Rover's suspension can be quite tired, having covered over 100,000 miles on the original springs, dampers and bushes.

The good news is that replacing and upgrading the Defender's suspension is straightforward and doesn't necessarily require specialist tools. But note that some Land Rover springs, including Discovery fronts, do need a spring compressor tool which needs to be used with great care.

The Land Rover should be raised by the jack, and set on the axle stands to work safely. The jack is also required to position the axle relative to the chassis, while the suspension components are removed and the new ones fitted. A vehicle ramp that allows the wheels to be free (such as a 2-post lift) with a transmission jack, is also suitable for this job.

The Defender 90 in this feature was being rebuilt for a client who had a change of heart. Originally, the project was to have been carried out on a tight budget using as many original parts as possible. Thus, old suspension had been refitted to the new chassis.

Happily, the owner realised the false economy of this and opted for new coil springs and dampers, as well as replacing the tired rear axle with a rebuilt disc-braked axle.

The new brief included a mild suspension lift and extended dampers with good all-round performance both on the road and when carrying heavy loads. The Pro Comp ES9000 dampers fit this bill very well and are known to have a long and durable service life.

A day or so before starting this job, soak all of the old nuts and bolts involved with a good quality penetrating fluid or spray to make it easier to undo them, given that they may have been assembled many years and miles ago.

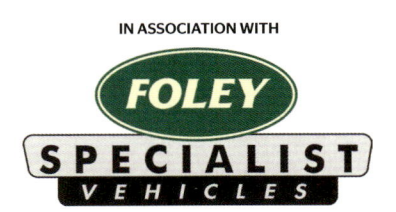

Removing the rear suspension

1. The Defender 90 is supported on axle stands or, in this case, a vehicle lift, with the trolley jack used to lift the axle after removing the road wheel.

2. As you raise it, the dampers prevent the axle from dropping to the limit of the A-frame. The spring is therefore still in place within the chassis mount.

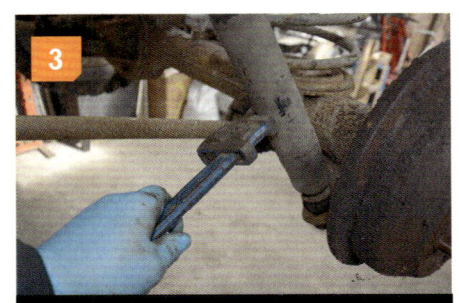

3. Hold the damper lower section with a Stillson wrench to prevent turning as the lower nut is loosened. Protect with cloth if the damper is to be re-used.

4. The lower damper nut is loosened with a 19mm socket wrench. As the nut is undone, the axle is dropping away from the chassis.

5. Before removing nuts completely, the axle is supported by the jack. Otherwise it would drop to the limits of the A-frame/chassis connection.

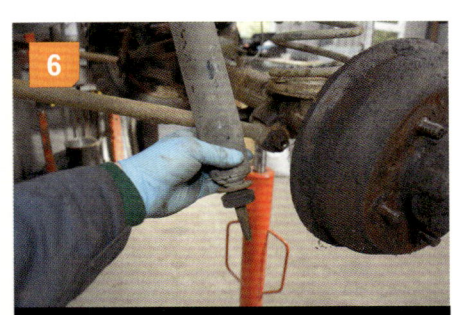

6. By compressing the damper upwards, or gently lowering the axle jack, the lower part of the damper is able to be pulled free of the axle.

7. The top damper mount is easier to unfasten due to clear access. The top nut is an M12 Nyloc, removed by a 19mm socket wrench.

8. Having released the lower mount first, the angle of the damper can be adjusted to allow it to be pulled free of the top mount with ease.

9. Now that the damper has been removed, lowering the axle means the coil spring drops free and clear of the top mount on the chassis.

10. Bolts holding the coil spring retainer plate and cup to the chassis can become quite rusty, so a soaking with penetrating fluid will ease removal.

11. The bolts are M10 through to either an M10 nut underneath, or a captive nut in the axle mount. A 17mm ring spanner is used to remove these bolts.

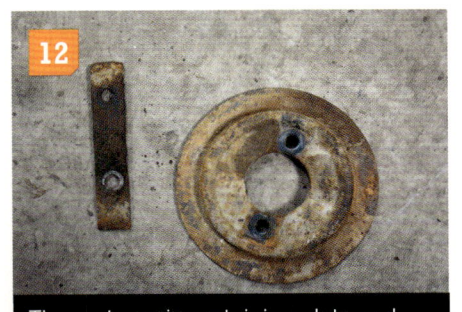

12. The rusty spring retaining plate and spring cup are sound enough to be cleaned up, painted and re-used. New galvanised replacements are cheap.

Suspension upgrades

Swapping the rear axle

THE ORIGINAL rear axle was an older drum-braked one. It was decided to change the axle for a refurbished disc braked version. With the suspension removed, this was the ideal time to do it, as half of the work to remove the old axle had already been done. The rear propeller shaft was removed ahead of time – the propeller shaft bolts and nuts are undone with a pair of 9/16 spanners (a special propshaft socket tool is available). After removal, the old axle was stripped of any remaining useful parts and drained of gear oil, before being consigned to the metal recycling pile. The oil was taken to the local collection point for recycling.

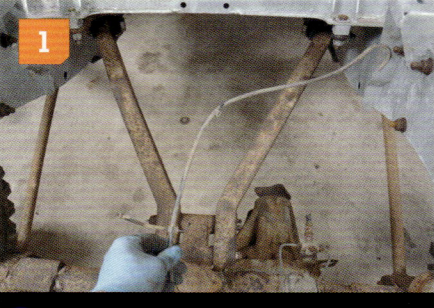

1 The axle breather pipe was attached to the A-frame with cable ties and clips. The clips can be re-used with new cable ties, when the new axle is fitted.

2 A large M20 castle nut clamps the A-frame ball joint to mount at the top of the axle. The split pin has already been removed.

3 The nut is loosened and removed using a 30mm ring spanner. A socket wrench with extension bar will also fit from below; pull the brake pipe clear.

4 With the castle nut removed, a stout smack with a heavy copper mallet is usually sufficient to break the joint from the axle mount.

5 The trailing arms can be released from the chassis mounts either by removing the M20 nut with a 30mm socket or the three M10 bolts and nuts.

6 With the A-frame ball joint pulled clear and the trailing arms released from the chassis bushes, the axle can be rolled out from under the chassis.

7 Each of the trailing arms is attached to its axle mount by a single bolt and nut. These are removed using a 24mm socket wrench and spanner.

8 The trailing arms required new bushes to match the fresh new chassis bushes. The old original bush was pressed out on the hydraulic bench press.

9 The new SuperPro polyurethane bushes are in two halves and use a special grease for all metal contact, both on the outside and inside

10 The metal inner bush is also coated with the supplied grease before being pressed by hand into the outer polyurethane bush in the trailing arm.

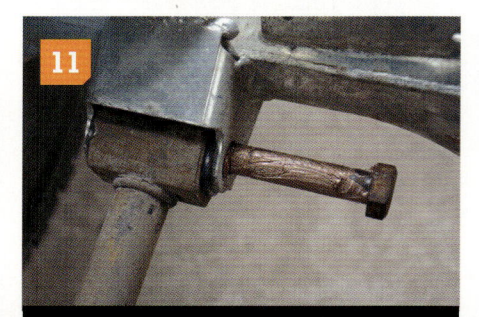

11 In order to prevent the trailing arm bolt and inner metal bush from binding in the years to come, apply copper grease.

12 The replacement axle is ready to be rolled under the chassis. (The old axle is being drained of oil prior to the differential being salvaged.)

13 The chassis bush also has an inner metal bush that is coated with the grease, before being pressed home into the polyurethane.

14 Also coated with copper grease, the end of the trailing arm is offered up to the bush on each side. The angle will make insertion difficult though.

15 To allow the trailing arms to enter the chassis bushes horizontally, the chassis is temporarily lowered on the ramp almost until the bump stops touch the axle.

16 The A-frame ball joint is aligned with the axle mount before being pressed into place. The axle needs slight adjustment laterally to achieve this.

17 The castle nut is tightened back up completely using the 30mm ring spanner, until the taper is firmly locked down into the axle mount.

18 We don't want the castle nut working loose and the A-frame disconnecting, so a new split pin is always fitted through one of the two hole options.

19 The replacement axle is now attached properly to the chassis and is ready for the new suspension to be added and the propeller shaft fitted.

20 The plastic axle breather hose is reattached to the A-frame and up to the chassis, using new cable ties through the original clips.

Suspension upgrades

Fitting the new rear suspension

WITH THE new rear axle fitted, the new blue Bearmach coil springs and Pro Comp dampers are installed. This is for the most part a reversal of the removal process, but it's more satisfying working with the new parts than old rusty parts.

Although providing a 2-inch lift, the new coil springs did not require spring compressors to fit them in place, as the drop on the axle was sufficient to get them in. After the dampers are fitted, the axle does not drop quite as far, so the springs need to be in place before the dampers are attached to the chassis and axle mounts.

1 This galvanised coil spring cup kit from Britpart is an inexpensive alternative to the old items and comes with new bolts, Nyloc nuts and washers.

2 The springs chosen are Blue Bearmach + 2-inch (50mm) lift springs. Here the spring is offered up to chassis and axle.

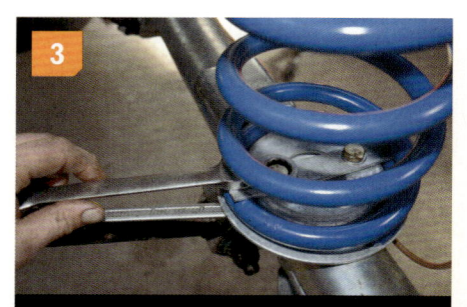

3 The coil spring is attached to the axle via the new galvanised spring seat, using the M10 bolts. 17mm spanners are used to tighten the nuts firmly.

4 The new damper kit comes with fresh bushes and washers for each end of the damper. Here the bush and washer are placed in the axle cup mount.

5 The damper is set into the axle cup, through the upper bush, and the bottom bush and washer fitted below, before being tightened.

6 Inner half of the damper top bush is fitted on chassis mount, then the damper, outer half of bush, washer, and a new M12 Nyloc nut (19mm spanner).

7 The Pro Comp extended dampers have this optional rubber gaiter fitted to keep out the muck and road grime. A cable tie secures it.

8 The Bearmach coil springs and Pro Comp dampers are a tried and tested combination and offer a great upgrade to the Land Rover.

Your Pride & Joy

Benefits available can include:

- FREE Legal Cover
- Club Member Discounts
- Agreed Value
- Green Lane & Off Road Cover
- Modifications Cover
- Limited Mileage Discounts

Great Insurance Policies for your Defender

Adrian Flux know how much you love your Defender, that's why we are dedicated to finding you a policy, tailor-made to your own personal requirements and driving history. Don't face an uphill struggle, call us today for a free, no obligation quote.

0800 085 5000
adrianflux.co.uk

Authorised and regulated by the Financial Conduct Authority

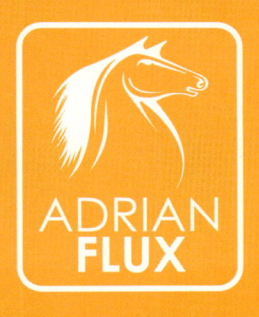

ADRIAN FLUX

Suspension upgrades

Renew front suspension

1. Access to the top of the front suspension is via the engine bay under the plastic cover on each inner wing, fixed with short self-tapping screws.

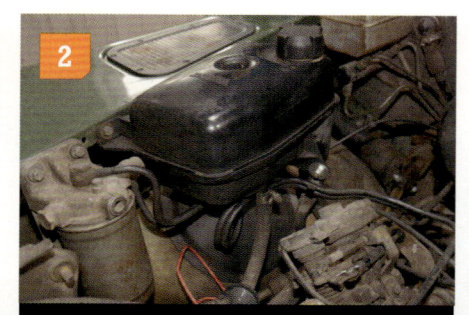

2. On the right side, access to the cover is restricted by the coolant header tank, which is bolted to the wing top and to a support on the inner arch.

3. The M8 bolts are removed with a 10mm socket. Holding the nut on the inside is tricky, but improve access by moving the fuel filter housing.

4. The header tank and the fuel filter housing have been unbolted and moved aside but still attached to their respective hoses.

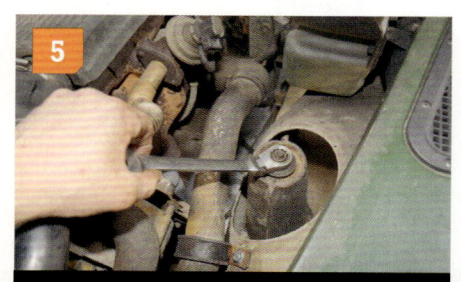

5. With the access covers removed, the nut at the top of the damper is loosened with a 19mm spanner. A 19mm socket wrench can also be used.

6. After the nut and washer are removed, the top bush may need to be pried off with a screwdriver if corrosion has adhered it to the turret top.

7. The chassis needs to be supported on axle stands or the vehicle ramp, with the axle supported and adjusted up or down by a suitable jack.

8. To remove the lower damper nut with a 19mm spanner, prevent the lower section from turning. These soft grip pliers prevent damage.

9. Now both damper nuts have been removed, the axle is lowered by the jack to allow the damper and coil spring to be withdrawn together.

10. The axle is dropped to almost the limit of the brake flexi-hose (without straining it), which allows fitment of a new +2-inch coil spring/damper

11. The suspension turret could be loosened to ease the fitting of the new dampers, which are very prone to extending out to their full length

12. The new Pro Comp dampers are each packed with a strap that keeps them compressed for shipping. This strap can be very helpful if left uncut.

94

WORK SAFELY:
Before starting work, support the vehicle securely on axle stands resting on a firm and stable floor. Ensure the wheels remaining in contact with the floor are chocked, and that the handbrake and gear engaged.

The axle will need to be gently raised and lowered with a jack in order to remove and refit the springs and dampers while the chassis is supported on stands.

Take great care not to inadvertently lift the vehicle from the support stands when raising the axle. Re-check that the chassis is still securely supported by the stands after raising the axle, and also before lowering the axle.

Whenever extended springs or other means of lifting the chassis are to be fitted, check that the brake hoses will cope with the full extent of suspension movement without being stretched. If in doubt, fit a set of longer hoses.

13 The fully extended damper is unwieldy to work with, particularly when the spring is added to the mix and the axle can't be dropped any further.

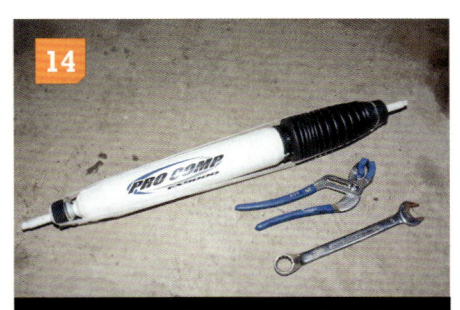

14 Inner washers/bushes are fitted, then the original packing strap is placed around the compressed damper, keeping it short enough to be fitted.

15 The compressed damper is placed within the new coil spring and offered up to the suspension turret and will easily slot on to the spring seat.

16 The damper's top shaft is now protruding through the turret hole. The new top bush and washers are fitted in place, to be followed by the nut.

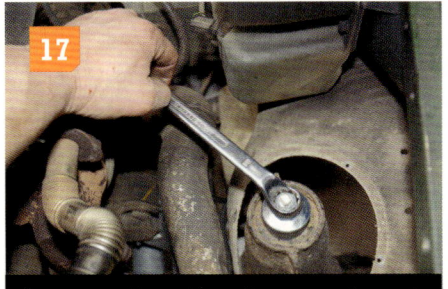

17 Generous thread length means the nut (19mm) is easily started without compressing the bush. Cut the packing strap, remove it and tighten fully.

18 The new outer lower bush is fitted with the new washer to the damper, through the gap between the spring seat and the axle.

19 Finally, the lower nut is fitted and tightened with a 19mm spanner. Again the lower damper will need to be held by a non-damaging pliers grip.

20 New coil spring and damper in place, just before the packing strap was removed. When back on the road, the spring will settle slightly in the top and bottom seats.

The Verdict

NEW suspension that is designed to give a lift over the standard equipment often gives a dramatic result because the old suspension may be tired and making the Land Rover body sit lower than when it was new.

The blue Bearmach coil springs and Pro Comp dampers have indeed given a pleasing lift to the Land Rover, which now looks much more purposeful, and it has more of that all-important ground clearance. The drive was now more comfortable and precise with no sign of the harshness experienced with some upgraded Land Rovers.

Rear crossmember swap

PART 1

Ed Evans explains what's involved in replacing a Td5 110's crumbling rear crossmember

ED EVANS

TOOLS REQUIRED:
Parts: Rear crossmember 110 Td5 'long leg', Britpart number DA4374

TIME:
6 hours

COST:
£260

DIFFICULTY RATING:
4/5

DEFENDER REAR CROSSMEMBER REMOVAL

THE REAR CROSSMEMBER is the most commonly replaced section of a Defender chassis. A bad one lets down the whole vehicle visually, but the loss of strength in this rear section usually means an MoT fail, even for minor corrosion. Structurally, it is a critical rigid link between the two main longitudinal sections. It's also the main structure supporting the towing brackets, so it undergoes a lot of push-pull and twisting stress even with a relatively light trailer attached to the vehicle.

It's rarely worth patching the rear crossmember because when corrosion shows itself in one area, you can be sure other parts of the crossmember are on the way out. The only real answer is to fit a new one, and they are readily available from aftermarket suppliers.

There are two basic types: the standard crossmember, and the extended leg version which incorporates the rear part of the main longitudinal frames of the chassis.

Usually, the extended type is needed because the ends of the main chassis corrode equally fast, leaving no good metal to weld the new crossmember to. So, if intending to renew the crossmember, it's essential to first make a critical assessment of the adjoining main chassis frame, and then buy the appropriate type of replacement crossmember to fit.

With such a substantial replacement part, the quality of welding needs to be first class, not only to retain the chassis frame's original torsional rigidity, but also to provide that safe anchorage for the towing gear. In this feature, Britpart's Steve Grant is doing the work and, as we follow him through, we'll see that it's quite an involved job.

IN ASSOCIATION WITH

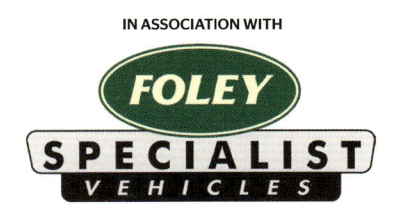

FOLEY SPECIALIST VEHICLES

Looking for trouble

BEFORE WE look at replacing the rear crossmember, let's go through the assessment of my own Td5 110's rear end, which has all the typical problems. This is a year 2000 model and the rest of the chassis is reasonably good and solid, showing only surface rust that needs protection before it becomes serious. Even the rear crossmember looked to be in reasonable condition at first sight. But any crossmember that has been patched in the past and subsequently re-painted over, as this has, is not going to be serviceable for long. It's also worth remembering that most corrosion starts inside where it's hidden, and works its way out.

1 At first it doesn't look too bad, especially with that relatively fresh layer of paint over it. But it's well and truly shot.

2 This old rectangular patch is a sure sign of trouble. A poke with a screwdriver next to that drop plate reveals more rot.

3 To the right of the tow plate there's another old, neat, patch with a hole next to it. Rust is bubbling under the paint.

4 Underneath the crossmember, below that first patch, terminal rust is evident. Worse, the main chassis (left) has a suspicious looking patch.

5 Rght side main chassis leg is rusted through underneath, so there's nothing to weld to. A new crossmember with extensions is needed.

WORK SAFELY:

When using an angle grinder with a cutting disc, wear thick gloves and a strong visor. Be aware of the machine's tendency to twist in your hand, and to kick back.

Extract as much fuel as possible from the tank before removing it, and mop up any spillage.

Two people, or a support jack or trolley jack are needed to lower the cumbersome fuel tank and its support plate.

When welding, wear flame resistant overalls, welding gloves and a good quality visor. Beware of hot material falling when working overhead.

• If working from the floor, ensure it is firm and level and that the vehicle is fully supported and stable.

Unbolting the rear crossmember

1 After soaking the rear nuts, the tow gear is unbolted. After that the towing electrics can be disconnected, before tackling more serious dismantling.

2 Underside bracket bolts are screwed into Rivnuts which can spin, so they are slackened gently to prevent them turning in situ.

3 The forward-running brackets of the tow gear are bolted to the main chassis. These recovery eyes are retained for rebuild.

4 An original rear step will be bolted into more Rivnuts inside the crossmember. These were seized so the step was left on for now.

97

Rear crossmember swap

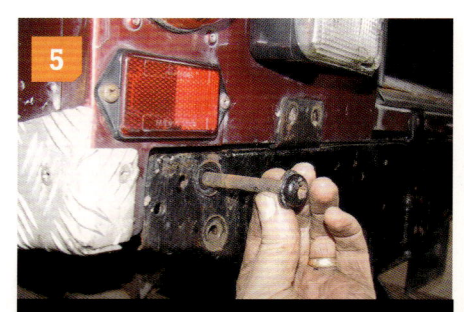

5 Two socket-head screws at each end of the crossmember are removed. They're screwed into the seat belt anchor frames.

6 Rear body bolts may come out using a socket or Torx bit (depending on model). All have nuts at back, outer pairs have captive nuts.

7 Mud flap brackets are detached from the body side and from the chassis. Exhaust pipe bracket at left side is unbolted from the crossmember.

8 The 110's fuel tank has to come out. So this strap over the top of the tank is unbolted from the chassis at each side.

Removing the fuel tank (rear mounted only)

1 After cleaning the connections, the fuel filler and breather hoses are removed (the breather is secured with a plastic tie on the chassis top).

2 Also, this additional fuel tank breather pipe under the left rear wing needs to be unclipped from the body panel.

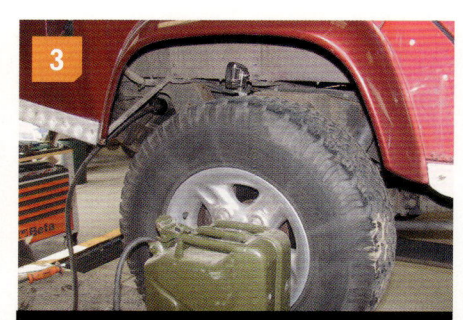

3 I'd run the fuel tank to near empty. Now the remaining fuel is pumped out from the tank's open filler pipe into a jerrycan.

4 Even empty, the tank and its support plate are awkward to handle. We place a transmission jack under for support.

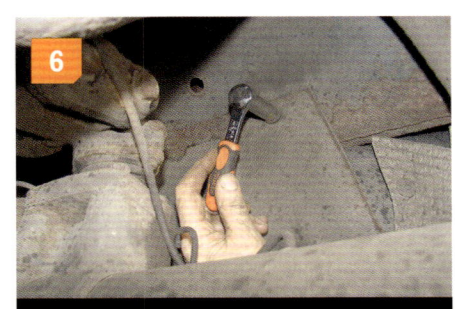

5 The rear of the fuel tank support plate is held by 15 AF nuts accessed through two holes in the rear crossmember.

6 The front of the support plate is held by two bolts to the chassis intermediate crossmember, just aft of the axle, as shown.

7 The tank and support plate are initially lowered at the front so we can reach in to disconnect the fuel pipes on top.

8 The four pipes (left to right: black, blue, green, white) are released by squeezing the connectors' push clips.

9 After disconnection, the pipe ends and tank connectors are plugged to keep dirt out. The wiring connector is also released.

10 Holding the tank, its support plate is lifted out, then the tank is lowered, feeding the hose. Upper steel strap (indicated) is lifted out.

Rear crossmember swap

Removing the chassis wiring

THE WIRING harness to the rear lamps runs through the chassis. So before we cut the chassis and rear crossmember off, we need to remove the harness to avoid the risk of accidentally cutting it or burning it when welding the new sections.

We'll disconnect the harness at the bulkhead, then pull it back through the chassis. But first we'll secure a length of the blue wire to the harness and feed that through with it so that, if the harness or the plugs get jammed inside the chassis on the way, we can pull it forward again with the wire to unjam it.

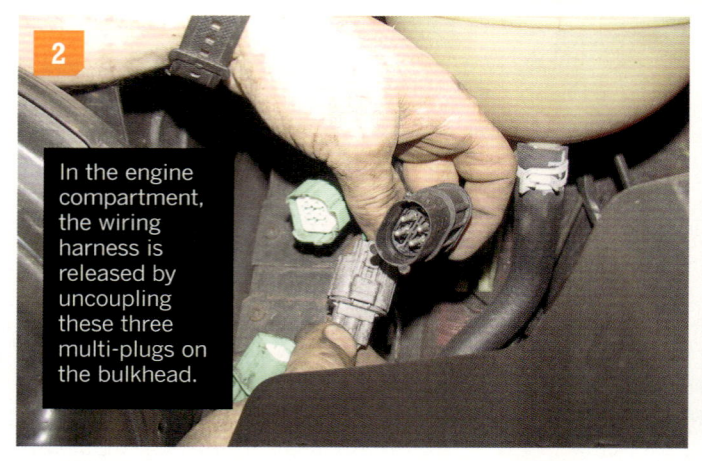

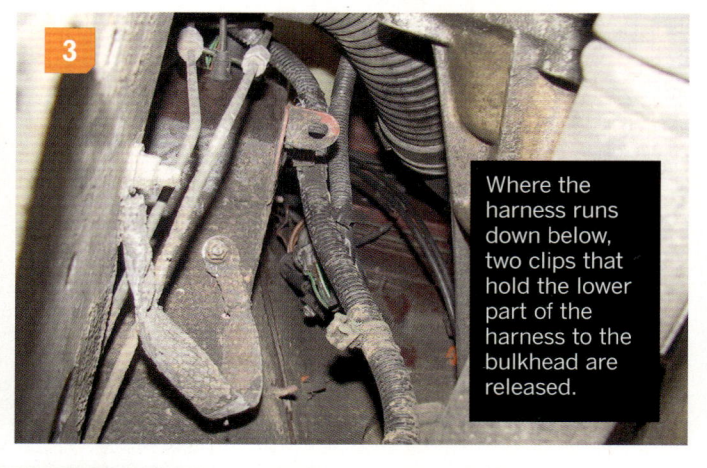

1 We begin disconnecting the wiring harness by unbolting these two earth cables from the side of the transmission, above the transfer box.

2 In the engine compartment, the wiring harness is released by uncoupling these three multi-plugs on the bulkhead.

3 Where the harness runs down below, two clips that hold the lower part of the harness to the bulkhead are released.

4 The harness is pulled down free, and the blue wire secured to it. The hole where the harness enters the chassis is arrowed.

5 We disconnect the harness from the rear lamps. Left lamp connections are behind this panel (station wagon seat base removed first).

6 All left side lamps are unplugged from inside the vehicle, except the indicator which has to be removed from outside to reach its connector.

7 Left and right electrical connectors are pushed through the floor and the harness unclipped from the top of the rear crossmember.

8 The harness is gently pulled out of the chassis from the rear, while feeding the blue safety cable in through the front hole.

100

Cutting out the rear crossmember

THE NEW REAR crossmember has forward extensions that replace the rusted ends of the main sections. These are supplied cut and opened slightly so their forward ends slide over the cut ends of the existing chassis.

The new crossmember has its position dictated by the rear row of body bolt holes to which it is fixed. We take measurements from the next crossmember back to the rear crossmember, and record the height of the ends of the rear crossmember, before cutting the rear end off the chassis.

1 The new Britpart rear crossmember (part number DA4374) includes forward extensions and body supports. We need to cut the chassis to suit it.

2 The old chassis is marked for cutting just forward of the upper body supports. The repair section will slide over the chassis past this mark.

3 Two bolts are refitted to hold the rear crossmember to the back body before using a plasma cutter to slice through the main chassis.

4 Steve also has to cut a hole rearward of the main opening, to cut the chassis' internal reinforcement inserts at these points.

5 The two body bolts are removed as the crossmember is lifted off. Temporary strut on new section (foreground) is to be cut after fitting.

6 In the cut ends of the chassis, internal stiffeners are seen. No rust inside! Cable to pull wiring harness through has stayed intact.

7 The result is an empty-looking underside, giving plenty of access for welding, and for other repairs we didn't expect.

IN PART 2 we will complete the rear crossmember replacement. But things don't quite go as planned. The trouble with taking things apart is that, usually, more problems are found hidden away, and that has to be turned to advantage by making the appropriate additional repairs while there is good access. There's certainly no long-term benefit in covering problems up again in the hope they'll go away. How to make a perfect job of fitting the new crossmember, and ensuring the whole rear end is good, will be revealed next time round.

Rear crossmember swap

Ed Evans explains what's involved in replacing a Td5 110's crumbling rear crossmember

PART 2
DEFENDER REAR CROSSMEMBER: REBUILDING

ED EVANS

TOOLS REQUIRED:
Parts: Rear crossmember 110 Td5 'long leg', Britpart number DA4374

TIME: 6 hours

COST: £260

DIFFICULTY RATING: 4/5

IN THE LAST PART we took a close look around the Defender's crumbling rear crossmember, then set about removing it, ready to install a new repair section. It's a sizeable job for several reasons:
- The main chassis side rails are usually corroded just forward of the rear crossmember, so these sections also need to be replaced because otherwise, there would be no good metal to weld on to. For this reason, we're fitting a rear crossmember with integral extension legs which replace the rusted rear ends of the main chassis sections.
- The main wiring harness to the rear of the vehicle passes inside the main right hand chassis rail, so this has to be disconnected and pulled through before the rear of the chassis can be cut off.
- And on later models and earlier long wheelbase variants, the rear-mounted fuel tank has to be removed to gain access to cut the chassis and weld everything safely.

All of this work was completed. Now we rejoin Steve Grant in Britpart's development workshop to install the new rear crossmember and rebuild the back end of the vehicle.

As we explained in the first installment, with the rear crossmember being such a substantial and critical replacement part, the quality of welding needs to be first class, not only to retain the chassis frame's original strength, but also to resist the forces imposed on it by the towing gear which is bolted directly to the crossmember and to those new rear chassis extension legs.

Here is the rusted original rear crossmember (fuel tank out), also showing holes and old patches on the main chassis sections.

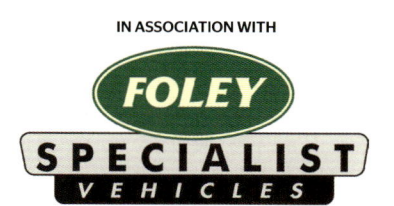

Fitting the new crossmember

1 After cutting the crossmember and rear chassis (March issue), we're left with two stubs on the main chassis, which the new assembly slides on to.

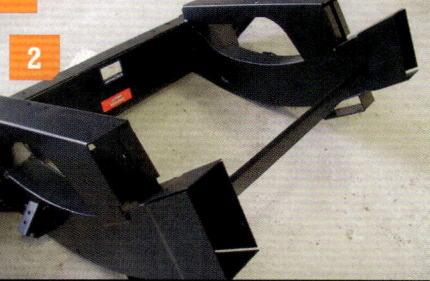

2 The new crossmember (Britpart DA4374). Open ends slide over chassis. Raised frames are Td5 body supports. Cross-strut is temporary.

3 With the rear chassis now cut away, the length of the repair section is accurately marked from the rear body edge to the chassis.

WORK SAFELY:
When using an angle grinder with a cutting disc, wear thick gloves and a strong visor. Be aware of the machine's tendency to twist in your hand, and to kick back.

Extract as much fuel as possible from the tank before removing it, and mop up any spillage.

If working from the floor, ensure it is firm and level and that the vehicle is fully supported and remains stable.

Two people, or a support jack or trolley jack are needed to lower the cumbersome fuel tank and its support plate.

When welding, wear flame resistant overalls, welding gloves and a good quality visor. Beware of hot material falling when working overhead.

4 The exposed ends are now very carefully marked all round and a final accurate cut made with the angle grinder and cutting disc.

5 The cut ends are then cleaned up and all surface rust ground off the outside to help achieve strong and clean welds, which are worth doing well.

6 Paint is cleaned off the repair section's open ends which slide over the chassis, so as not to contaminate the weld with foreign material.

IN ASSOCIATION WITH
FOLEY SPECIALIST VEHICLES

Rear crossmember swap

7 Before the new section is tried in position, the separate cross rail with rear body mounting flanges is bolted on, to ensure everything lines up.

8 The trial fit looks good. The open ends slide snugly over the existing chassis, and the rear flanges align with the rear body bolt holes.

9 But on the right side, the top of the repair section is trimmed back slightly to keep the weld away from those fuel pipes above.

10 Now supported on blocks, with the rear lightly bolted to the body, the open ends are clamped and tapped to the chassis, and tack welded.

11 The rear body flange bolts are tightened after checking the new rear crossmember is perfectly aligned with the body on each side.

12 Contact points between the body and the body support structure on the chassis are checked. Thicker rubber pad will fill this slight gap.

WORTH CHECKING: Steve noticed the wiring harness to the fuel filter's water sensor was trapped between the body and chassis, possibly from new. A crow bar helped lift the body enough to pull the harness free. Here it is, freed but flattened.

13 The repair section is finally secured by tightening the flange rail bolts using a socket and extension up through the crossmember.

14 With the repair section held by rear bolts and front tack welds, the top and outer sides of the joints are welded from the wheel arches.

RECONNECTING THE ELECTRICAL HARNESS

If you want to be authentic by putting the main wiring harness back through the chassis, simply feed the tug wire through the new chassis section before welding, and use it to pull the harness back through later. But this is difficult because there will be an internal step inside where the old rear section was cut off. Routing the harness on top of the chassis is easier, quicker, and more practical.

15 Then the insides of the chassis legs and the underside are tackled from underneath the vehicle to complete the welding.

When pulling the harness out of the chassis (March issue) we attached this tug-cable to it in case it snagged.

"Remember that quality welding is essential when undertaking this work"

16 Several protective coats of paint are added. Tow gear bolt holes are greased, and the steel band over the top of the fuel tank is in position.

17 New section is fully welded along the sides, top, bottom, and along the split corners fusing the welds through to the chassis.

Rear crossmember swap

EXTRA REPAIR: Carefully check everything that becomes accessible when the fuel tank is removed. In particular the next chassis crossmember moving forward. This section butts up to the front of the fuel tank and corrodes badly, so it's worth checking and repairing while the tank is out.

The crossmember corrodes along the bottom of this rearmost edge, and along the underside shown here.

After cleaning back to sound metal, Steve forms an angled plate and tack-welds it into position.

Continuous MIG welds along each seam provide a strong joint, restoring rigidity to the crossmember.

Drain holes are drilled underneath at each end of the repair plate. Water can get in and may need draining out.

Rebuilding the vehicle

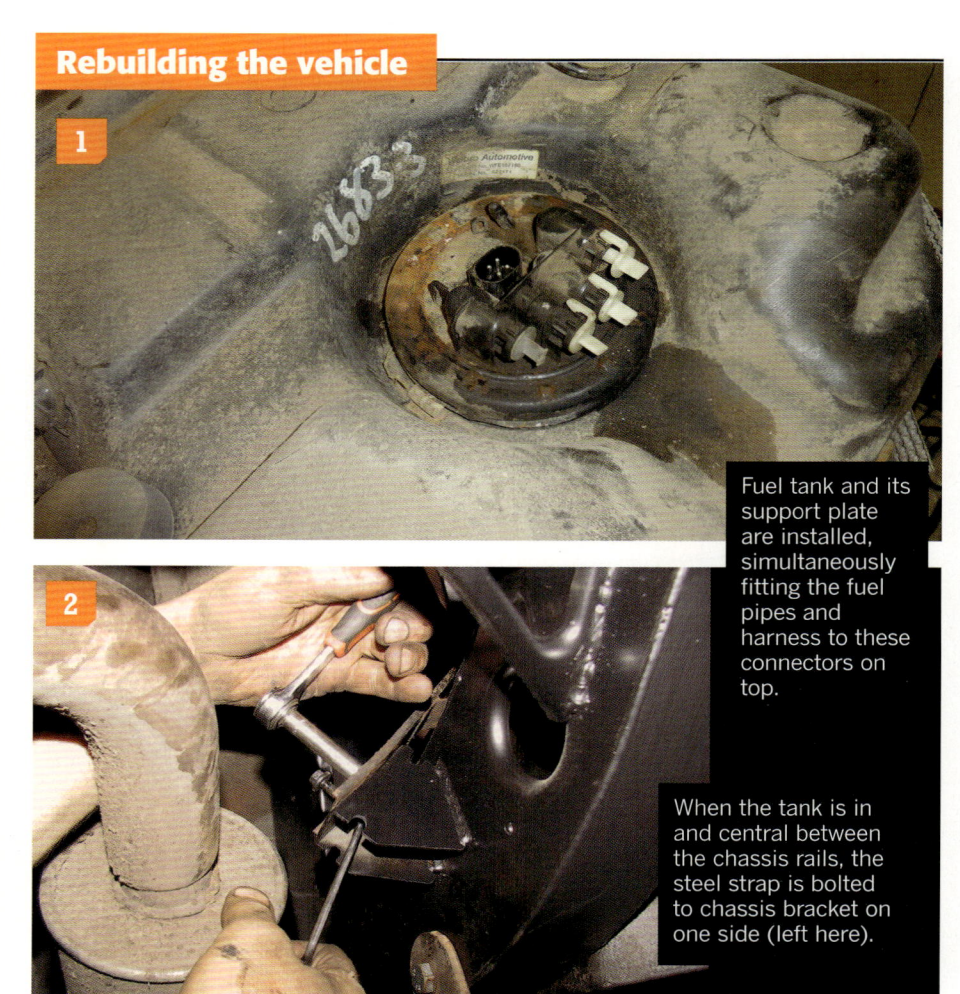

1 Fuel tank and its support plate are installed, simultaneously fitting the fuel pipes and harness to these connectors on top.

2 When the tank is in and central between the chassis rails, the steel strap is bolted to chassis bracket on one side (left here).

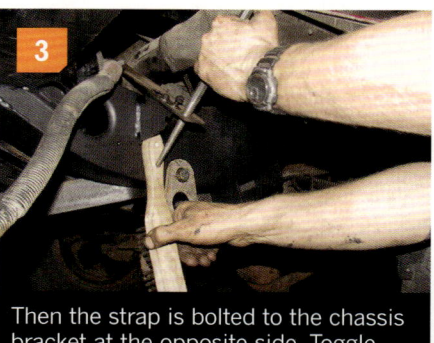

3 Then the strap is bolted to the chassis bracket at the opposite side. Toggle bar stretches it down to align the bolt holes.

4 The tow gear is bolted on, having first loosened the two lower arms to enable them to be aligned with the forward chassis bolt holes.

5 Wiring is reconnected. We secured the main harness along the top of the chassis rail, rather than inside it, dipping down for this outrigger.

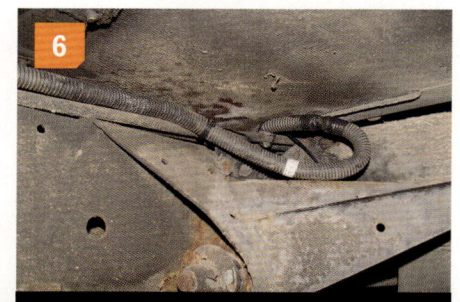

6 Here, it heads under and up to the bulkhead. This routing means it's accessible for repair/test, and easily moved for future chassis weld repair.

"FOR THOSE WHO DARE TO GO OFF TRACK"

Headline sponsors

01480 220 185
www.lancasterinsurance.co.uk

LANCASTER INSURANCE

Policy benefits, features and discounts offered may vary between insurance schemes or cover selected and are subject to underwriting criteria. Lancaster Insurance Services is a trading name of Insurance Factory Limited who are authorised and regulated by the Financial Conduct Authority (No. 306164). For mutual security, calls are recorded and may be monitored for training purposes.

Steering swivels overhaul

Section through a typical swivel hub assembly

Labels (clockwise from top): Brake disc; Stub axle; Upper swivel pin; Bearing; Axle casing; Oil seal; Inner swivel housing (ball); Bearing; Lower swivel pin; Outer swivel housing; Hub; Dust cap; Halfshaft; Drive flange; CV joint

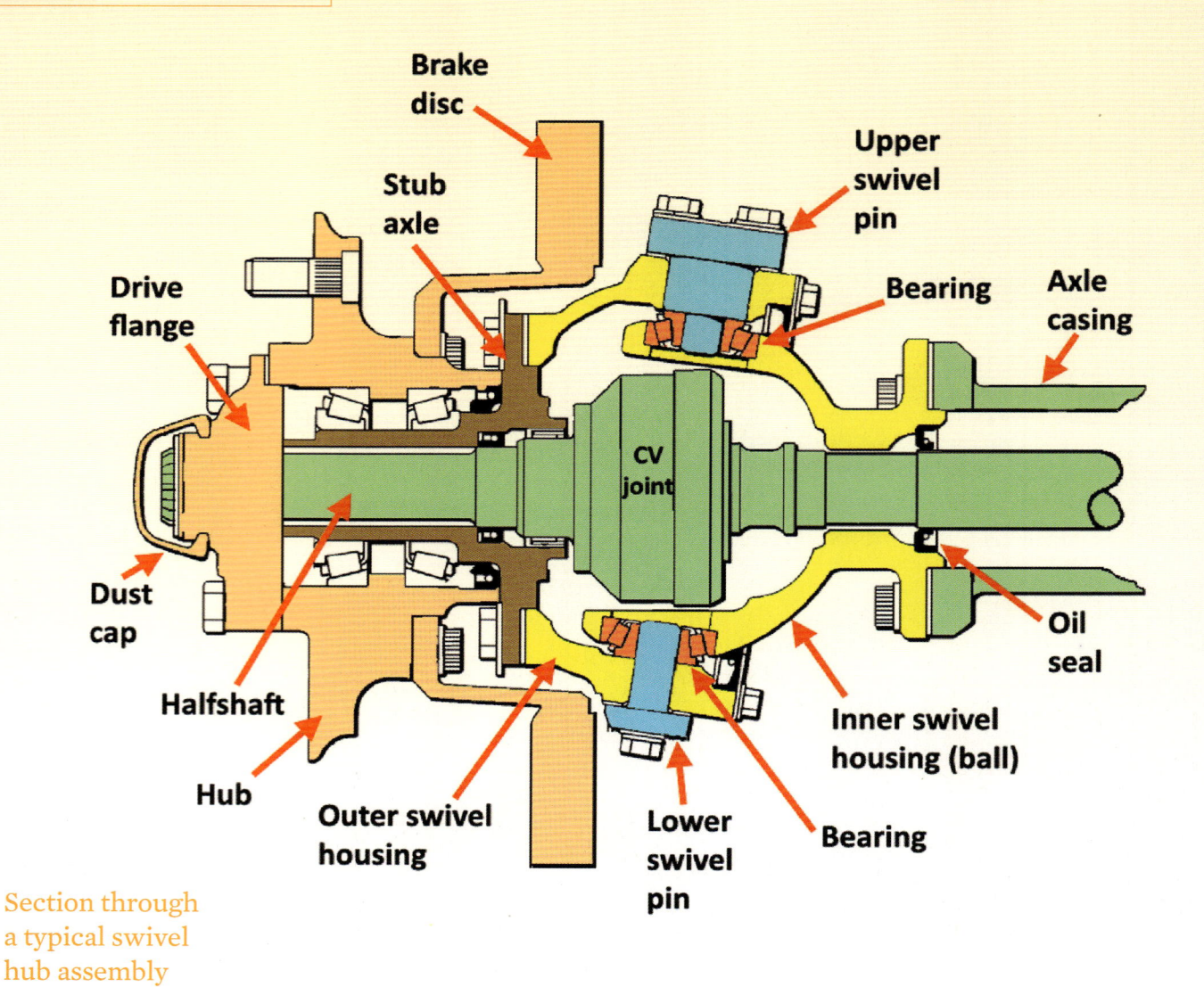

STEERING SWIVELS OVERHAUL

DAVE BARKER

TOOLS REQUIRED:
Jack and axle stands; hub nut socket (52 mm); 13, 14 and 17 mm double hex spanners; 8, 17, 19, 27 mm spanners and sockets; circlip pliers; pry bar and general workshop tools

TIME:
5 hours

COST:
£110

DIFFICULTY RATING:
4/5

CONTACT:
Maddison 4x4, Water House Farm, Station Road, Topcliffe near Thirsk, YO7 3SG. Tel: 01845 587407. Web: www.maddison4x4.com

THE SWIVEL assembly on a Defender can require overhauling or replacing due to wear that can be caused by a number of reasons. The exposed part of the swivel assembly (the ball) can wear, corrode and pit with age, damaging its oil seal. That allows swivel grease (or oil) to leak out, or water and dirt to get in, all of which damages the upper and lower swivel bearings, ultimately wearing the swivel pins. This often results in vague steering, vibrations, steering wobble at speed, and excessive play at the front wheel.

The owners of the Defender shown here had noticed the signs of damage on the inner swivel ball itself, plus a front wheel wobble at speed. An inspection found excessive play in the front nearside assembly when grasping the raised wheel, indicating a worn swivel pin or bearings, and damage on the swivel ball. It was agreed that both swivel housings (inner and outer), the bearings and the top pins should be replaced.

PARTS:
Rather THAN buying individual parts, a full Swivel Housing Kit is available (part number DA3179) for Defender VIN XA onwards (non-ABS), otherwise check parts against your VIN. The kit includes swivel housing, swivel pin bearing, gasket, seals, plate, joint washers, swivel pin kit, shims and swivel grease. The complete kit cost around £110 including VAT. It's recommended you use a thread lock on some bolts; Land Rover recommends using Loctite 270.

CONTACT:
The work was carried out by Maddison 4x4, Water House Farm, Station Road, Topcliffe near Thirsk, YO7 3SG. Tel: 01845 587407. Web: www.maddison4x4.com

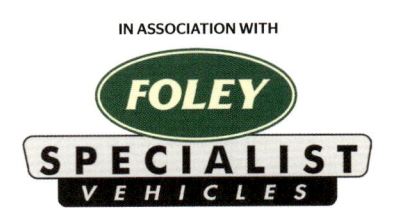

Dismantling the Swivel Housings

1 Note excessive wear and damage to the ball of the inner swivel housing, with grease leaking through the oil seal. Both sides were equally worn.

2 Loosen the wheel nuts, jack the vehicle and secure the Defender on suitable axle stands, then remove the road wheel.

3 Remove the split pin, then the castellated nut from the track rod end, split the ball joint and disconnect the drag rod link from the swivel housing.

4 Repeat the process on the track rod link, remove the split pin and nut then split the ball joint and remove the track rod from the swivel housing.

5 Undo and remove the two swivel pin securing bolts, and remove the bracket that holds the brake pipe in position, then replace the swivel pin bolts.

6 Remove the two bolts that secure the complete brake caliper assembly to the hub assembly, then lift the caliper off the disc and secure it.

7 Remove the plastic dust end cap and, using circlip pliers, remove the circlip and shim from the end of the driveshaft.

8 Remove the five bolts from the drive member (flange) and remove the drive member from the hub and driveshaft, this may need to be pried off.

9 Once the drive member has been taken off, remove all traces of the old gasket from the mating faces, as a new gasket will be fitted later.

10 Using the correct size hub nut socket, undo and then remove Athe hub's locking stake nut from the outer halfshaft.

11 Once the nut has been removed, you can now remove the outer bearing and the spacer from the hub assembly.

12 Once they have been removed you can now pull the hub and brake disc assembly off the end of the stub axle/drive shaft.

Streering swivels overhaul

13 Undo the six bolts that secure the stub axle to the swivel housing as pictured, then remove the bolts and front plate ring.

14 Next, remove the stub axle by pulling it off the swivel housing. Once removed, check the stub axle shaft for any signs of wear or damage.

15 Scrape off and remove all traces of the old sealing gasket from the mating face of the swivel housing; you will need a new gasket later.

16 Now, the complete constant velocity joint and front half shaft assembly can be withdrawn from the front axle tube through the swivel housing.

17 Once the constant velocity (CV) joint and halfshaft has been removed, check the CV joint for any signs of internal wear or damage in the parts.

18 Undo the seven bolts securing the inner swivel bearing housing (swivel ball) to the end of the front axle tube, and remove it from the vehicle.

19 Undo and remove the upper swivel pin, then undo and remove the swivel ball retaining plate which secures it to the swivel pin housing.

20 Once the retaining plate has been undone and removed, you can remove the inner swivel housing ball from the outer swivel pin housing.

21 Remove the worn bearing from the lower swivel pin and check the housing for debris from broken bearings. Clean the housings.

WORK SAFELY
If using a lift or ramp, before lifting the vehicle, ensure that it is rated to lift the weight of the vehicle and is in serviceable condition

Ensure the vehicle is securely on the ramp especially if it's a wheels-free post ramp

If using a jack, after lifting the vehicle always secure it on axle stands. Always ensure the vehicle is stable and secure and is safely chocked, braked and in gear on a level firm surface

Wear eye protection when removing and fitting circlips

Rebuilding the assembly

1 The replacement parts include the new inner swivel housing, oil seals, retaining plate, bearings and a new upper swivel pin.

2 Carefully press a new oil seal squarely into the inner swivel housing flange until it fits flush. Ensure the seal's lip faces away from the ball.

3 Fit the new swivel bearing outer races into the new inner swivel ball, using a suitable drift to carefully tap the races squarely into the recess.

4 Lubricate the new upper swivel bearing with suitable grease, then carefully fit it into the new race you fitted in the inner swivel ball housing.

5 After lubricating the new lower swivel bearing with suitable grease, fit the bearing onto the lower swivel pin not being replaced.

6 Carefully position the new inner swivel housing into the outer swivel housing, and check that the lower pin and bearing align with the inner swivel ball.

7 Fit the new upper swivel pin, shim(s) and gasket into the housing, and replace the two securing bolts. Tighten to 78 Nm.

8 Using a spring balance, check the force required to move the swivel is between 1.16 and 1.46 kg. Add/remove shims to achieve correct pre-load.

9 Apply some grease between the lips of the new swivel housing oil seal then carefully fit the seal squarely into the outer swivel housing.

10 Fit the new swivel retaining plate and joint washer over the oil seal and onto the inner swivel housing. Tighten the 7 bolts to 11 Nm.

11 Fit the rebuilt swivel assembly with a new gasket onto the end of the axle tube. Apply thread lock to the bolts and tighten evenly to 73 Nm.

Steering swivels overhaul

12 Slide the halfshaft and CV joint assembly into the front axle tube. When the splines are engaged, push it fully into the differential.

13 Fit a new gasket and slide the stub axle into position over the axleshaft. The stub axle should be located with the flat at the top.

14 With the stub axle positioned correctly on the swivel housing, apply thread lock to the bolts, then fit the bolts and tighten evenly to 65 Nm.

15 Refit the hub assembly and inner bearing; then the outer bearing and hub nut. Tighten to 210 Nm, check the end float, then stake the hub nut.

16 Fit the drive flange with new gasket. Use a flange bolt to pull the drive shaft outward to refit the washer and circlip. Fit the dust cap.

17 With the circlip correctly refitted, fit the bolts that secure the drive flange to the hub assembly, and tighten to 82 Nm.

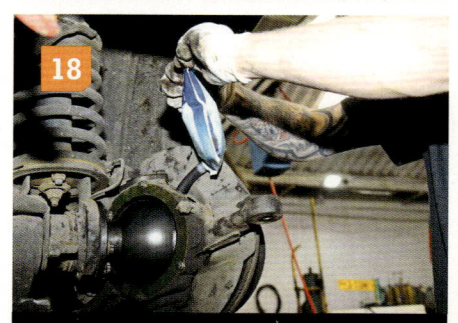

18 Remove the filler plug from the swivel housing and fill the swivel with grease using a one-shot swivel housing grease. Refit the filler plug.

19 Refit the brake caliper to the hub assembly, refit the drag rod link and the track rod link, tighten the securing bolts and refit the split pins.

20 Once you have replaced one side move onto the other side. Both are identical and both swivel housings are replaced in the same way.

TWISTED®
ANTI-ORDINARY

Twisted Automotive has one mission: to take the iconic LandRover® Defender® and re-engineer it to be the very best vehicle it can be.

www.twistedautomotive.com | Thirsk, North Yorkshire | +44 (0)1845 574 990

Fuel tank replaced

FITTING A NEW FUEL TANK

It's a good plan to replace a rusty fuel tank before it starts to leak. Dave Barker shows how

DAVE BARKER

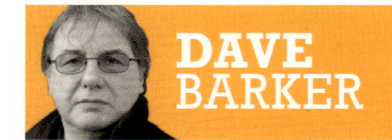

TOOLS REQUIRED:
General workshop tools, 13 mm, 14 mm, 15 mm, 16 mm spanners and sockets, pry bar, a funnel and clean container to drain fuel into

TIME:
1-2 hours

COST:
£90

DIFFICULTY RATING:
1/5

CONTACT:
The work was carried out by Maddison 4x4, Water House Farm, Station Road, Topcliffe near Thirsk, YO7 3SG. Tel: 01845 587407
www.maddison4x4.com

THE OWNER OF this 1994 300Tdi Defender 90 with over 110,000 miles on the clock, spotted a wet patch of diesel on the bottom of the fuel tank. A closer inspection found a large section of badly flaking and very corroded metal around the centre seam of the tank, from where diesel had been seeping out, but only when the tank was more than half full. One temporary option was to do nothing and just not to fill the tank more than half full until there was time to replace the tank. But this risks spillage which, apart from the cost of wasted fuel, creates a serious skid hazard on the roads. The only real option is to replace the old fuel tank right away. In this case, it hasn't done bad service after 22 years. In fact, it's probably well overdue, considering this Defender had its chassis replaced several years ago.

Replacing the fuel tank is not difficult. The hardest part of the job is going to be undoing the bolts securing the old tank to the side of the chassis where it is exposed to the elements. In this case, the bolts were not badly corroded or seized as they had been replaced a few years back when the chassis was replaced. The other potential problem area is undoing the pipe unions on the fuel supply and return pipes where there is a risk of snapping the ends of the pipes where they go into the tank. Due to age, the pipes are often corroded but, with care, you should manage to undo them without snapping them. If not, the parts are easily available and not expensive to replace. The other difficult part is removing the tank from the vehicle. It's a tight fit between the chassis rail and the sills. Once the securing bolts are removed you should lower the front of the tank and then twist it towards the chassis, you should then be able to remove it from the vehicle.

Removing the old tank

1 Diesel was found to be leaking out of the fuel tank from a corroded section along the tank's centre flanged seam.

2 Run the fuel as low as possible before starting the job. Undo and remove the drain plug and drain remaining fuel into a clean container.

3 Remove the right side seat cushion and seat box cover to expose the fuel tank with sender unit (left), and fuel supply and return pipes.

4 Disconnect the two electrical wires that are connected to the fuel gauge unit, note which wire goes to which connection – it's best to label them.

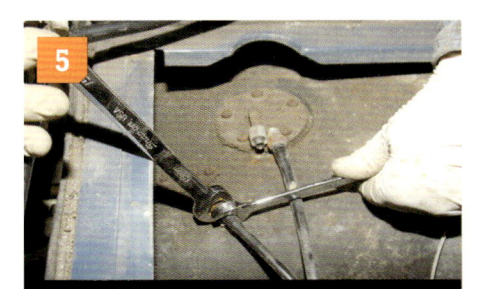

5 Using two spanners, release the fuel supply pipe union (right) and the spill return pipe (left) and disconnect from the fuel tank.

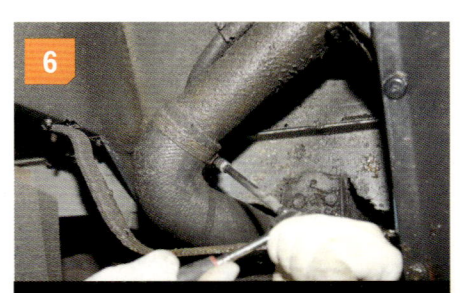

6 In the wheel arch, undo the hose clip securing the large rubber pipe to the metal stub pipe which is attached to the fuel filler inlet.

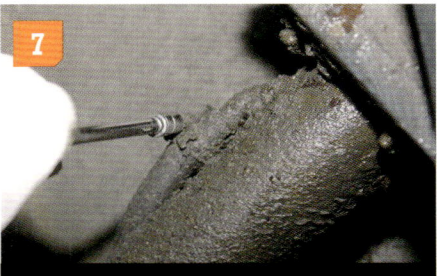

7 After releasing the main hose, undo this hose clip securing the smaller rubber pipe to the breather stub on the fuel filler supply pipe.

IN ASSOCIATION WITH **FOLEY SPECIALIST VEHICLES**

Fuel tank replaced

8 Once the hose clips have been undone, with some deft twisting, both the fuel filler and breather hoses will come off corroded pipes.

9 Working at the rear of the tank, undo the two nuts from what should be captive bolts securing the rear of the tank in position.

10 At the front of the tank, undo the nut and bolt that is securing the tank to the front mounting bracket located on the chassis.

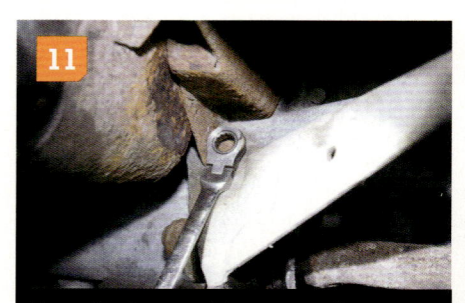

11 You will also need to remove the mounting bracket from the chassis. This is secured to the chassis with three bolts and nuts.

12 Once the nuts and bolts have been undone and removed, you can manoeuvre the mounting bracket out from the chassis.

13 Let the front of the tank drop down a little, then twist it sideways. This should allow you to lower it, and remove the tank from the Defender.

Swapping the tank fittings over

1 Before removing the tank's fittings, a few carefully aimed blows to the flange with a mallet can help to crack the corrosion holding the flange screws.

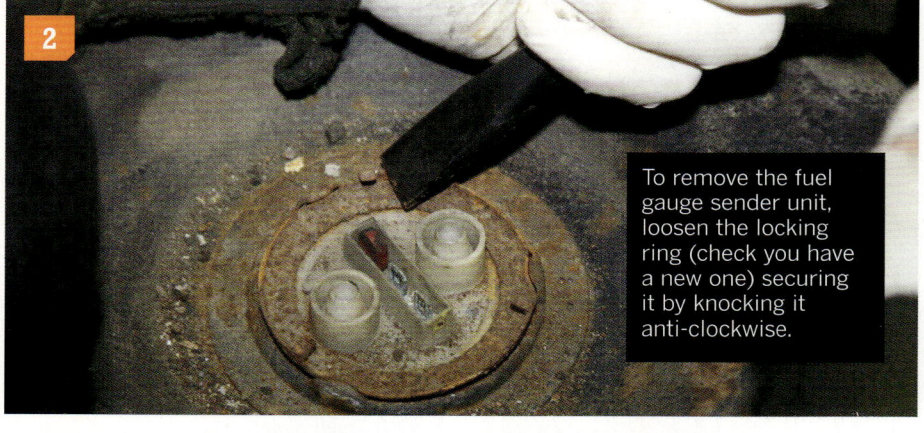

2 To remove the fuel gauge sender unit, loosen the locking ring (check you have a new one) securing it by knocking it anti-clockwise.

3 Once the locking ring has been loosened and removed, the fuel gauge sender unit can be lifted and carefully worked out of the tank.

4 Remove the five securing screws that hold the fuel supply pipe unit into the tank, then lift the unit out ready to fit into the new tank.

116

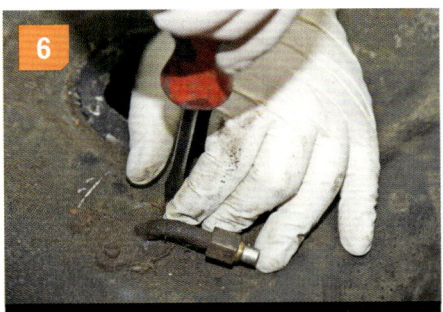

5 The replacement fuel tank being fitted to our 1994 300Tdi Defender 90 is ESR2242 (1986 to 1998). Expect to pay around £90.

6 Similarly, carefully remove the two screws securing the fuel spill return pipe unit into the old tank and remove it. Keep these parts clean.

WORK SAFELY: Ensure vehicle lifting equipment such as ramps, lifts, trolley jacks and axle stands are correctly rated for the job and in serviceable condition.

Ensure vehicle is securely supported before working.

Wear eye protection and protective gloves or barrier cream and particle filter when dealing with airborne dust and particles.

7 Seat the unit on its seal, then fit a new locking ring and tighten clockwise by hand. Tap the ring further to lock it into position.

8 Apply a new conventional gasket or use gasket sealant on the mating face of the fuel supply pipe unit, and on the spill return pipe flange.

9 Fit the old fuel supply pipe and spill pipe unit into the new tank, checking they're pointing in the correct direction, then tighten the screws.

10 Remove the rubber fuel filler pipe and breather pipes from the old tank, clean the ends inside, and fit then to the new tank.

Fuel tank replaced

Installing the new tank

1 Lift the new fuel tank into the Defender chassis. This needs to be done by lifting the rear end of the tank into position first.

2 With the tank supported in position, refit the two nuts and washers onto the captive bolts to hold the rear of the tank to the chassis.

3 Secure the front mounting bracket to the tank using the bolts and rubber bushes collected during removal, then attach it to the chassis.

4 Once the bolts are tight, clean inside the ends of the filler and breather pipes and slide them onto the filler stubs, and fit new hose clips.

5 Reconnect the fuel supply and spill return pipes onto the supply and spill stubs from the tank, carefully tightening the pipe unions.

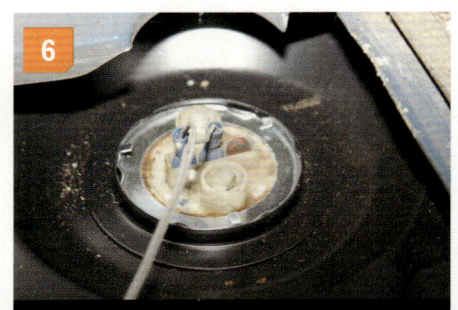

6 Reconnect the two electrical wires onto the fuel gauge unit. Check you reconnect them the correct way round, referring to notes or labels.

7 Before finishing the job and filling the new fuel tank, check that the drain plug is correctly tightened and the seal correctly seated.

8 Double check that all of the securing bolts, hose clips and fuel pipes are correctly tightened and secure, and then fill the tank.

9 Before or after fitting, protect the fuel tank with sealant, Waxoyl or Dintrol protective products, especially around that middle flange joint.

Bearmach
PARTS FOR LAND ROVERS
Est.UK1958

10,000 Parts and accessories available from our website

SELECT 4 COLLECT
Stockist Collection Service
Select 4 Collect
Choose your favourite local stockist to collect your order from

3 Year Warranty
On Bearmach own-brand parts and accessories

10% OFF
YOUR FIRST ORDER
USE DISCOUNT CODE: **LRMDEF10**

Subject to Bearmach's Terms and Conditions. 10% discount does not apply to clearance stock. Cannot be used in conjunction with any other offer.

Buy Parts & Accessories for Land Rovers at
www.bearmach.com

PANORAMIC KITS FROM £499.00

VGS Vehicle Glazing Specialists
BESPOKE DEFENDER PRIVACY GLASS RANGE

NOW AVAILABLE DEFENDER 90 PANORAMIC ROOF £699 INC VAT & DELIVERY

WORLDWIDE SHIPPING AVAILABLE

dave@vgs.uk.com | Mobile: 07772018940

www.vehicleglazingspecialists.com

Chassis swap

PART 1
FITTING A NEW CHASSIS

The chassis is the weak point on early Defenders, so the best way to prolong their life is to fit a new galvanised frame. Trevor Cuthbert demonstrates the fast-track method on a 300Tdi 90

A DERRY MAN asked if I could deliver a new Defender 90 chassis from Richards Chassis in Doncaster and replace the chassis on his 300Tdi, I visited the owner to assess the work. I was quite surprised to find a pristine, low-mileage Defender which didn't look like it needed a new chassis any time soon.

But owner, Mervyn, had bought the Land Rover as his very own retirement present, and wanted to preserve it for many years of fishing and shooting ahead. A new chassis would be the basis of its intended long life. To speed up the job, the body would be lifted and refitted as one complete assembly, saving time and work in unbolting components and realignment.

Preparation and initial assessment
The first stage is to check underneath to see if other parts need replacement, and to spray the nuts and bolts with a penetrating oil to make dismantling faster and smoother when the work starts. The Defender recently had new bushes and an A-frame ball joint, so much of the suspension bolts were rust-free. All wheels were removed, plus the bumper and grill, steering guard and floor mats. Inside, the battery was disconnected, earth lead first, then the engine coolant drained by releasing the bottom hose.

Body bolts
The key to removing any Land Rover body is to identify every bolt holding the body to the chassis mounts, and remove each at the appropriate time. The other half of the job is disconnecting every other electrical, fluid and physical connection between the two.

Some of the body bolt locations are obvious, like the five pairs of M8 bolts

TREVOR CUTHBERT

TOOLS REQUIRED:
Standard workshop tools. Lifting gear or two-post ramp. Suitable cross beam

TIME:
Up to 2 days

COST:
up to £1254

DIFFICULTY RATING:
4/5

CONTACT:
Trevor Cuthbert Land Rovers
07890 868929, info@trevorcuthbert.com

Richards Chassis Ltd
01709 577477, www.richardschassis.co.uk

IN ASSOCIATION WITH

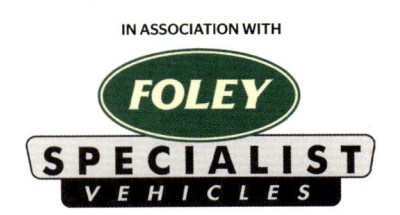

FOLEY SPECIALIST VEHICLES

1 After the spare wheel was removed, the bolts holding the back of the body to the rear cross member were first to be removed, being the most accessible.

2 Raising the Defender a few feet in the air on the two-post ramp gives a comfortable working height for removal of the bumper and road wheels.

3 The fuel filler had been attached to the body with M6 stainless steel bolts, which were easily removed with a pair of 10 mm spanners.

4 The rubber mat, trim, gear shifter and hi-low knob are all that need to be removed. The transmission tunnel and floor panels can stay in place.

5 Handbrake cable is detached from the lever by removing the clip and clevis pin. It is tucked out of the way around the transfer gearbox.

through the mounts on the rear cross member to the back of the body tub. The outer pair of bolts on each side are held by nuts on the inside, which need to be held with a 13 mm spanner in a spot that's just reachable by feeling around blindly. The remaining three pairs of bolts are held by captive nut plates affixed to the tub and are usually easy to remove. Care should be taken not to round the spanner flats with all nuts and bolts where things look a little tight or rusty.

At the dismantling stage I prefer to use six-point hexagon sockets, rather than bi-hexagonal sockets, as they are less likely to tear the soft edges of the nut head and make them round.

On a Defender 90, working forward from the rear, you will find body bolts at the seat belt mounting points at the front of the tub section, where an M8 nut and bolt hold a chassis bracket to the vertical face of the inner seatbelt mounts on each side. These two bolts are often the ones that are overlooked and only discovered when attempting to lift the body and then finding it won't separate.

An easy way to find them is to look in line with the more obvious outrigger bolts. These are the bolts connecting the tub to the chassis and to the outer seat belt mounts; on a 90 chassis the outrigger is tubular and has only one pair of M8 bolts on each side (on a 110 there are two pairs).

These outrigger bolts can be quite corroded, being in the direct line of fire from the rear wheels. However the nut heads are easily accessible and can be split with an angle grinder if necessary. Beware that on the right side, the outrigger bolts are very close to the fuel tank and filler hose so great care must be taken when cutting in this area. No open access to the fuel tank should be allowed: if in doubt, cover up and look for any signs of fuel leakage. The chances are that if your chassis needs to be replaced, the fuel tank might show signs of fuel leakage. The correct type of fire

121

Chassis swap

6. Long bulkhead body bolts run through the bulkhead outrigger and were stubborn and needed this long breaker bar on a socket to turn them.

7. This seized bolt head on this chassis-to-body bracket was split with the angle grinder and the remains knocked off before punching the bolt out.

8. The brackets to the front of the bulkhead on each side are bolted with long M8 bolts through the chassis. A 13 mm socket and spanner loosens them up.

extinguisher (dry powder) should also be at the ready. Another pair of body bolts that are easy to overlook are the little M6 bolts that hold the lower edge of the seat box to chassis brackets underneath. The heads of these are found in cut outs in the floor plates. Being in this area means the heads are often soft with rust and the nut underneath is difficult to get a 10 mm spanner on to. I prefer to mark the head of the bolts with a centre punch and drill out the head, starting with a 4 mm drill bit to a depth of about 5 mm. Following with an 8 mm drill bit will have the head off fairly easily and the remains of the bolt will drop through.

The bulkhead outrigger bolts are long M12 bolts, holding the foot of the bulkhead, on each side, to the chassis. The long length of these means they can become stubborn, as rust may have built up somewhere along the length, making them tight. I generally spray penetrating fluid at each end and work them back and forth with a socket to loosen the rust. Further spraying as they begin to move also helps. I don't remove these bolts all the way, until I'm ready to lift the body, as the bulkhead can drop slightly when the bolts come out.

In front of the bulkhead there are brackets on each side, which support the bulkhead and rear of the wing assembly. The brackets can be seen from within the front wheel area, where two long M8 bolts run right through the chassis. A 13 mm socket and a spanner on the inside will have these bolts remove quite easily.

At the very front of the chassis there are the final three M8 bolts on each side. These are best left until the radiator and frame have been removed. There are two on each side holding the inner wing to the chassis and another one on each side, fixing the bonnet slam panel supports to the chassis.

All systems disconnect

Working systematically around the Land Rover, every connection between the body and the chassis needs to be released. For

9. These M10 bolts hold the radiator frame brackets to the slam panel on each side. Normally there are captive nuts on the underside for easy removal.

10 After removing the viscous fan (32 mm flat spanner) and its shroud, the intercooler is removed first, making it easier to get the radiator out.

11 Looking down – with the radiator frame removed – the slam panel supports are unbolted from the chassis using a pair of 13 mm spanners.

12 A small chassis bracket holds the metal power steering pipe and the rubber hose feeding the power steering pump. Use an 8 mm and a 10 mm spanner.

13 Cutch slave cylinder has been unbolted from the bellhousing. It will be tied to a convenient point at the foot of the bulkhead.

14 There are three electrical connections between engine and bulkhead. The glow plug feed wire on the left was removed from the rearmost plug (7 mm spanner).

example the fuel filler neck is held to the body with four M5 bolts (or M6 on the vehicle shown here). With these removed, the filler neck is pushed behind the bodywork, and the filler cap refitted to keep dirt out. There is also a breather hose you need to remove as it loops through a hole in the body.

The gear knobs are removed and the main shifter is unbolted, although it is not necessary to remove the transmission tunnel and floor plates. Also in the cabin, the handbrake cable needs to be disconnected and there may be an electrical connection here too for the warning light. On later Defender models, there will be a control unit for the EGR valve which needs to be unplugged and the wiring loom pushed through the seatbox cover. This cover can then be removed, allowing easy access to disconnect the speedometer cable from the transfer gearbox. It is easier, and wiser, to disconnect the speedo cable here rather than upset the instrument panel unnecessarily.

The battery cables are pushed through out of the battery box. The positive cable will stay attached to the engine, while the earth cable will later be disconnected from the chassis and gearbox. At the rear, the inner covers for the lighting clusters need to be removed to allow the wiring loom to be disconnected from the lights

Chassis swap

15 The engine EGR electronic control unit is located under the middle front seat. It is unplugged and the loom pushed down through the seatbox cover.

16 The speedometer cable is detached from the transfer gearbox by taking out the special clip, held by an M6 stud and nut. A small 10 mm socket just fits.

17 Difficult bolts, such as the seatbox to chassis bracket bolts on each side, are best to be simply drilled out – rather than struggling in a confined space.

18 The front brake pipes on each side were detached at the flexible hose. A container hung on the coil spring is used to catch the draining brake fluid.

19 The rear of the body will be supported by a stout length of steel tube, across the width. Steel plates will be welded to the ends to prevent it rolling.

20 The body is slowly lifted by the two-post ramp in very small steps, each time checking the clearance and looking for missed connections.

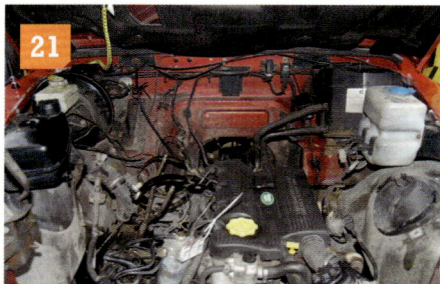

21 Particular attention and checking at the engine bay is crucial, as there are so many connections – it would be very easy to miss a small cable or hose.

22 Once everything is clear and disconnected, the body is fully raised clear on the ramp, allowing the rolling chassis to be wheeled out.

WORK SAFELY
Disconnect battery cables (earth first) before work commences.

Wear googles, gloves and hearing protection when grinding, cutting, drilling and hammering.

Wear a bump cap when working underneath the vehicle.

After lifting, lower the body to a safe position as soon as possible.

With the body now lowered to a safe position, we're ready to start swapping the mechanical components over to build up the new rolling chassis.

and trailer plug and pushed down through the body to the chassis. It's worth making notes of wiring connections to aid refitting, which is faster than having to look up wiring diagrams.

Where they are fitted, side steps support brackets are unbolted from the chassis, although the steps can be left bolted to the sills.

The remaining disconnection work will take place in the engine bay where a thorough and systematic approach is required with careful checking before any attempt is made to lift the body.

Some systems can remain largely intact. For example, the fuel filter housing can be unbolted from the wing (or the bulkhead in earlier models) but remain connected to the injection pump with a cable tie used to hold it to the engine at some convenient location. Likewise the power steering system can be left intact at this stage by unbolting the reservoir from the inner wing and tying it to the engine. When everything has been disconnected, check again. Did you remember the throttle cable? What about the vacuum pipe to the brake servo? There will probably be something still attached. On the plus side, if the body is raised very slowly, constant checking will probably find a remaining missed connection, before cables, pipes or hoses are stretched or damaged. It is vital to patiently take your time.

Body lifting

We've heard of numerous ways to lift a body from a Land Rover chassis without the luxury of a two-post ramp. Some are good, others dangerous. Ultimately, the only way to carry out the lift is by using proper lifting equipment such as block and tackle sets, cranes, chains, shackles and lifting strops that are in serviceable condition and rated for the load they'll be lifting. Structures from which any lifting gear is suspended must be capable of taking the load. Before lifting the body in one piece, ensure all doors are closed.

With my two-post ramp, lifting the body was very simple for this Defender 90. The front pads were lined up under the feet of the bulkhead, taking care not to foul the bulkhead outriggers on the chassis. At the rear, the lifting pads were kept outside the body area and a heavy steel pipe – with flat plates welded at each end for stability – was run through the gap between the tub and the chassis, just behind the rear wheels. The lifting pads then caught the protruding ends of the pipe on each side.

Then it was a matter of hitting the lift button on the ramp at intervals, lifting 50 mm or so at a time while checking in between lifts that all parts were properly disconnected, but without reaching or leaning under the suspended body. It is also important to listen carefully as the body raises – one can often hear if anything is awry, even over the drone of the electric motor. For example, I had the steering column unbolted at the power steering box, but not disconnected. There was a sudden clang as it dropped, causing momentary alarm – but thankfully no damage.

With anything raised up on a ramp (or by any other means) it is always important to take great care around the raised load, and not to venture under it. As soon as the body was clear, I pulled the rolling chassis out from under the body, then lowered the ramp until the body was just off ground level and could not be dislodged.

Next time

The body will stay in position until the next stage of the job is completed: dismantling the old chassis and building the parts up onto the new frame. I'll be covering that job in Part 2.

Chassis swap

PART 2
FITTING A NEW CHASSIS

Trevor Cuthbert continues our Defender re-chassis project by stripping the old chassis and transferring the parts to the new frame

TREVOR CUTHBERT

TOOLS REQUIRED:
Standard workshop tools, Engine crane or lifting gear, angle grinder with metal cutting discs

TIME:
Two days

COST:
up to £1254

DIFFICULTY RATING:
4/5

CONTACT:
Trevor Cuthbert Land Rovers, tel: 07890 868929, info@trevorcuthbert.com.
Richards Chassis Ltd, tel: 01709 577477.
BLRC, tel: 02897 519736, www.blrcvehiclespecialist.co.uk

THE OWNER OF the pristine low-mileage 300Tdi Defender 90 had ordered a heavy-duty galvanised replacement chassis from me to replace the original frame which was showing signs of its age. It would certainly need a new rear cross-member soon. In part one of this series in last month's LRM, I inspected the vehicle, looking for potential problems before working through all of the disconnections and finally lifting the body off as one complete assembly using the two-post vehicle lift. In this issue, we look at preparing the new chassis, and then transferring the complete running gear across to build up the new rolling chassis.

Galvanised and painted
Most of the new Land Rover chassis manufactured by Richards Chassis, are fitted straight from the galvanising process. The shiny layer of zinc on the chassis will protect it for many years to come and, to some owners, the visible galvanised rear cross member is a badge of honour. Another school of thought is that the visible signs of a galvanised chassis makes the Land Rover even more attractive to vehicle theives – and therefore it is important to, as a deterrent mechanism, have the chassis painted. And many owners of special Defenders and most classic Series vehicles prefer to

1 The new galvanised chassis is completely painted with an etch primer prior to receiving a coat of black chassis paint – a special paint for metal.

2 The etch primer dries to a dark grey colour, making it easy to check over the whole chassis to ensure no areas have been missed.

3 Before lifting the Land Rover body, almost all connections to the engine had been removed. The power steering pipes were all that remained to disconnect.

4 When lowering the heavy engine and gearboxes, safer control of the crane's hydraulic release valve is attained by using pliers to turn the valve.

paint the chassis black to preserve the vehicle's original appearance.

In this case, owner Mervyn asked me to paint his new chassis, before fitting it to his Defender, both to suppress the fact of the new chassis, and to protect the galvanised layer, thus prolonging the chassis life even further.

While the new galvanised chassis would appear to be an ideal surface to apply black paint to, it needs to be properly primed with etch primer, otherwise the new paint will simply peel off. Etch primer is a paint that is designed to physically bond itself to the substrate to which it is applied. This is achieved by combining an acid with the paint so that the acid microscopically etches the surface of the metal, forming a physical and chemical bond between the two. In most cases a colour will be added to the etch primer so that it remains visible during the painting process. The Tractol 729 Single Pack etch primer used on Mervyn's chassis was light grey in colour, becoming dark grey as it dried. I used Dulux Trade Metalshield Gloss Finish paint for the final black coat.

Engine out

The engine plus the main and transfer gearbox (R380 and LT230) combination were almost ready to be lifted from the old rolling chassis. Early on, when the Land Rover was up on the ramp, I had removed the nuts from below the engine mounts on the chassis and the gearbox mounts on the gearbox crossmember. These need an 18 mm socket on a long extension to reach them from below. The 300Tdi Defender arrangement for the engine and gearbox mounts is very convenient, where the stud comes through the mount vertically (rather than at an angle on earlier models), allowing the lump to be lifted without hindrance.

The power steering reservoir had been detached from the inner wing and was tied to the engine. To keep the power steering system largely intact, with all of the fluid retained, I removed the pipes running to the steering box and immediately tied them up to the engine, with the ends higher than the reservoir so that the fluid would not flow out. This left only minor drips of fluid from the steering box after the pipes were removed. All open ends were tightly covered to prevent dirt getting inside.

The engine and transmission was now ready to be lifted in one piece. I used a short chain across the lifting eyes on the engine (attached using small shackles) and a long hooked chain wrapped around the transmission brake area and the left side gearbox mount. Both chains were looped over the hook on the engine crane.

5 The engine, R380 gearbox and LT230 transfer gearbox were lifted from the chassis as one unit, the engine crane extended no further than the one tonne position.

127

Chassis swap

6 — An 8 mm spanner is used to hold the top of front damper and prevent it from turning, as the M10 nyloc nut is removed using a 17 mm spanner.

7 — Four nuts hold the front turrets to the chassis, with the turret ring below. These normally need a 13 mm socket to undo them, but these were 12 mm nuts.

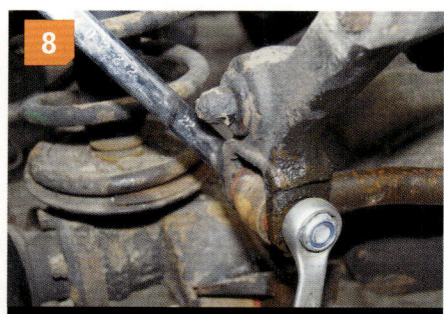

8 — The panhard rod is attached to the front axle and the chassis to prevent lateral movement between the two. Here it is being removed using 22 mm spanners.

9 — The chassis bracket for the panhard rod is bolted to the chassis at two points by long M12 bolts, here being removed with 19 mm spanners.

10 — On each side of front axle, flexible brake hoses are fixed to the small brackets on the chassis. They need a 16 mm and a 17 mm spanner to undo them.

11 — The radius arms on each side require a big 30 mm socket or spanner to remove the nuts. A recent rebush meant these nuts were fairly easy to remove.

12 — The front of the chassis is propped up on axle stands, allowing the axle to be rolled out from underneath, with much still attached to it.

13 — The axle is immediately transferred over to the new chassis, which gets it out of the way and begins the rebuild process. Note the height of the chassis.

14 — With the chassis low, the radius arms enter the chassis brackets at the horizontal, making it easy to refit the bushes, washer and 30 mm nut.

The crane needed extension to reach the best-balanced lifting point but, to keep it stable, I did not extend it further than the one tonne setting. Nonetheless, with the heavy lump lifted in the air, I was quick to get the chassis rolled out and the engine lowered to the ground.

Front axle change over

The front dampers were detached from the suspension turrets by removing the M10 nut from the top of the dampers. To do this, the centre is held by an 8 mm spanner, while a 17 mm spanner turns the nut. The centre can slip easily from the small spanner because there is not much material to hold against the force of the large spanner, but I just got the nuts off without having to use more brutal methods. The turrets were then removed from the chassis, leaving the front suspension free of the old chassis.

The panhard rod was loosened from the bracket that attaches it to the chassis, and from the steering box bracket by removing the large bolt. Two 22 mm spanners are needed for this but the bolt was free, as the bushes had all recently been replaced.

The front radius arms were pretty easy to detach from the chassis too, as new bushes had been recently fitted to them. The large nut on each side was new and a 30 mm socket wrench soon had them off.

WORK SAFELY
Wear safety glasses, gloves and hearing protection when grinding, cutting and drilling.

Ensure lifting gear and chain are in excellent condition and take great care with suspended engine and gearboxes. Lower to a safer height as soon as possible.

Wear gloves and safety boots for general work.

15 The chassis is now raised up by the trolley jack, making it easy to fit the coil spring and get the damper through the aperture.

16 Before the turrets are refitted, the threads on the damper get a liberal coating of copper grease to ease future removal when they need to be changed.

17 There is no engine and gearbox mass to compress the front springs, so these old weights push the chassis down enough to get a nut on top of the dampers.

18 It is correct procedure for these locking tabs to be fitted on the outside of each of the washers on the four M12 power steering box bolts.

19 A stout length of grey twin-and-earth electrical cable is easy to run through the right side chassis rail, from the aperture at the rear to the front.

Finally, the flexible brake hoses were detached from the chassis, and the axle was ready to be rolled out. I jacked the chassis up and removed the front coil springs and pushed the dampers down to clear the turret mounts and, therefore, the axle was free.

The axle was immediately fitted to the new chassis alongside, rolling it underneath and lowering the chassis to allow the radius arms to go through their chassis mounts at a shallow angle. This makes it easy to get the bushes in place and get the nuts on again. When the nuts were fully tightened, the chassis was raised up from the axle in order to refit the coils spring (not forgetting to put the turret rings in place) and refit the turrets.

The power steering box was transferred over to the new chassis, along with the panhard rod bracket. I find that, if the top bolt for this bracket is not fitted, the panhard rod can be attached to the bracket easily, with no twist in the bushes. Then the bracket can be pivoted on the middle bolt by applying turning force with a large spanner (32 mm) over the top, to get the top bolt through.

Chassis wiring loom
I have made the mistake in the past of fitting the rear top damper mounts to the chassis before running the chassis loom through the right-hand side chassis rail.

This means that there are three bolts through the chassis, for the loom to catch on. To get the loom though the chassis rail, I run a length of stout grey electrical cable through first.

This has enough stiffness to be pushed through, with flexibility to be fed through the hole at the rear and fished out through the hole at the front. Some yellow insulating tape on the end makes the cable easier to see through the hole – it is usually resting at the bottom of the rail and needs to be hooked with some wire and caught with the long-nosed pliers.

The chassis loom is then attached to the electrical cable with insulating tape and gently worked through the chassis.

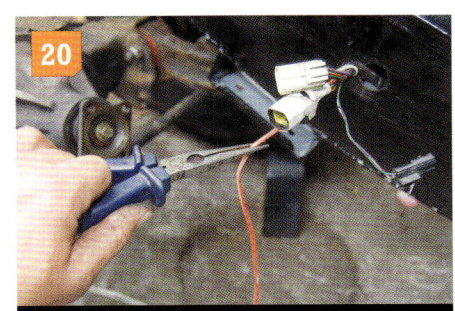

20 Chassis wiring loom is carefully pulled through the rail and plugs gently teased through tight aperture. Original rubber grommet will be refitted.

Chassis swap

21 The old rear upper damper mounts have been removed from the original chassis and bolted to the new chassis using original M10 bolts and new nyloc nuts.

22 There was around 15 litres of diesel left in the fuel tank, which was drained off into a jerry can for future reuse in the new fuel tank.

23 The fuel lift pipe and return pipe are removed from the top of the fuel tank and are immediately hung up to keep them clean for the new tank.

24 The fuel gauge sender unit and float are also perfectly serviceable and will be fitted to the new tank. This unit must also be kept clean.

25 After the gearbox cross member was removed from the old chassis, corrosion build-up could be clearly seen. The chassis is actually holed in places.

26 The rear axle is released from the chassis by removing the trailing arm nuts and unbolting the A-frame from the chassis. Tip chassis to clear the wheels.

The plastic connectors are fiddly to get out through the hole, but just be patient.

Fuel tank out

The fuel tank was not leaking but was quite blistered with rust and would need to be replaced soon, so Mervyn decided he'd like me to fit a new one.

Consequently the old one was not removed from the chassis. However, the remaining fuel was drained off while the fuel supply, return pipes and the sender unit were removed from the top of the tank and hung up to keep them clean.

Gearbox cross member

The gearbox crossmember is attached between the chassis rails by three M8 bolts on each side going through the chassis, as well as an M10 bolt at the leading edge on each side.

The small bolts were taken off with 13 mm spanners (one of these bolts clamps the earth cable to the chassis) and 17 mm spanners were used on the larger bolts. The cross member then needed to be knocked out with the copper mallet.

There had been a build-up of rust flakes between the chassis rails and sides of the crossmember; in fact, the chassis was completely holed by rust in a couple of areas behind the crossmember. Fitting the gearbox crossmember to the new chassis was easier; it was a snug fit but definately not too tight. The bolts were first cleaned up with a wire brush, particularly the one that clamps the earth cable.

Rear axle

The rear axle is held to the chassis by trailing arms on both sides – similar to the front radius arms, with 30 mm nuts on the ends, plus the A-frame that attaches to the top of the axle at one point and attaches to the chassis mounts at two points.

I removed the large bolts that hold the A-frame to the chassis mounts, and also

27 New chassis is raised at the rear using engine crane lifting at the middle cross member, and the rear axle is rolled into place – as my dog, Luna, looks on.

28 The front mounting bracket for the fuel tank, from the original chassis, is bolted to the pre-drilled holes in the new chassis. Use M8 nuts and bolts.

29 Access is tight for rear tank mounting points, so Britpart captive bolts make fitting simpler. A 13 mm ratchet spanner is quickest for the M8 nuts.

30 The new fuel tank is bolted in place on the front mounting point and the two at the back. Reinforced adhesive tape over the apertures keeps out dirt out.

31 The new rolling chassis is now ready for the engine and gearboxes. They are lifted again by the engine crane and the chassis rolled under them.

removed the radius arms bolts. The dampers had already been disconnected from their top mounts, and the rear coil springs remained attached to the axle.

The only other connection between the rear axle and the chassis was the single flexible brake hose. This I cut through in the middle, as it was perished and will be replaced with a new one.

The old chassis was raised in the air at the back and the axle rolled out. The new chassis was lifted at the back using the engine crane, to allow the axle to be refitted. This is quite convenient, as the crane offers easy height control when lining up the axle.

The old chassis was propped against the wall on its side, to allow easy access to the A-frame brackets (which needed the bolts to be cut off due to rust) and to the front and rear mud flaps for removal.

Fuel tank in
A new Britpart fuel tank – hastily delivered by BLRC – was fitted to the new rolling chassis, using new captive bolts at the rear, and the chassis bracket at the front. The other furniture for the tank has yet to be fitted, but it can be accessed from under the driver's seat after the body has been refitted.

Meanwhile the apertures in the tank are all sealed using heavy reinforced tape to keep dirt and foreign material out.

Engine and transmission back in place
Finally the engine and gearbox combination were reattached to the engine crane and raised in the air. The new rolling chassis was pushed underneath the lump and it was lowered down in to place. Again, the vertical mounting studs made getting the four attachment points in place very simple – all it takes is gentle and gradual lowering, while pushing the engine a little to direct it home.

Coming up in Part 3
Trevor completes the job by refitting the body assembly, reconnecting the systems and checking through to confirm that all is up and running correctly.

32

131

Chassis swap

PART 3

FITTING THE NEW CHASSIS

The end is in sight as Trevor prepares to reunite the Defender 90 body with the rolling chassis

TREVOR CUTHBERT

TOOLS REQUIRED:
Standard workshop tools, Engine crane or lifting gear, angle grinder with metal cutting discs

TIME:
Two days

COST:
up to £1254

DIFFICULTY RATING:
4/5

CONTACT:
Trevor Cuthbert Land Rovers, tel: 07890 868929, info@trevorcuthbert.com.
Richards Chassis Ltd, tel: 01709 577477.
BLRC, tel: 02897 519736, www.blrcvehiclespecialist.co.uk

THE BUSINESS of replacing a chassis in a Defender 90 is relatively straightforward using the correct tools, lifting equipment, a methodical approach and common sense for when things become a little tricky. So far in this build, the job has progressed as reasonable and smoothly as expected – helped by the fact that the Land Rover is a well-maintained example with recent work carried out, such as the replacement of the suspension bushes and the A-frame ball joint.

I have a similar job coming up on a 110 County Station Wagon and, in contrast, this will be a very different proposition – the chassis on this one is heavily corroded with most of the fixings to match.

The ease or difficulty of replacing the chassis is considerably affected by the condition of the vehicle.

The body shell of the Defender 90 had been detached from the rolling chassis, by removing all of the body mount bolts and releasing every connection between the body and the chassis – electrical links, fluid links and mechanical links. With the body then safely raised on the two-post ramp, the chassis was rolled out and everything was transferred over to the new chassis.

With the new rolling chassis nearly complete, reuniting the body and the chassis is largely a reversal of the first process. Rather than describe every single reconnection (which will be pretty clear if you've done the first half of the job on your Land Rover), I will cover the points that proved to be tricky, plus some useful tips along the way.

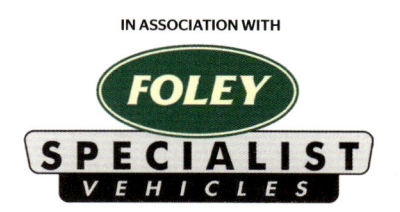

IN ASSOCIATION WITH
FOLEY SPECIALIST VEHICLES

Preliminary work

Before I could progress with lining up the new rolling chassis under the raised body shell, there were some final checks to carry out, and the fittings on the new fuel tank had to be dealt with (although this could be done later through the aperture in the driver's seat box). The fuel lift pipe, return pipe and fuel gauge sender had been hung up in the workshop out of harm's way. They were all in good condition and could be reused, with only the addition of new sealing gaskets and a new retaining clip for the fuel sender. The fuel return pipe is held to the tank with a pair of set screws, new ones having been supplied with the new Britpart tank. A cork gasket was fitted between the tank and the pipe mount and the screws tightened down fully. The lift pipe was replaced in a similar manner, although the mount is a larger circular affair, with five set screws holding it in place, again with a new cork gasket fitted. The float on the fuel gauge sender needs to be carefully fed into place in the tank, and the top of the sender sits on a new rubber gasket. The sender is fastened to the tank by a circular clip that is turned into three wedged lugs to lock it in place. This needs to be done correctly or the tank will leak.

1 New gaskets are required to seal the fuel gauge sender, fuel lift pipe and fuel return pipe to the new fuel tank so no fuel or vapour leaks will occur.

2 The fuel gauge sender unit is seated in place on the new gasket and the retaining clip is forced around into place, wedging firmly in three locations.

3 Breather pipe needs to be disconnected to allow the body to lower into place. It will then be threaded through and connected to the body fitting.

4 One of the studs on the exhaust down pipe flange sheared during removal. To reattach, the remaining stud was cut away, the flange drilled and a bolt fitted.

5 All body brackets, such as these to the lower front of the bulkhead, were coated with copper grease. This provides rust protection and helps them to slide into place.

WORK SAFELY
Safety glasses, gloves and hearing protection when grinding, cutting and drilling.

Ensure lifting gear and chain is in serviceable condition and take great care with suspended engine and gearboxes. Lower to a safer height as soon as possible.

Wear gloves and safety boots.

Chassis swap

> It's difficult to steer the chassis into its aligned position under the suspended body. It was roughly aligned and fine adjustment carried out using a trolley jack.

6

7 As the body is lowered, the rear mounts are first to engage. Alignment is pretty close, and a gentle nudge of the body gets it perfect.

8 This is a spare bulkhead outrigger bolt I keep for forcing final bulkhead alignment; the end has been ground to a blunt point to find its way through.

9 As soon as the bulkhead outrigger bolts are through the chassis and bulkhead foot, they are tightened in place, with any packing washers inserted first.

1 If the bulkhead outrigger bolts are particularly stubborn, packer washers can be inserted without removing the bolt, by cutting a slot out of each them.

2 These spacers were originally fitted between the rear body and the tubular outrigger on the left. The same number of spacers were now needed.

3 Both difficult to see and difficult to reach, the rear tub brackets bolt securely to the inner seatbelt mount. Don't forget them.

Body/chassis alignment and bolting

When lifting the body from the chassis for the first time, I should have marked the floor with the positions of all four tyres. This way, aligning the new rolling chassis under the supported body would have been simple. Instead, I had to guide the chassis into place by eye and by trial and error. Lifting the chassis at one end or the other with a trolley jack helps to fine tune the location but it took a fair amount of time to get it right. Of course marking the floor would only work for fixed lifting equipment, like the two-post ramp.

Due to the way in which the two-post ramp lifted the Land Rover body (not perfectly level) the rear was first to come back in contact with the new chassis mounts. The rear of the body had been lifted using a large stout steel tube across the rearmost lifting pads on the ramp; the pads having a convenient groove in them for the steel tube, with no risk of the tube slipping off. I had the alignment pretty close at this stage – slightly off at the rear and perfect at the front. A gentle controlled shove of the body at the rear had the holes at the back of the body aligned with the five mounts on the rear cross member. I put a couple of bolts through at each side to hold it stable at the rear, before moving forward and lowering more. The forward body mounts from the front lower part of the bulkhead slide down the outside of the chassis rails on each side. By bending these out slightly, they cleared the rails with no problem and yet again I put one bolt through on each side to further stabilise the reunion.

The key body to chassis bolts – and potentially the most difficult – are the bulkhead outrigger bolts. These are a pair of long M12 bolts that run through the bulkhead outrigger on the chassis and through the foot at the bottom of bulkhead on each side. The left side bolt went through quite easily after a firm thump with the copper mallet. On the right side, alignment was out by around 4 mm. This can be due to normal build tolerances or a bit of flexing of the body/bulkhead when the body was removed from the old chassis. I've also seen this problem when mating a new bulkhead on its own to a new or existing chassis, and my solution involves the use of an old bulkhead bolt. The bolt was ground to a dull point on the bench grinder. It was taped through the bulkhead outrigger, until the point just engaged with the bulkhead foot. The point just engages with the offset bulkhead foot and then, with the persuasion of a hefty lump hammer, the bolt is forced through, the point forcing the bulkhead foot into alignment as it progresses. Once the old pointed bolt is all the way through, another good bolt is tapped through from the other side – quickly at the point of alignment – knocking out the old bolt and the attachment is complete (another good bolt can be knocked through again from the other side, to get the threaded end towards the rear).

On this particular Defender 90, there were originally three washers between the bulkhead outrigger and the bulkhead foot on the right side, placed there at the factory for body alignment purposes. With the new chassis in place, it seemed that two of these washers would be needed for the same reason. Rather than removing the left side bulkhead bolt again, a slot was cut in the washers to slip them over the bolt in the space to be filled. As the bulkhead bolt was tightened again, the slots in the washers were turned to be out of line with each other to even out the clamping forces of the bolt. The other body to chassis bolts (mostly made up of M8 bolts) were very straightforward to get back in place with alignment being virtually spot on.

The brackets from the chassis to the inner seat belt mounts are adjustable; after the M8 bolt to the seat belt point was tight on each side, it is important to remember to tighten the two slider bolts

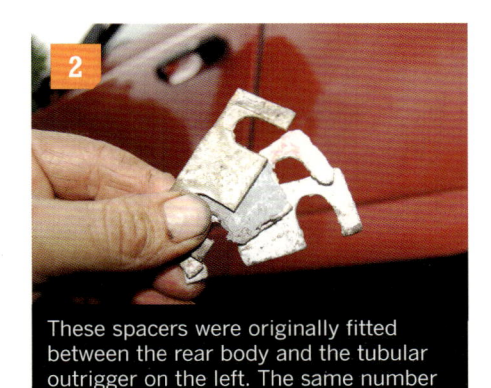

Chassis swap

4 The chassis loom on the right side needs to be fed through the rear of the tub, to reach the rear lamp cluster. The left side is easier, with fewer cables.

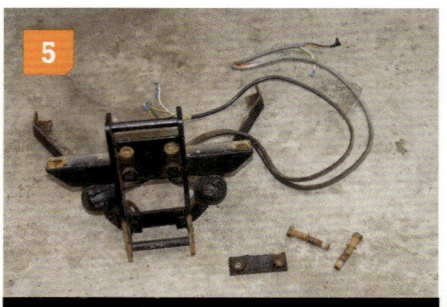

5 All accessories need to be refitted to the Land Rover. Most Defenders will have a towing bracket of some description. Some will also have steering guards.

6 The rear flexi brake hose needed to be replaced. Here the vice grips are holding the flimsy mounting bracket, while a 15 mm spanner is used to unscrew it.

7 Only a small section of brake pipe to the rear needed to be replaced. A professional crimping tool ensures an excellent flare every time.

Connecting up

The chassis wiring loom to the rear light clusters was fed through the holes in the rear tub, the right side being tricky due to the number of circuits that are located here. Extra systems are connected at the right, such as rear wash-wipe and heated rear window, whereas the left side normally only has the lighting loom to contend with.

Other items that need to be refitted include the towing bracket and electrics, the front bumper and any guards, such as the steering guard that had been fitted to this Land Rover. The mudflaps were not refitted because the brackets were quite rusty and the flaps were showing their age – I figured that owner Mervyn would want to fit new ones in due course.

The braking system needed to be reconnected. This was a simple matter of tightening up the front brake pipes to the flexi hoses attached to the chassis at the front. The brake pipes here were in good condition, having been recently replaced. At the rear, a new flexi hose was required between the axle and the chassis, and a new section of copper brake pipe was made to replace a damaged section (the end had seized to the old flexi hose and it twisted and weakened at the time of removal). With the brake pipes all

8 A vacuum brake bleeding kit makes bleeding the brakes quick and easy. Compressed air creates the vacuum, and new brake fluid is sucked through.

9 All ramp work is complete, and attention now turns to connecting and checking the engine bay systems. A methodical approach is imperative.

10 Looking down from the top of the radiator into the engine bay at the right, the lower oil cooler pipe is reconnected to the radiator.

11 Looking down on the power steering box in the engine bay, the steering linkage has been reattached and the locking bolt tightened up using a 13 mm spanner.

12 The fuel filter housing is bolted back on to the inner wing on the right side. There are captive rivnuts in the wing to make this job quick and easy.

13 The throttle cable is re-attached to the fuel injection pump, taking care to route the cable correctly from the bulkhead to the pump, with a smooth passage.

14 The viscous cooling fan is fixed back in place, using a 32 mm flat spanner. Remember that the thread is a left-hand one and tightens opposite to normal.

15 The original engine coolant was relatively new and was saved in this clean oil drainer. Here Matthew lends a hand, topping up the header tank, as I check the bleed points.

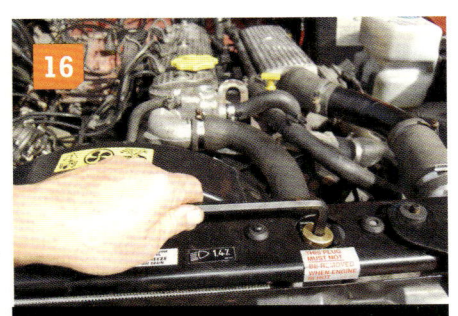

16 The radiator fills with coolant and the air is expelled at the top. When completely filled, the plug is refitted and tightened with a 10 mm Allen key.

17 When the thermostat housing is full, this plastic plug is replaced. As it is relatively fragile, I like to tighten it using a 21 mm spanner and a screwdriver together.

reinstated, the braking system was bled using a new bottle of Dot 4 brake fluid.

Starting at the hub furthest from the brake fluid reservoir (the back left wheel) and working progressively through the closer hubs, each brake calliper was bled using a Sealey vacuum brake bleeder kit. This device uses compressed air to create a vacuum in the chamber, which pulls the brake fluid through the pipes via a hose attached to the bleed nipple. It is excellent for one-man operation, and normally achieves a good firm brake pedal at first bleeding. However, I always check corners a second time to ensure that all air is out of the braking system.

The final stage of the job was to work through all of the connections in the engine bay, starting with the most inaccessible areas and working outwards. The first of these was the steering linkage and the pinch bolts. This is a crucial safety area and must be done correctly. A quality thread lock solution was applied to the threads on the pinch bolts to ensure that they could never work loose. With the radiator refitted, the bottom oil cooler pipe was reconnected using a 24 mm spanner, followed by the radiator and intercooler cowling and then the remaining coolant hoses and oil cooler pipe. All other reconnections in the engine bay were straightforward and a fairly simple matter of reversing the removal process. However it is very important to be methodical and check everything at least twice – there is so much going on in an engine bay that it would be easy to miss something.

In the cab, the hand brake was reconnected using access through the middle seat box aperture. The speedometer cable was reconnected to the transfer gearbox through this location as well, and the gear shifter was refitted, tightening its M10 nut with a 17 mm ratchet spanner. Finally, all of the interior trim and gear knobs were refitted. Other than pouring fuel into the new tank, the final task to complete was to refill the cooling system, bleeding the air out in the process. Coolant was poured in to the header tank with plugs removed from the radiator and the thermostat housing. As soon as the coolant filtered through and filled the radiator, the plug was replaced as the coolant began to overflow from the top. Further filling had the same effect at the thermostat housing and that plug was also replaced.

Back in commission
The Defender's engine started immediately, because there was still fuel in the injection pump. There wasn't even a single misfire as fuel was sucked up through the lift pipe.

A happy Mervyn collected his Land Rover and reported no problems during the 64-mile drive back home to Derry.

18 Handbrake cable is routed through the seat box and reattached to the handbrake. A new split pin is fitted because the old one was fragile.

19 Final fit out in the cab includes refitting the gear shifter, using a 17 mm spanner and reattaching the battery cable. All removed trim is replaced too.

20 Mervyn (pictured looking ecstatic) collected his Land Rover and he reported no problems during his 64-mile drive home.

Fit a fuel tank guard

Steel fuel tanks are tough, but they're vulnerable off-road. Protect them with a guard – which is simple to fit, as Trev explains...

FIT A FUEL TANK GUARD

TREVOR CUTHBERT

TOOLS REQUIRED:
13mm spanners and socket wrench
Drill with 8mm bit
Trolley jack or transmission jack

TIME:
1 hour

COST:
£125 fuel tank guard

DIFFICULTY RATING:
2/5

CONTACT:
BLRC Tel: 02897 511763

MY FRIEND Matthew Spoerri owns a Defender 90 that is used mainly for weekend fun with local offroad clubs, such as the Northern Ireland Land Rover Club. He keeps it well maintained and constantly strives to make it as capable as possible and well protected against breakdown. This is because over the years we have had occasion to do in-field repairs or – worse – recover one of our Land Rovers home on the back of the trailer.

This winter, Matt wanted to carry out some maintenance and improvements to the Defender, and the first of these was to protect the fuel tank which he always feared was going to get badly bashed in the course of his off-road driving.

The fuel tank on a Defender 90 is mounted on the centre right (viewing from the driver's seat) of the Land Rover on models up to the end of 300Tdi production in 1998. For the Td5 and TDCi models (1998 onwards), the fuel tank is mounted at the rear. Both locations have their vulnerabilities and there is an extensive array of protection solutions available from aftermarket suppliers to prevent physical damage from rocks and tree stumps, and on ramp-over exercises.

Matt's 90 is from the 1980s and has been retro-fitted with a 200Tdi engine, so the fuel tank is of the centre-mounted variety.

Our local Land Rover specialist, BLRC, has plenty of underbody protection for all Land Rover models and they supplied the heavy galvanised steel tank guard to be fitted here.

This particular tank guard is a good design from the fitting point of view. It bolts to the chassis in a very convenient way, needing only two 8mm holes to be drilled in a support bracket near the front radius arm mount where it is attached with two M8 bolts. The centre mount uses an existing bolt on the chassis rail, while the rear of the guard hangs firmly from the tubular outrigger via two U-bolts.

The job of fitting the tank guard takes around an hour and is a very worthwhile addition to a Land Rover that's used off-road. We took the time to clean the tank and coat it with underbody sealant first, as the guard forms a new mud trap. Such a trap holds moisture and therefore increases the chances of premature rusting of the fuel tank but, knowing Matthew, he will be clearing out the mud at every opportunity anyway.

IN ASSOCIATION WITH

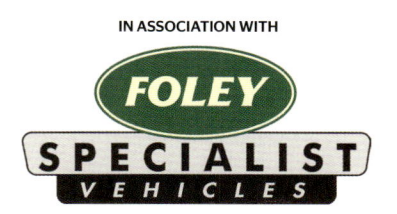

FOLEY SPECIALIST VEHICLES

1 The main clumps of mud and dirt were scraped away from the fuel tank and the bracket, and then a stiff brush was used to clean the rest off.

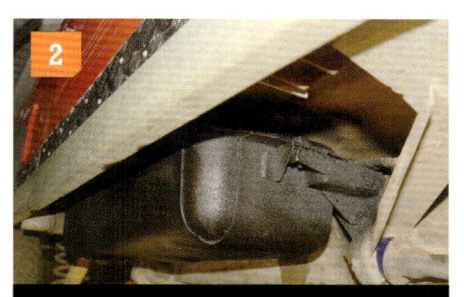

2 A liberal coating of underbody sealant was sprayed over the underside of the fuel tank, getting it well into all of the nooks and crannies.

3 Dents and damage to gearbox crossmember illustrates just how vulnerable fuel tank is, in its location at the centre of the Land Rover.

4 The heavy-gauge steel fuel tank guard has been galvanised for rust protection. It is a well-engineered and very strong piece of underbody armour.

5 Fitting such a heavy piece of steel is best carried out by two persons. If using a vehicle lift, this transmission jack will take the strain.

6 Front edge of the tank guard is bolted to this radius arm mount's reinforcing strut on the chassis, through two 8mm holes drilled in vertical face.

7 The tank guard is offered up to the chassis using the transmission jack. The job could also be done on the driveway with two people.

WORK SAFELY
The job of fitting a heavy piece of steel, such as a tank guard, is best carried out by two people for safety reasons.

Otherwise, the job can be done by one person using lifting gear such as a trolley jack on the ground, or using a transmission jack if the Land Rover is on a ramp.

It is important to wear appropriate protective clothing, particularly safety boots when working with heavy objects and heavy tools.

The main thing to be wary of when fitting the tank guard is working with such a weight in an essentially overhead position. The job can be done on the ground, as the Land Rover has enough ground clearance.

8 The guard is slightly tilted on the jack, and is almost aligned with the support bracket on the chassis. It will be easy to get the bolts in place now.

9 The rear of the tank guard hangs from the tubular outriggers, using a pair of U-bolts. These 51mm exhaust clamps will do the job very well.

Fit a fuel tank guard

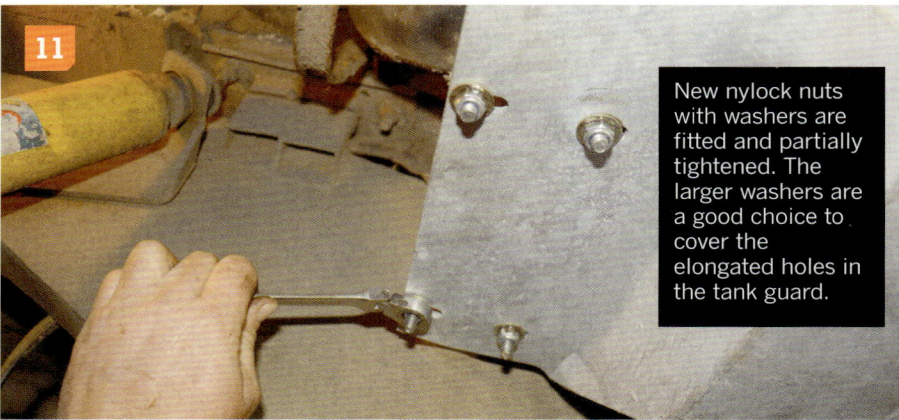

10 Now that the front bolts are in place, the jack is used to push the rear up close to the tubular outriggers, to get the U-bolts through.

11 New nylock nuts with washers are fitted and partially tightened. The larger washers are a good choice to cover the elongated holes in the tank guard.

12 The centre mounting bracket picks up one of the existing bolts that is present for the transfer gearbox mount which passes through the chassis rail.

13 The two front M8 bolts holding the new fuel tank guard to the chassis bracket are now fully tightened, again using large washers and new nylock nuts.

14 The sloped design of the front of the tank guard should allow the Land Rover to better skid over obstructions, rather than becoming snagged on them.

15 The new tank guard, plus existing rock sliders and front differential and steering protection, completes the armour for this well-guarded Defender 90.

140

Richards chassis

Unit F2
Swinton Bridge Industrial Estate
Whitelee Road
Swinton
Mexborough
S64 8BH

We can now fit your new chassis!!!
Please contact us to discuss your requirements

DISCOVERY 2 CHASSIS NOW AVAILABLE

Futureproof your Landrover with a Richards Chassis

Tel: 01709 577477   Fax: 01709 577442
Web: www.richardschassis.co.uk   Email: info@richardschassis.co.uk

Rear axle rebuild

PART 1
REBUILDING A REAR AXLE

Discovery and Defender rear disc-braked axles are usually repaired as the parts wear. But when the axle casing itself is worn out, it's time for a full rebuild

TREVOR CUTHBERT

TOOLS REQUIRED:
Standard workshop tools, Hub box spanner or socket, 52mm deep impact socket, Bolt Grip nut remover sockets, starter set or full set

TIME:
Three hours

COST:
DIY, no cost to dismantle

DIFFICULTY RATING:
2/5

THE INTRODUCTION of the Discovery and later Defender models brought improved axles. Gone was the rear drum-braked axle in favour of disc brakes front and rear, and the differentials (and therefore the half shafts) on later Discovery 1 and 300Tdi Defender 90 became 24-spline instead of the earlier 10-spline versions.

However, some improvements came to the last production of the previous model as new parts and tooling came on stream. A good example is the last of the 200 Tdi Defender 90 models which benefited from rear disc brakes and 24-spline differentials. This was the case on a 200 Tdi 90 I'd purchased as an engine donor for a project. The rear disc-braked axle was not needed and was in poor condition, so it was stored for future repair at some point.

The main issue with this axle was the axle casing itself – the structure to which the stub axles, the hubs, the brakes, half shafts and the differential are all assembled. The casing was heavily rusted to the point where one of the lower spring seats had fractured and was missing, with the coil spring simply resting on top of the casing. The radius arm brackets were also severely weakened by rust. Likewise, the anti roll bar brackets were weakened and holed and large chunks of rust had accumulated where the bump stops contact the axle. All in all, it was a pretty bad case, and although many of the brackets can be replaced by welding new items on, the casing itself was probably too weak in key areas for this to be a satisfactory solution.

The whole axle might have been considered scrap but for the fact that the hubs and brakes seemed to have been well maintained and the differential was in good condition. So when a job came up that called for a Defender 90 disc-braked axle, I dug the old 200 Tdi one out of storage to rebuild it with a new casing.

The strip-down
The first task was to drain the axle of gear oil (EP90) by removing the drain plug from the lower right of the differential area. A drain plug wrench can be used, but the end of a half-inch drive socket wrench fits perfectly after any dirt is

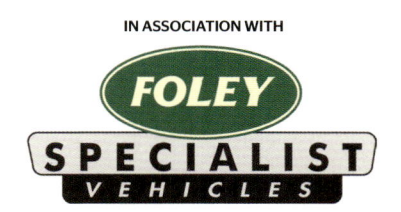

1 First clue that the axle casing is rotten is the absence of a spring cup. Chunks of flaky rust came off where the bump-stops meet the axle.

2 In the area where the axle bracket for the spring cup was missing, the axle casing is too corroded to have any chance of making a successful weld.

3 The anti roll bar mounts, whether needed or not, are also badly corroded and extremely weak. The axle casing would be dangerously weak.

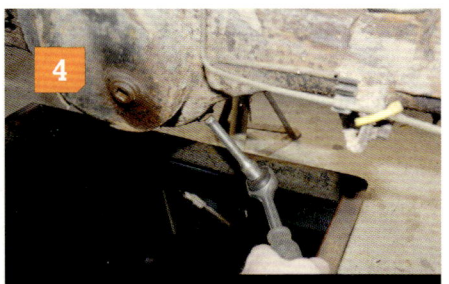

4 The drain and filler plugs are reasonably free and the oil looks clean enough, suggesting the axle has been given regular maintenance.

5 The rear brake pipe's T-piece connector is removed from the bracket above the differential. It may be reused if it proves to be in good condition.

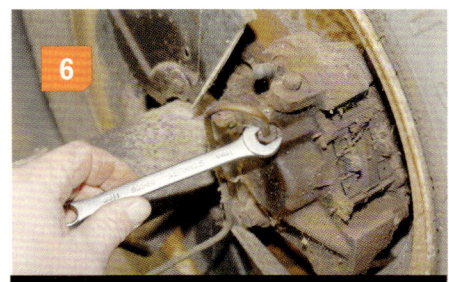

6 At the brake callipers, the brake pipes are undone using an 11mm open-ended spanner, and the pipes removed from the axle.

7 The half shafts are located to the hubs by five M10 high tensile bolts on each side, removed using a 17mm socket, here with an impact wrench.

8 The half shaft flanges are usually adhered to the hub by gasket and gasket seal, but are easily levered free with a pry bar or similar.

9 Half shafts can then be fully withdrawn from the casing, which has the effect of freeing up the rear differential for removal from the axle.

10 Nuts holding rear differential to axle are the same size as propeller shaft nuts. Here they are being removed with a 9/16th propshaft socket.

11 With all of the nuts removed the rear differential needs to be pried away from the axle casing, evenly all around to avoid it jamming on the studs.

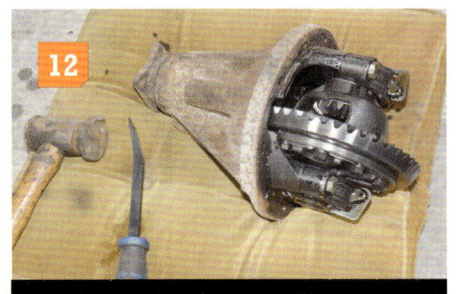

12 When removing a heavy differential without help, a soft cushion or similar protects it from damage, should it be allowed to fall from the axle.

Rear axle rebuild

13 With differential removed, as much of remaining gear oil as possible can be drained from the axle casing by tipping it appropriately over the drain pan.

14 Replacement axle casing does not have these studs fitted, so originals can be reused by tapping them out, using a soft copper headed hammer.

15 The studs are serrated where they sit in the flange. They'll be cleaned in the parts washer and their condition will then be checked before re-use.

16 The A-frame ball joint needs to be removed from the axle casing. Here looking up from below, the split pin is pulled out from the castle nut.

17 Castle nut is loosened with a 30mm ring spanner, then bashed with a copper mallet to break joint between the ball joint and the axle mount.

18 Any other reusable parts, such as this plastic clip for the brake pipes, are removed from the axle casing. This will be refitted to the new casing.

"The axle is stripped to its component parts"

poked out of the square hole.

Using an 11mm spanner, the brake pipes were removed from the brake calliper on each side. The brake pipe T-piece was unbolted from the mounting bracket over the differential and the brake pipes removed. New brake pipes will be made when the axle is finally fitted to the Land Rover.

The axle halfshafts are held to the hub by their drive flange with five M10 bolts which can be removed using a 17mm socket and possibly an impact driver. With a little leverage, the flange will come free of the hub and the complete half shaft can be withdrawn from the axle. The splines on the half shafts were in good condition and can be re-reused.

Once the halfshafts are disengaged from the differential, the differential can be removed from the axle casing. It is held by ten nuts on 3/8" UNF studs in the casing, removed by a 9/16" spanner or socket.

There is a special 9/16" propeller shaft socket tool available, which is ideal for removing differential nuts.

A few gentle taps with a soft mallet breaks the seal to the axle casing, and the differential is pulled evenly from the axle using a little leverage where necessary. Like the half shafts, the differential is in good condition and can be fitted to the new axle casing without the need for any servicing. The differential studs are also saved from the old axle casing for re-use with the new casing, following a good clean up.

The axle is propped on an axle stand to allow one of the road wheels to be removed, giving access to the brake calliper, which needs to be unbolted and lifted off, to allow the hub to be removed. The brake callipers will be inspected and either serviced with new pistons and seals, or replaced with new callipers – depending on how bad they are. New brake pads will be fitted as a matter of course.

The large hub nuts are removed with a 52mm hub (box) spanner or a deep socket. They are both threaded normally. As the hub is withdrawn from the stub axle, the wheel bearings come with it as one assembly and will be taken out for inspection and re-greasing.

The hubs turn free and true on the axle, and the bearings appear in good condition and have probably been replaced not too many miles ago.

The bolt heads holding the stub axle to the casing look like they will be challenging due to the ravages of rust, but they come out relatively easily, except for one that shears off and one that becomes rounded.

A Bolt Grip socket of the appropriate size for a 17mm bolt head soon has the rounded bolt removed. These sockets have a reverse spiral flute design which securely grips the rounded head, and are excellent for stubborn or heavily-painted nuts and bolts.

The sheared bolt doesn't matter because the old axle casing will be discarded and all new bolts will be used to fit the stub axle to the new casing.

Now that the axle is completely stripped down to its component parts, everything will be inspected to determine the need to repair or replace, and an order will be placed for new bolts, seals and gaskets.

■ In Part 2 we will be completely rebuilding the axle components on to a new axle casing, in readiness to be fitted.

19 After removing the brake pads, the bolts holding the calliper to the axle are released using a bi-hexagonal 13mm socket with breaker bar.

20 The tabs on the lock washer are levered back from the hub's outer lock nut and the inner adjuster nut, leaving them free to be unscrewed.

21 The outer lock nut is extremely tight and using this hub-nut box spanner it's difficult to apply any real torque on such a shallow nut.

22 But 24-volt impact wrench with Sealey 52mm deep impact socket makes short work of removing the lock nut – a worthwhile investment.

23 Now the lock washer and adjusting nut are removed, and the hub can be lifted off the axle, complete with its bearings.

24 Most stub axle bolts are removed with a 17mm socket. Others need a Bolt Grip socket. Alternatively, cut with the angle grinder.

WORK SAFELY

When working on an axle that has been removed from the vehicle, ensure it is secured on a sturdy support and cannot slip or rotate off, causing injury.

Oil drained from the axle should be taken to a recycling centre for safe disposal.

Wear barrier cream or gloves to protect skin from oils.

Wear thick gloves when scraping down and working near sharp and rusted edges.

If an angle grinder is to be used, wear thick protective gloves and face/eye protection.

25 The six bolts are removed, allowing the stub axle to come free of the casing. The mount plate is rusty but the stub axle may be useable.

26 The rear axle now completely stripped down to component parts. Everything will be cleaned and inspected to determine re-use or replacement.

Rear axle rebuild

PART 2
REBUILDING A REAR AXLE

Trevor Cuthbert concludes his Defender rear disc-braked axle rebuild with a swathe of new components

TREVOR CUTHBERT

TOOLS REQUIRED:
Standard workshop tools, hub box spanner or socket

TIME:
Three hours

COST:
Costs: brake discs and pads kit £36, stub axles kit £48, brake callipers £60, bolts and gaskets £12, gasket sealer £2, axle oil £9, brake pipes, fitting and hose £12, galvanised spring-seat kit £22

DIFFICULTY RATING:
2/5

MY SPARE Defender 90 rear axle had been stripped to replace a badly corroded axle casing. The trailing arm and spring cup brackets on the casing were too rusted to do their job; likewise new brackets couldn't be welded on.

A new axle casing costs over £2500 from Land Rover, but good used ones can be found online from £150. Luckily, I had a good used one in storage. The previous owner had shotblasted the casing and had it bright zinc plated as an experiment, so when he offered it for sale for £50, I snapped it up.

For now, the axle casing was set up on a pair of heavy axle stands for the initial job of building on components and assemblies. It will then have road wheels fitted for moving it as it becomes heavy and less manageable. All of the fixings had been cleaned up to determine which were re-usable.

The studs were re-fitted to the axle casing to hold the differential assembly on. These are 3/8 UNF and were in good condition and pressed through from the inside. An old 3/8 nut was spun on to each stud with a 9/16 socket on the impact gun to seat the stud and pull in completely into position.

Hubs and Discs

THE STUB axles were re-usable but, as a new stub axle kit only costs around £30, it made sense to order a pair, as the bolts and seals would have to be ordered anyway.

The brake discs and stub axles had a thin layer of protective oil, which I removed with brake cleaning spray. The stub axles were fitted to the axle casing using new M10 bolts with a fresh gasket, and gasket sealant applied. The bolts were tightened to 100 Nm.

The assembly of the hubs and bearing depends on the axle and vehicle specification and the combination of new parts used. Always refer to the workshop manual for your vehicle for the particular assembly procedure.

In this case, the hub bearings were inspected and found to be in good condition and all that was needed was to repack each bearing with grease to be refitted to the hub.

The bolts holding the old brake disc to the hub were loosened fairly easily, using a breaker bar on a 14mm socket wrench, with a pry bar across the wheel stud to prevent rotation. Then a few taps with the hide and copper mallet had the brake disc free from the hub. The inner oil seal was removed and discarded, allowing the inner wheel bearing to be removed, inspected, and re-packed with grease before being refitted.

A fresh oil seal was then tapped in place, before the new brake disc was set on to the hub. As the disc is tapped into position, it's important to make sure that the bolt holes are correctly aligned with those on the hub.

The bolts were cleaned with a wire brush and thread-lock solution applied to the threads. They were then tightened with a torque wrench to 72 Nm.

With the new brake discs and the wheel bearings fitted, the hubs were offered up to the stub axles. The hub's inner adjuster nut was fitted to the stub axle and tightened up by hand. It was then tightened up to 60 Nm torque, before being backed off by 90 degrees. The nut was then retightened to approximately 10 Nm (essentially just past hand tight). Here, the feel of the hub when spun on the stub axle comes into play – check if it's binding, or whether it is free to turn without any lateral play in the hub.

The lock washer is then fitted, followed by the outer lock nut. This nut is tightened to a torque setting of 90 Nm before the lock washer is bent over both nuts to prevent loosening.

2 The studs that hold the diff to the casing are pushed through the casing from inside and pulled into position using an old nut, which is then removed.

1 The replacement axle casing is set up on sturdy axle stands to be worked on. All of the other components will gradually be built on to the casing.

3 New brake discs, brake callipers and brake pads were required, as the old items were well past their best. New stub axles will also be fitted.

4 A selection of fresh gaskets is now required for the various fittings we are working on Sealant will be used on all the mating surfaces.

5 A new inner oil seal is fitted to each of the stub axles. This oil seal meets the raised section on the half shaft to prevent gear oil leaking into the hubs.

Rear axle rebuild

6 A small bead of sealant is applied and smoothed before the gasket is put in place. The other mating surface on the casing is treated similarly.

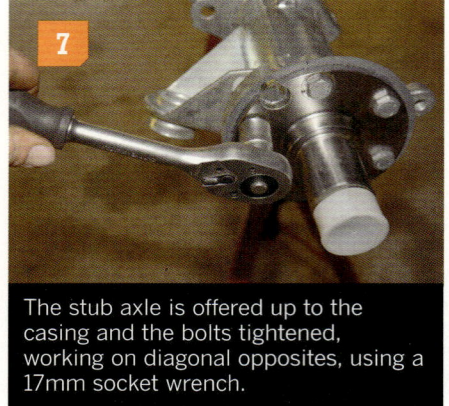

7 The stub axle is offered up to the casing and the bolts tightened, working on diagonal opposites, using a 17mm socket wrench.

8 Five bolts on the back of the hub holding the brake disc need a socket and breaker bar to release the worn and rust-pitted disc.

9 Old disc is tapped off with a mallet. Inner oil seal is pried out and the inner bearing cleaned, checked and greased before refitting with a new seal.

WORK SAFELY
The torque settings mentioned here apply only to the particular axle being assembled. Always refer to the workshop manual for the correct settings for your vehicle/axle.

When working on an axle that has been removed from the vehicle, ensure it is secured on a sturdy support and cannot slip or rotate off.

Wear barrier cream or gloves to protect the skin from oils.

10 New brake disc is tapped on to hub. The bolts aare cleaned, and thread-lock fluid applied before fitting and tightening using a 14mm bi-hex socket.

11 The outer wheel bearing is also in fine condition and is refitted, after it has been thoroughly cleaned and repacked with fresh grease.

12 The hub is pushed home on the stub axle with the wheel bearings in place. The inner thrust washer is pushed on, then the adjuster nut.

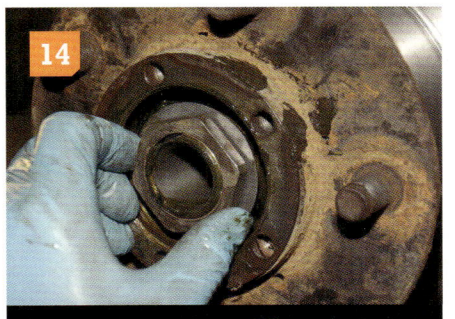

13 The new lock washer (right) is placed on the stub axle, before the outer lock nut. The original nuts are re-used, after cleaning.

14 A hub box spanner, or 52mm impact socket is used to tighten the outer nut, locking it in to the inner nut, with the lock washer sandwiched between.

15 After the nut is tightened, the lock washer is bent over the edge of both nuts using a large screwdriver to prevent movement.

Diff and Halfshafts

TO FIT THE differential assembly a new gasket is used, with gasket sealant on either side after the mating surfaces have been cleaned.

The differential might need some persuasion to fit over the studs, with careful and precise alignment, but in this case it slotted home easily first time. The diff is held by 3/8 UNF Nyloc nuts, tightened with a 9/16 socket wrench.

With the differential in place, the drive shafts were refitted to the axle with new sealed gaskets on each side. Tighten the new OEM drive flange bolts to 65 Nm.

1 The differential is now fitted to the axle casing, with a new gasket and sealant applied to the mating surfaces, and new nylon locking nuts.

2 The half shafts are fed through the hub into the axle casing and engaged with the diff. It takes a little wiggling to get them home and in place.

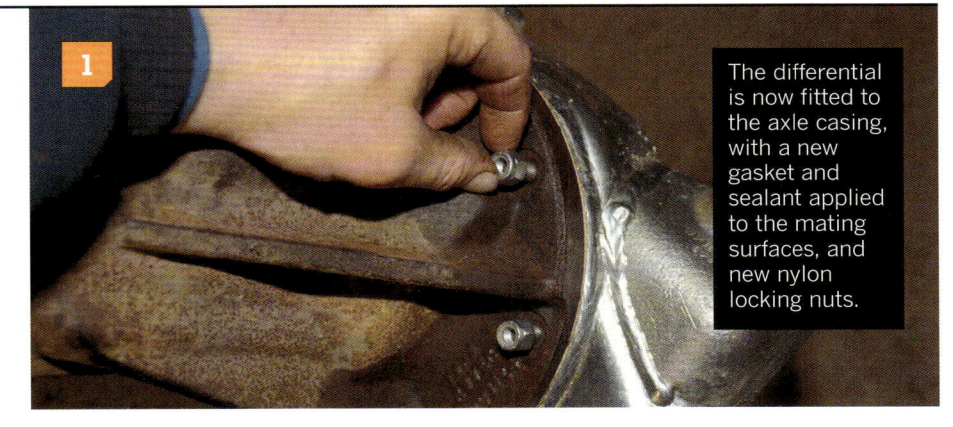

3 As with the stub axle bolts, new OEM quality M10 bolts are being used for the half shafts. These too have thread-lock material pre-applied.

4 The five driveshaft bolts on each side are tightened with a 17mm socket. Again the pry bar is used on the wheel nuts to hold the hub firm.

Rear axle rebuild

Final Preparation

THE REAR AXLE will soon be fitted to a Land Rover, so a new brake pipe T-piece was attached using an M6 bolt, and a new brake flexi hose was fitted to the front of the T-piece (17mm spanner). New brake pipes from the T-piece to the callipers were made using a flaring tool, and fitted with an 11mm spanner.

The axle needed 1.7 litres of oil, the plug being removed with a 1/2 socket drive. A new axle breather collet was fitted to the casing, into which a breather hose will be connected when the axle is fitted to the Land Rover.

When the finished rear axle is fitted into a Defender 90, it will give good service for many more miles to come.

1 Fit callipers using new bolts, and with the dust shield bracket held under the bolt heads. Tightened with a 14mm bi-hex socket wrench.

2 With calliper pistons pushed back, new brake pads are installed. Smear a trace of copper grease on the non-friction side to reduce possible problems.

3 Anti rattle springs are fitted, then the retaining pins are pushed through, and the ends of the pins are bent to keep them in position.

4 This galvanised rear spring seat kit now available from Britpart and comprising the seats and the retaining plates will help prevent rusting.

5 The old T-piece for the rear brakes had damaged threads. A new one with new flexi hoses is fitted to the bracket on the diff.

6 New copper brake pipes were cut, flared and bent to shape for the rear axle. The male ends are tightened into the T-piece with an 11mm spanner.

7 EP90 is poured into the axle until it is level with the fill hole and is just beginning to drip out. The filler plug is then fitted and tightened.

8 This later type axle casing is not threaded for the breather pipe banjo bolt. Instead this brass collet snaps into the 10mm hole to take the breather pipe.

9 The rear axle is complete and is now a "turnkey" assembly, with all ancillaries fitted. It is ready to be installed in a Land Rover and ready for work.

MM 4x4 Independent Land Rover Specialists

UK's largest Land Rover Centre for Parts, Accessories, Service and Vehicle Sales all under one roof

Parts & accessories for all Land Rover models
UK Next Working Day Delivery - Worldwide Export
Seen it cheaper elsewhere? Let us know!

Come and visit us! Just off junction 5 or 6 of the M5

Call or Click or Swipe!

Brands: BORG & BECK · ExMoor Trim · EBC BRAKES · Hi-Lift · MINTEX brake pads · K&N · AllMakes4x4 · BRITPART · ARB 4x4 Accessories · WARN · TerrafirMa · ProTrac · Warrior Winches · WIPAC · Bearmach · TIMKEN

A FAMILY BUSINESS CELEBRATING OUR 67TH YEAR!

OVERSEAS CALLS: +44 1905 451506
EMAIL: parts@mm-4x4.com

Tel: 01905 451506
www.mm-4x4.com

MM4x4
Droitwich Road
Martin Hussingtree
Worcester
WR3 8TE

---

choosePLATES

Ensure your number plates reflect the value of your Land Rover

- Fully legal and compliant
- Customisable design at no extra cost
- Durable number plates with 5 year guarantee
- Create your unique design online, choose font, flag, border

www.chooseplates.co.uk

Fitting a door latch

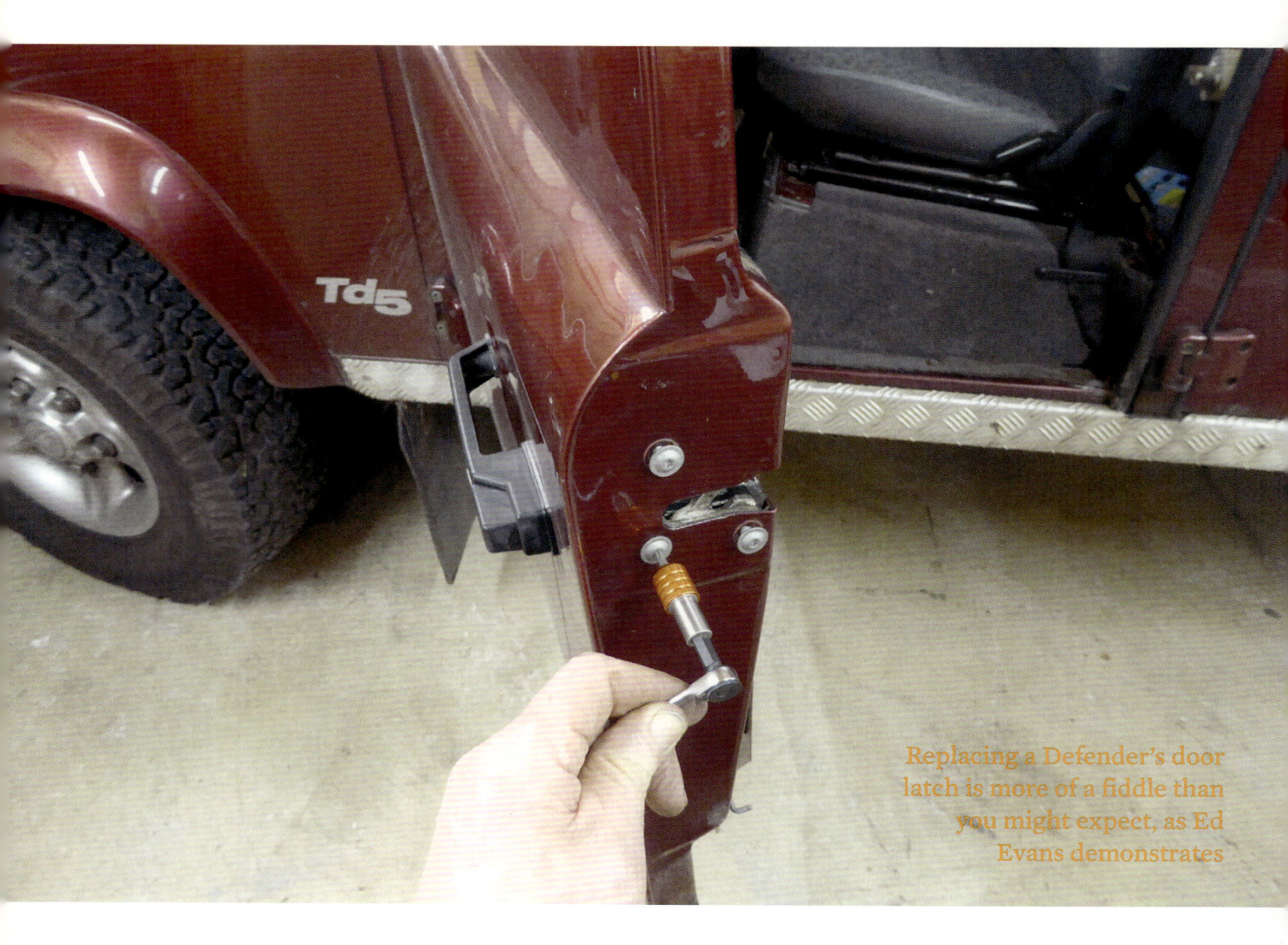

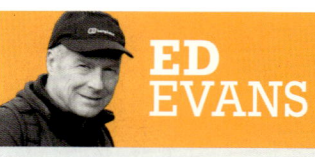

Replacing a Defender's door latch is more of a fiddle than you might expect, as Ed Evans demonstrates

ED EVANS

TOOLS REQUIRED:
General workshop tools

TIME:
1 hour

COST:
£25-30

DIFFICULTY RATING:
2/5

HOW TO REPLACE A DOOR LATCH

DEFENDER DOORS often don't shut in the way the door of a normal car or later Land Rover would be expected to. But before blaming a faulty latch, there are a few other points to check which can all affect whether the door shuts flush with the bodywork or fails to latch onto the striker in the door frame, or even latches onto the striker too tightly.

Check the condition of the door frame's rubber seal for kinks, distortion, swelling or breaks. If the seal is protruding at one point, examine the metal flange that the seal sits on, straightening any damage using pliers or a mallet and wood block. Test for play in the door hinge pins by trying to lift the rear end of the door up and down while it is open.

If hinges are worn, the door and the latch will be permanently out of alignment with the body and striker. Finally, if your door still only latches with a hard shove, consider that the window frame may just need bending out a tad to allow the latch to move inward sufficiently to hold onto the striker.

If all that is in order, or you know there is physical damage to the latch inside the door frame, then it's time to fit a new one. Replacing the latch is fairly easy, but it's important to disconnect and reconnect the components in the correct order. It also helps, after disconnecting each control rod, to refit its spring clip back onto the rod so it cannot become misplaced.

In the time between finding a problem with closing a door, and getting around to fix it, remind your passengers to push only on the external handle. Many people try to close an awkward door by pushing hard on the door panel, which simply puts dents in the soft aluminium.

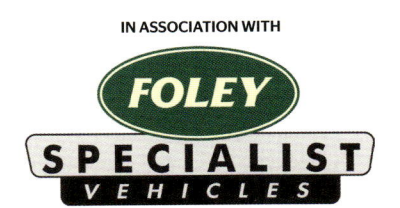

Removing the latch

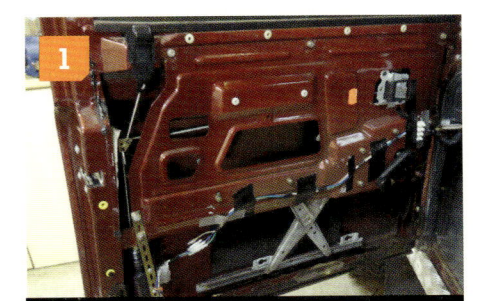

1. Remove the internal door pull handle and door card screws, then gently prise the securing plugs free to release the card, exposing the door shell.

2. Remove the plastic condensation barrier, then lower the window glass and ease the two clamp bolts (5/16 AF) to release the glass from the regulator.

3. The glass can now be lifted up and secured using adhesive tape over the top of the frame (use paper to protect the paintwork).

4. Release the door lock motor link (if fitted) from the latch. This one is a crude aftermarket fitment – normally there is a clip to release.

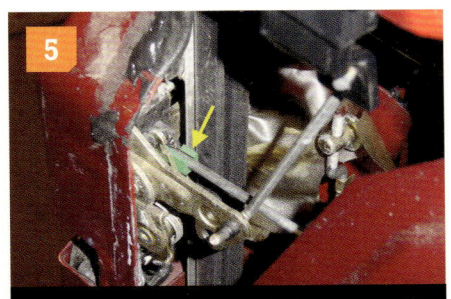

5. On top of the latch, push the green clip down to release the internal handle rod. Operate the handle and the link will pop free.

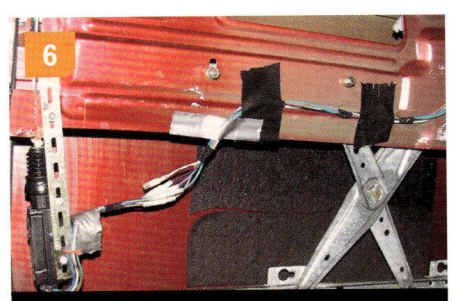

6. Before releasing the door reinforcement panel, any central locking and electric window harness will need to be released from it.

7. The door reinforcement panel can be detached after removing the six securing bolts as well as one nut at the front edge.

8. Remove all the fasteners except the lower front one, so the panel will hinge down, giving full access to the latch area.

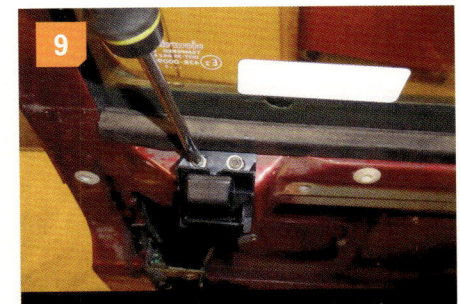

9. Remove the two screws that hold the internal lock button assembly, and carefully unclip it from the door casing (it's a bit delicate).

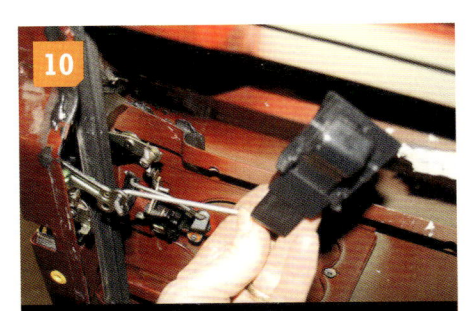

10. Turn the lock button and rod through 90 degrees to disengage the rod from the latch, noting the small bush in the link hole.

11. Disconnect the control rod from the exterior handle's lock lever by releasing the clip, then turn through 90 degrees to disengage from the latch.

12. The vertical rod connecting the external handle's push-button to the latch can now be unclipped at the handle, leaving it attached to the latch.

IN ASSOCIATION WITH
FOLEY SPECIALIST VEHICLES

Fitting a door latch

13 The rearmost window runner is released by removing two self-tapping screws fitted through the runner, to allow the latch to be manoeuvred out.

14 The latch is held into the door casing by these three screws which should release easily using a quality driver bit.

15 The latch needs to be turned through 90 degrees to work it around the window runner, and it can then be withdrawn sideways.

Fitting the new latch

1

2 The new latch is a straight forward replacement, but first, a couple of parts need to be transferred from the old latch.

The green clip (centre of pic) for the internal door handle rod needs to be transferred to the new latch before fitting.

3 Likewise, the control rod from the handle push-button lever to the latch needs to be transferred over to the new latch.

WORK SAFELY
Remember to always disconnect the battery earth before starting any DIY work.

Wear eye protection when releasing and fitting spring clips, in the event that they fly off and cause damage.

Be aware of sharp edges on the internal door frame parts, you could get a nasty surpise.

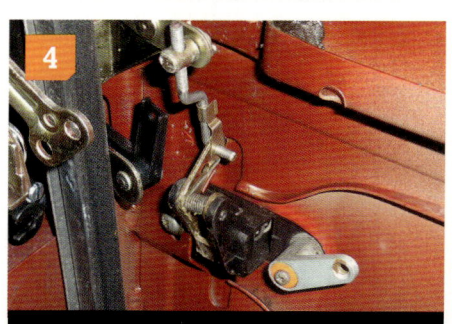

4 Fit the latch and add the external handle release rod first, adjusting its length if needed, then connect the remaining links, and reassemble.

154

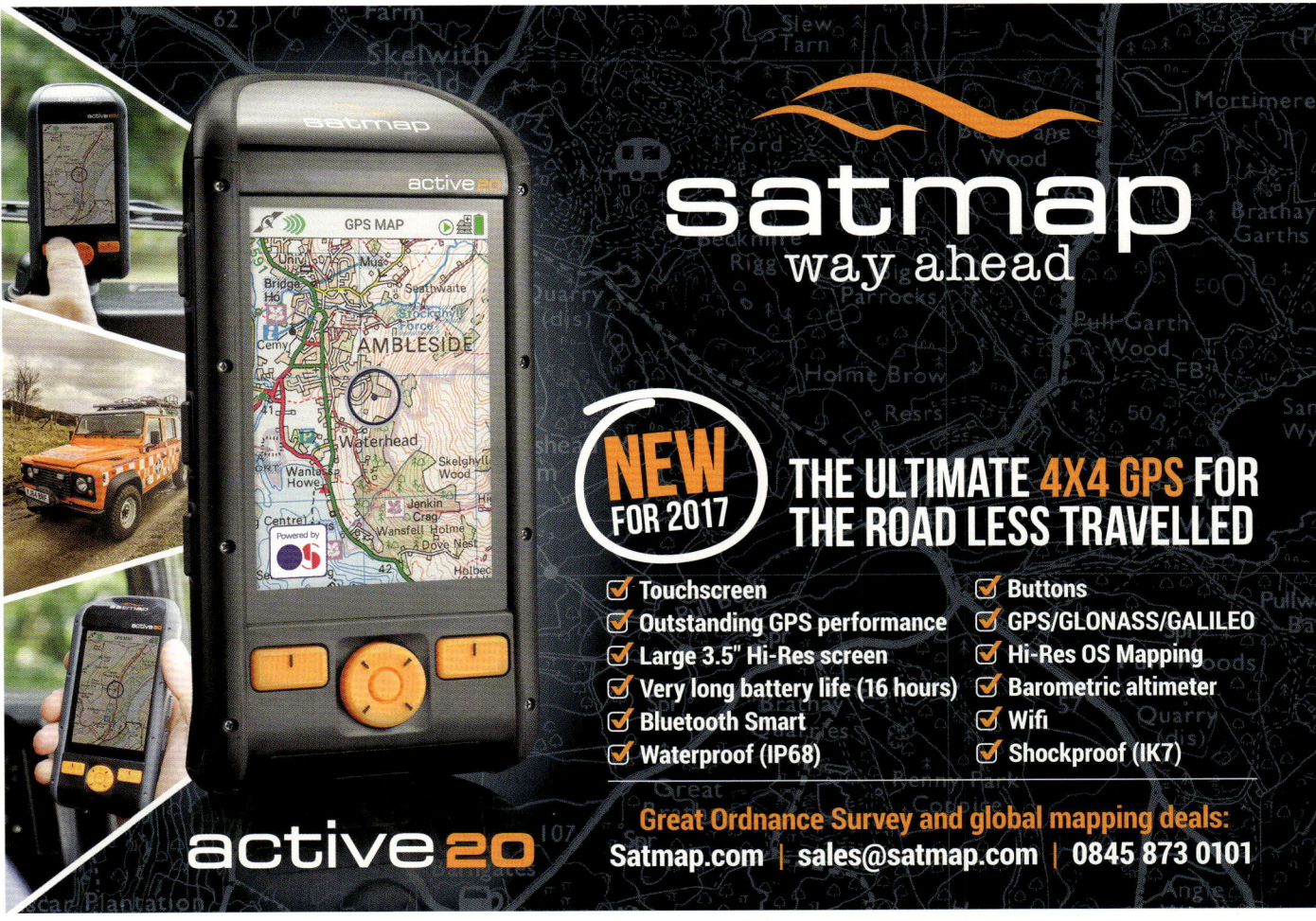

satmap
way ahead

NEW FOR 2017

THE ULTIMATE 4X4 GPS FOR THE ROAD LESS TRAVELLED

- ✓ Touchscreen
- ✓ Outstanding GPS performance
- ✓ Large 3.5" Hi-Res screen
- ✓ Very long battery life (16 hours)
- ✓ Bluetooth Smart
- ✓ Waterproof (IP68)
- ✓ Buttons
- ✓ GPS/GLONASS/GALILEO
- ✓ Hi-Res OS Mapping
- ✓ Barometric altimeter
- ✓ Wifi
- ✓ Shockproof (IK7)

Great Ordnance Survey and global mapping deals:
Satmap.com | sales@satmap.com | 0845 873 0101

active 20

Premium Quality
Lifetime Warranty

Best SELLER

NEW LIFT Technology
Uprated Intercooler

Defender TD5 / 2.4 / 2.2 Tdci with & without air con

£398 Buy online now at www.allisport.com

e: sales@allisport.com
t: 01594 826045

🇬🇧 Made in Britain

Price shown excludes vat and is correct at time of publishing.

ALLISPORT

Silkstone 4x4

Celebrating 31 years

Telephone: 01226 386920 Mobile: 07984 774 448

0959 Defender 90, Chawton white, grey trim, boost alloys, tow pack, 1 owner, 58,000 miles, **£16,500 No VAT**

1161 110 County Station Wagon, Galway Green Metalic, Boost alloys, Black cloth trim, 31,000 miles, FSH, **£23,995 inc VAT**

98R Land Rover 90, 300TDI Hard Top, Alpine White, 1 owner, 28,000 miles **£18995 No VAT**

15.15 Land Rover 110 Utility XS Station Wagon with full adventure pack, Fuji White, full leather, very high spec, 1 owner, 54,000 miles FLRSH **£28,995 +VAT**

0606 Land Rover Defender 90 TD5 Truck Cab, in Belize Green with black roof & spats, high spec, 90,000 miles, 2 owners. **£15,600 inc VAT.**

10/60 Defender 110 High CAP pick up with Stainless steel dropside body in silver, 42,000 miles 2 owners **£15995+VAT**

Anchor Farm, Elmhirst Lane
Silkstone, Barnsley,
S Yorks, S75 4LD.

open 6 days
Please visit
www.silkstonereclamation.co.uk

Please visit our website for more stock

Brake discs

BRAKE DISCS RESURFACED

Replacing brake discs can involve considerable time and money, but a re-face can be a cost-effective cure for judder, vibration and corrosion. Dave Barker explains

DAVE BARKER

TOOLS REQUIRED:
This is not a DIY job, simply because specialised equipment is required

TIME:
2 hours

COST:
from £30. Parts and costs: From around £30 per pair, plus new pads. Cost depends on the vehicle and size of the discs being skimmed.

DIFFICULTY RATING:
5/5

CONTACT:
Station Auto Services, who carried out the work shown here. Contact them at Unit 6, Carlton Minottt Business Park, Carlton Miniott, Thirsk YO7 4NE. Tel: 01845 524934. Email:stationautoservice@tiscali.co.uk

LESS THAN 5000 miles ago I replaced all the brakes on my Defender. As well as fitting new discs and pads, I also replaced the calipers. Recently, however, the Defender started to suffer from juddering when braking. The problem was diagnosed as a warped disc, or more than one. But, with no signs of damage, we were uncertain which disc was causing the problem, though I suspected it was the rears.

The warping could be due to a disc or discs getting very hot at some point, and then suddenly cooled. Other reasons for brake judder or vibration can be disc/hub run out or, with older discs, corrosion or even a thickness variation in the disc. Whatever the cause, my bad case of brake vibration needed to be fixed.

With my discs showing little sign of wear, instead of replacing them, it was suggested that I had them re-faced by taking a skim off the surface on each side. I wouldn't normally have considered this option because I expected the cost of having discs re-faced to be far more than the cost of replacing them, especially with aftermarket brake discs being so reasonable. However, when you add the labour cost of fitting new discs on a Defender, especially the fronts, it does work out cheaper to have them skimmed.

And on, say, a Range Rover where a genuine brake disc is listed at over £83 then provided your discs are not worn, having them re-faced is an even more cost-effective option, as it is for high performance vehicles with vented, cross slotted and drilled discs. Re-facing can also be useful on vehicles that are not used all year and laid up, often resulting in the disc brakes becoming rusted through lack of use.

The equipment used to resurface my discs is known as a Pro-Cut On-Car Brake Lathe. As the name suggests, it resurfaces the discs on the vehicle, taking into account any run out, and ensures the disc is matched to the hub and machined at 90 degrees to the axle. The complete caliper assembly first needs to be removed, which is a relative easy job, then the Pro-Cut is attached to the hub by means of an adaptor. The machine then auto-adjusts itself for lateral run out of the disc, before a manual first rough cut is taken off the disc, cutting inwards, and normally removing around 0.1 to 0.2 mm off the disc. Once that is complete the Pro-Cut machine is set to automatic mode and it then works outwards with a fine cut, again taking off 0.2 mm, making a total cut of around 0.3 to 0.4 mm. The Pro-Cut On-Car Brake Lathe is approved by leading manufactures including Land Rover, and also by brake component specialist, EBC, if a customer has brake vibrations after fitting EBC pads and discs. In my case, we first resurfaced the rear discs because we suspected they were causing the juddering. But during a subsequent road test the brake vibration had only improved slightly, so it was decided to re-face the front discs as well. Doing that cured the juddering completely. Hopefully, I can now look forward to several years of vibration and judder free motoring.

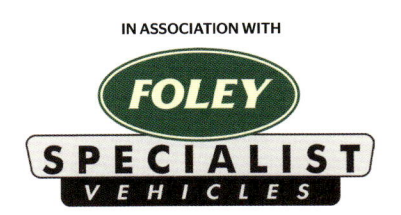

Because of the specialist equipment needed, this job is not a DIY prospect. This feature shows what can be done and how a commercial garage would carry out the work. Not all defective discs can be reclaimed in this way, and there are limits on the remaining thickness of the disc after surfacing work has been carried out. So a well worn disc may already be too thin to be re-faced.

A good repairer with access to the appropriate specifications will advise what, if anything, can be done to restore the discs in a safe manner, and whether the process is applicable to your particular Land Rover model.

1 The Defender is lifted off the ground for a full brake inspection prior to any remedial work being done.

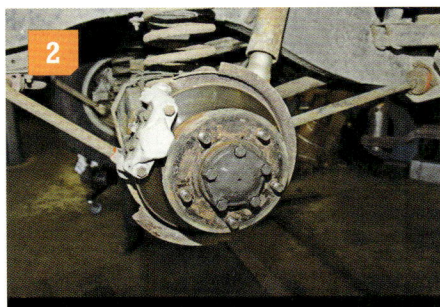

2 The rear wheels were removed and the discs inspected for signs of damage that could be causing the vibrations, but no damage was seen.

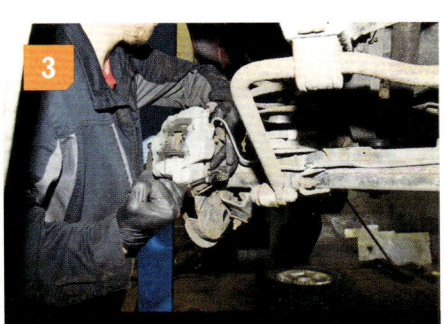

3 Before the disc can be resurfaced the brake caliper assembly is removed and supported safely out of the way.

4 Before attaching the equipment, the face of the hub is cleaned of dirt and any corrosion to ensure the Pro-Cut lathe is aligned correctly.

5 The Pro-Cut lathe is attached to the Defender's hub via a special adaptor, ensuring correct alignment to the hub.

Brake discs

6 Once fitted, the lathe automatically self-adjusts and centres itself alongside the vehicle's hub, with the cutting tool meeting the disc.

7 The cutting tool is set just in from the outer edge (inboard of any lip), and both sides of the disc will be cut together.

8 The lathe then cuts outward to the outer edge (removing the lip), before the operator makes a rough cut inwards to the centre of the disc.

9 This first manual rough cut, moving inward to the centre, normally machines around 0.1 to 0.2 mm off the disc.

10 Once the rough cut is complete a smoothing pad is fitted and the cutting tool adjusted before the machine is set to automatic cut.

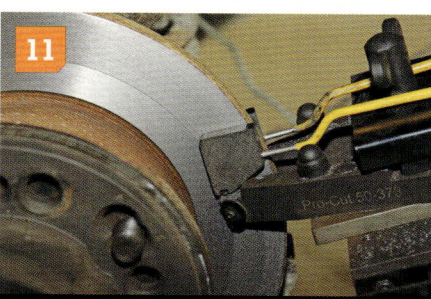

11 With the Pro-Cut lathe adjusted, it automatically makes a finer cut (again 0.1 to 0.2 mm) from the centre towards the outside edge.

12 After the first disc has been resurfaced, the Pro-Cut lathe is removed and attached to the opposite side hub to machine the right side disc.

13 The Pro-Cut lathe is now working upside down on the opposite hand brake disc, cutting and re-facing it in the same way.

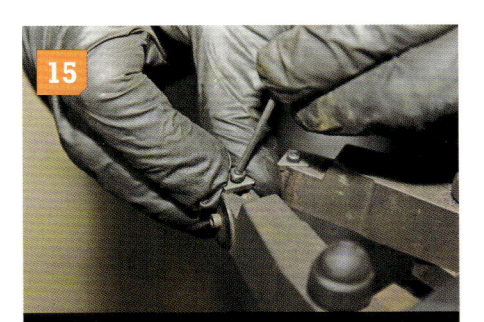

14 After machining, and refitting the calipers with new pads a road test showed only a slight reduction in vibration, so here we start the front discs.

15 Before the Pro-Cut lathe is fitted to the front discs, the cutting tools are checked and rotated so a fresh cutting edge is used.

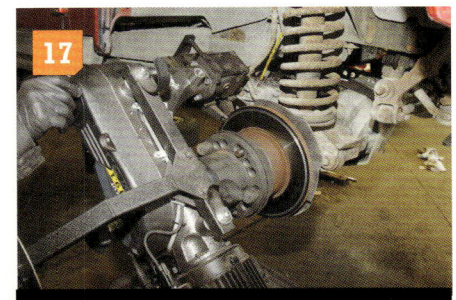

16 Again, the front hub face is cleaned of corrosion and dirt to ensure correct alignment, and the adaptor is bolted on ready to accept the Pro-Cut.

17 Once more, a first manual rough cut is made followed by an automatic fine cut with each cut taking around 0.1 to 0.2 mm off the disc.

18 This is some of the material removed from the discs. They are now running true with new pads fitted all round, and the Defender is vibration-free.

Fit new cappings

REPLACING CORRODED CAPPINGS

Replacement of damaged Defender rear body cappings is easier than it looks. Trevor Cuthbert shows how (and swaps a roof at the same time)

MY DEFENDER 90 Td5 is a well-maintained hard top. The body tub cappings and the rear corner cappings are painted steel components. Eventually during production, these were no longer supplied in galvanised form, except for pick-up models where the cappings were constantly exposed and vulnerable. All of the early Ninety and One Ten models had galvanised cappings which were left unpainted, imparting a characteristic Land Rover appearance that was carried on from the Series III before it – and dates back to the Series I. The cessation of galvanised body and corner cappings was possibly a cost-cutting exercise, although it could be argued that it happened so that body-coloured paint would stick properly in the age of ever-increasing colour co-ordinating. Whatever the reason, painted body cappings and corner cappings usually begin to show unsightly rust. This often first appears at the weld in the capping, but the rust can take hold anywhere, very quickly.

I like the traditional Land Rover look: the rear quarter lights, galvanised cappings and white roof. My own Defender was beginning to exhibit rust on the body cappings, physical damage and rust on the corner cappings, and the body-coloured roof panel was damaged from above at the rear, resulting in a loosened and vibrating inner strengthening rib. The roof panel has also been subject to an after-market colour matching exercise, so white paint was showing through where the green paint was peeling.

The job of replacing the body cappings requires the removal of the van side panels (or window side panels in the case of a Station Wagon). This can be done by removing all of the fixings from the side panel, and by releasing the roof fixings sufficiently to be able to work the side panels out.

The roof needs to be able to move upwards enough to allow the side panel to lift clear of the circular raised portions of the body capping. For example, on a 110 Station Wagon, it may help to unbolt the top of the B-post from the roof panel to allow the movement required. However, as this Land Rover was getting a replacement roof panel, the cappings replacement would be carried out with the roof fully removed and then the sides taken off in turn.

Breaking down a hard top Land Rover in this way to get at the body cappings is straightforward, mainly involving nuts, bolts and screws. But there's an adhesive seal to break along the top of the windscreen frame (and this needs to be resealed), and care has to taken with interior lights wiring and the washer water supply to the rear door jet.

There were a number of interesting differences with the roof panel. The factory-fitted 2005 roof had captive nuts all around the van sides' interface, whereas the earlier 300Tdi roof panel uses nuts, washers and lock washers in the traditional way. The later roof panel has subtle raised rib pressings on the outside of the roof, while the earlier panel is completely smooth. As a traditionalist, I probably would have fitted one of the early Ninety ribbed roof panels, had I been able to source a perfect undamaged example somewhere.

Another interesting experience was the effect that rusted clamp bolts (the main fittings that hold the van sides to the body tub) had on the panel gaps. Particularly at the two rear corners where the severity of the rust had pushed the corners up, creating a worse-than-usual panel gap. This was easily remedied by using new clamp bolts.

Land Rovers are easily tailored and customised to their owners' taste. I am certainly very pleased to have deleted most of the rust from mine in the body and corner cappings areas and added a more traditional look, imparted by the galvanised components and the nice new white roof itself.

IN ASSOCIATION WITH

FOLEY SPECIALIST VEHICLES

TREVOR CUTHBERT

TOOLS REQUIRED:
Cordless drill, 5mm short shank drill bit, 10mm, 13mm spanner and socket, screwdrivers, sealant gun, file

TIME:
1 day

COST:
From £90. Shot blasting £20, Galvanising £55 minimum charge (other parts were included in the batch), quality silicone sealant £11, secondhand roof panel £150, rivets £3

DIFFICULTY RATING:
2/5

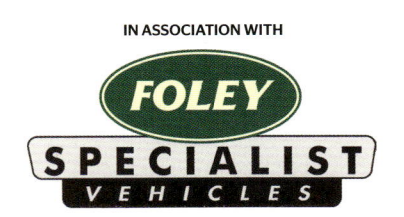

1 We're changing the post-manufacture colour-co-ordinated roof panel at the same time as the cappings. Read on for more on this.

2 Roof panel has been damaged, which has dislodged this internal central strengthening rib. The spot welds and adhesive bonds are fractured.

3 The rear corner cappings have received typical damage, ripping them from the body panels. And they are beginning to rust in the damaged areas.

4 The body tub top cappings are beginning to rust and rivets have been displaced. The gap to the van sides at each corner is also uneven.

5 The interior trim around the windscreen frame is removed – these side mouldings are held by two self-tapping screws.

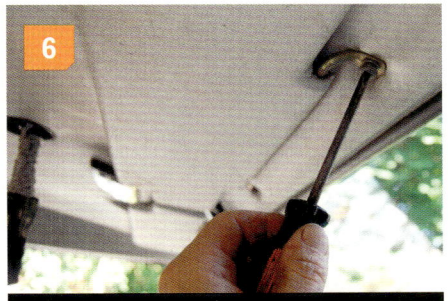

6 The Defender's front head lining is partly held in place to the roof panel by the sun visor fixings on each side, as shown here.

7 The head lining is also held by a series of plastic fasteners. These are re-usable if theya re properly – and carefully –removed.

8 With the fixings removed the headlining drops and is withdrawn after the interior light is unplugged (it remains fixed to the lining).

9 There is a large self tapping screw to be removed at the top of the windscreen frame on each side; this frees the frame from the roof panel.

10 There are also a series of M6 bolts to be removed using a 10mm ratchet spanner. The corresponding nut is a captive nut plate within the roof panel.

Fit new cappings

11 The roof panel is easily lifted off by two persons, as although large and bulky, it's not particularly heavy. The next job is to remove the side panels.

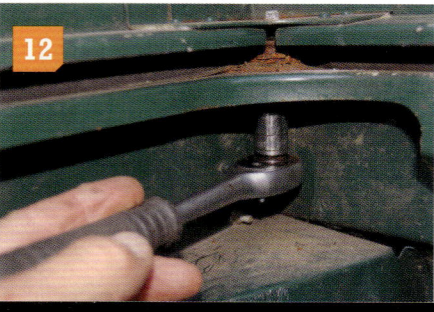

12 At the rear corners of the body tub and at the front of the panel at the door, an M8 nut is removed with a 13mm socket wrench to free up the body sides.

13 On either side of the tail door frame, M6 bolts are removed with 10mm socket and spanner, leaving the bracket attached to the body tub for now.

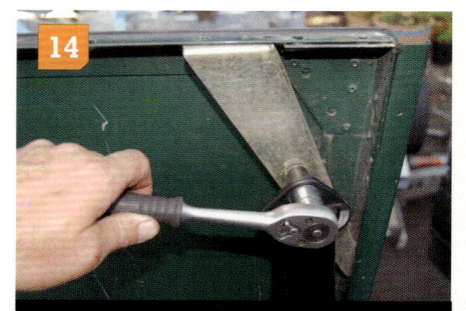

14 Top mounts of the seatbelts are unfastened to free up the van side. In this case a 17mm socket wrench is used on the bolt head.

15 Looking under the lower edge of the van side, the cause of the uneven fit can be seen. This clamp fitting has rusted and expanded, lifting the panel.

16 With the van side removed and out of the way, the body tub capping is fully exposed and ready to be de-riveted from the Land Rover.

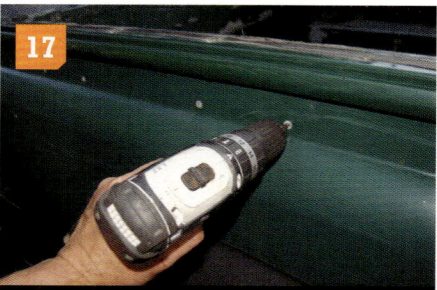

17 The rivets holding the cappings are drilled out using a 5mm short-shank drill bit. Longer drill bits fracture easily. Take care the drill does not slip.

18 When all of the rivets have been drilled out, the capping will be loose on the rear body tub. Angle it upwards slightly to remove it.

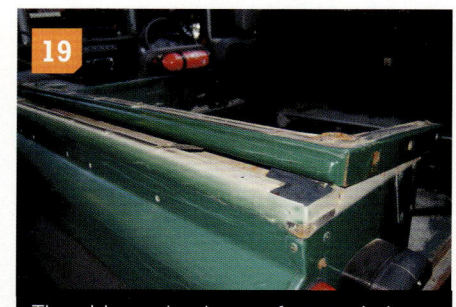

19 The old capping is now free, and given that it is not too heavily corroded, it will be sand blasted and galvanised for re-fitting to the Land Rover.

20 Prior to drilling out the rivets from the corner cappings, the light fittings need to be removed and unplugged from the wiring harness.

21 Angle plates are also drilled out for replacement. Exposed primer paint may need touching in if new cappings don't fully cover it.

WORK SAFELY:
Wear eye protection when drilling

Beware of sharp points of zinc (drips on galvanised parts) before filing

Get some help for lifting the roof panel (not heavy but cumbersome)

Connect electrical tools via an RCD and ensure leads cannot become trapped or damaged

ACCESSING THE CAPPINGS WITH THE ROOF ON

The rear body sides can be removed with the roof panel in place. It requires careful easing up of the panel to clear the raised sections of the cappings.

There's plenty of space to work when the side panels with the rear quarter sections have been lifted out.

This is a typical example of the rusting that occurs under the body-coloured paint on non-galvanised body cappings.

Fitting the new cappings

1 Fitting the new or re-galvanised components is a straight forward job of riveting them in place using a "long tong" riveter with 5mm x 13mm rivets.

2 Original plastic clips, into which the light fittings are screwed, have been saved from the old corner cappings and are pressed into the new part.

3 Just as it is important to take care drilling out the old rivets, one must be very careful not to allow the riveter to slip and damage the paintwork.

4 Replacement roof from an older 90 is undamaged and is a direct replacement. Sides and roof are built on in reverse order of dismantling.

5

6 Now with a white roof panel and galvanised body cappings, the Land Rover has a different appearance. All can be colour matched again, but I personally prefer this look.

The Big Picture

There's something very welcoming about an open garage door – especially when there's a Defender inside, with its bonnet open. Who can resist a peek into the inner workings of our favourite Land Rover?

We can't think of anything better than working on the vehicle that is so often described as a giant Meccano kit. And that's what this magbook is all about.

The workshop (and Defender 90) pictured here belongs to Ed Evans, who explains how to create your own perfect Land Rover service bay, starting on page 60. Ed is also technical editor of Land Rover Monthly, so make sure you don't miss his inimitable advice, in every single issue.

IN ASSOCIATION WITH

FOLEY SPECIALIST V E H I C L E S

Fit Cruise Control

FITTING CRUISE CONTROL

Defender TDCi is a practical motorway cruiser, so an aftermarket cruise control kit is a logical upgrade. Ed Evans reports.

ED EVANS

TOOLS REQUIRED:
General workshop tools, soldering iron, wire cutters/strippers, multi-meter optional, Torx 30 driver

TIME:
2-3 hours

COST:
£475

DIFFICULTY RATING:
3/5

WITH SO MANY TDCi Defenders comfortably plugging long distances on main roads and motorways, it's surprising that they weren't all factory fitted with cruise control, considering it's been available on every other model since the mid-nineties.

Cruise is not just a luxury to take some of the stress out of driving, it's also a practical tool that can help you avoid speeding tickets without continually checking the speedometer needle, and it can be easily adjusted and reset to whatever speed is preferred, or to whatever speed limit is encountered.

Yes, £475 plus your time seems a high cost, but a couple of fines, a speed awareness course and higher insurance premiums come close...

Installing this kit involves connecting in to sections of the vehicle's wiring system – to the brake and clutch switches and to the speed sensor circuit at the back of the instrument panel. It's important that the connections are soldered and insulated. Apart from these connections, the cruise control electronic module is simply connected using multiplugs on the supplied wiring harnesses. When all that kit is tucked away inside the facia, all that shows is the smart new column stalk.

When driving, cruise control is automatically de-activated when the brake or clutch pedal is pressed, and will remember the previously set speed. Vehicle speed can be increased by holding the RES/ACC (resume/accelerate) for more than 1 second, or tapping the button to increase speed (thus adjusting the set speed) in increments of 0.6mph. The SET/COAST button decelerates the vehicle in a similar way.

The cruise control kit is available for all TDCi Defenders, but the wiring colours are connected differently according to whether the vehicle is a 2.2-litre or 2.4-litre model.

Here, in the Britpart workshop, Steve Grant is installing the system on a 2.2 TDCi, so the wiring colours shown here do not apply to the 2.4 version, though in every other aspect the installation is the same, and the colour coding is clearly shown in the instructions.

Preparation

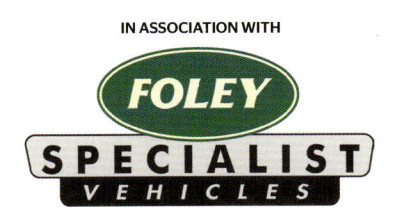

1. After disconnecting the battery earth lead, we begin by removing this lower trim from under the instrument panel. All the screws are size 30 Torx.

2. The upper trim is held by two screws at the back. Two front clips are released by pushing the trim up, then forward, at the front.

3. Two more Torx screws hold the instrument panel at the front. When they are removed, the panel can be tilted forward to reach behind.

4. At the rear of the instrument panel, the multiplug is disconnected by first pressing its lock button, then levering the black tab (arrowed) across.

5. The instrument panel is now lifted clear and placed in safe storage. A connection will be made to the multi-plug later.

6. Down below, the right hand speaker is removed. The control unit for the system will eventually be located inside here.

Connecting to the clutch switch

1. The yellow wire for the clutch switch is fed up through the speaker hole, together with the purple lead for the speed sensor connection.

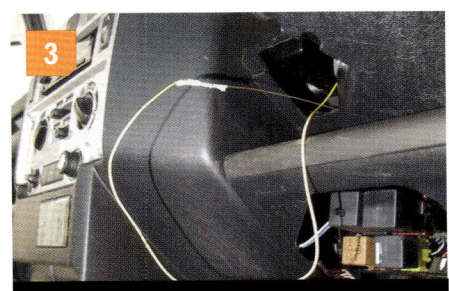

2. From inside the engine bay, the end is snipped off a spare stub grommet and a length of MIG welding wire is fed through.

3. The yellow wire is fed behind the fascia, past the steering column then taped to the welding wire and pulled into the engine bay.

4. The black/white wire to the clutch switch is bared and the yellow wire twisted through it, and the joint is then soldered.

5. The new soldered joint and all cables are reinsulated by winding with soft adhesive insulating tape, and the switch plug reconnected.

167

Fit Cruise Control

Accelator connections

1. The multiplug is unclipped from the accelerator pedal. Access is easier if the small black steel shield in front is bent up a little.

2. The bonnet release handle is released by removing the two bolts from its mounting bracket. The cable remains attached.

3. The new black accelerator harness is fed up behind the footwell trim and brought out at the top of the trim for the moment.

4. The connectors laying over accelerator pedal in the previous picture, are now connected to the socket on the original accelerator harness.

5. Higher up, on the multiplug we detached from the instrument panel earlier, a small screwdriver is used to prise the connector block out.

6. We access this connector block because we have to connect to one of two red/black wires, and this is the only way to identify them.

7. We need the red/black wire from pin 13. Only 14 and 30 are marked, but our wire is to the right of pin 14, on this 2.2 TDCi (connector inverted here)

8. The purple wire from the control unit is soldered to the black/red (speed sensor) wire, and the joint insulated. Bonnet release is refitted.

BRITPART CRUISE CONTROL KIT

The unit provides all the functions found on most Land Rover cruise control systems, and the new column stalk looks like an original part of the vehicle. The kit has Britpart part number DA7480. Recommended retail price £475.

The kit includes electronic control unit, harnesses with connectors, the cruise switch for the steering column, cable ties, instructions and owner's manual with diagnostic trouble-shooting guide.

Connecting to the brake switch

1 The blue wire from the control unit's white plug is joined to the red from the lower plug, between the plug and the in-line fuse.

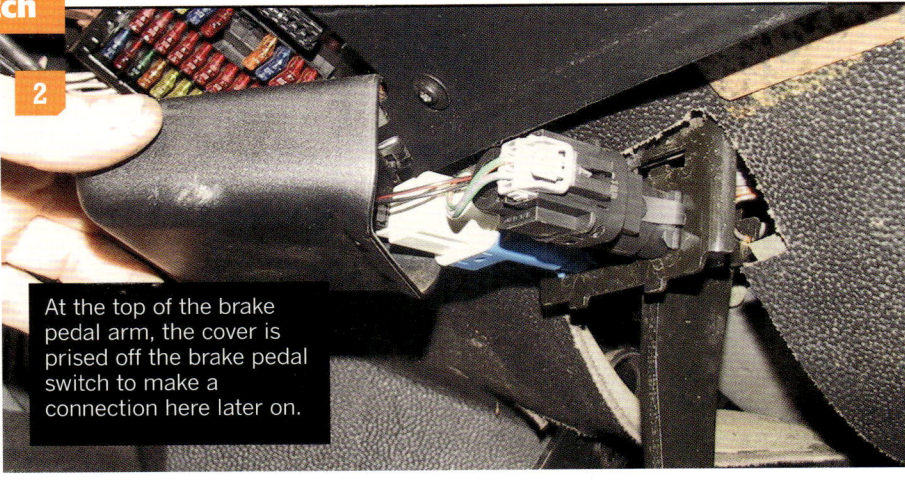

2 At the top of the brake pedal arm, the cover is prised off the brake pedal switch to make a connection here later on.

3 The red wire and the white/brown from the control unit are spliced into the green/orange and green/purple respectively on the brake switch plug.

4 After soldering and insulating the joints, the brake switch multi-plug and cover will be refitted, completing the wiring.

WORK SAFELY
Disconnect the battery earth lead before starting work.

Take care when drilling to ensure the drill cannot slip, causing damage or injury. Wear eye protection.

Take care when using and placing soldering iron

When using a soldering iron, take care to avoid touching the heated parts on other cables and trim. Switch it off betweeen tasks.

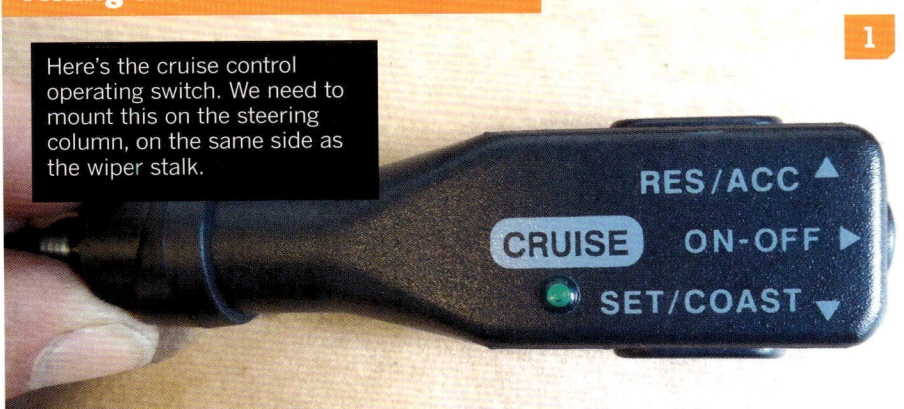

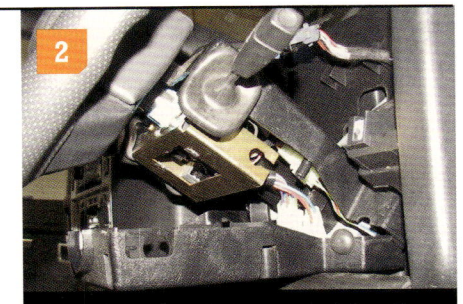

Fitting the driver's control stalk

1 Here's the cruise control operating switch. We need to mount this on the steering column, on the same side as the wiper stalk.

2 After removing six screws holding the steering column trim, the bottom half is lowered, exposing the steel bracket with slotted hole.

3 This hole position in the bracket is marked on the bottom trim, and the trim is drilled 10 mm and cleaned up with a file.

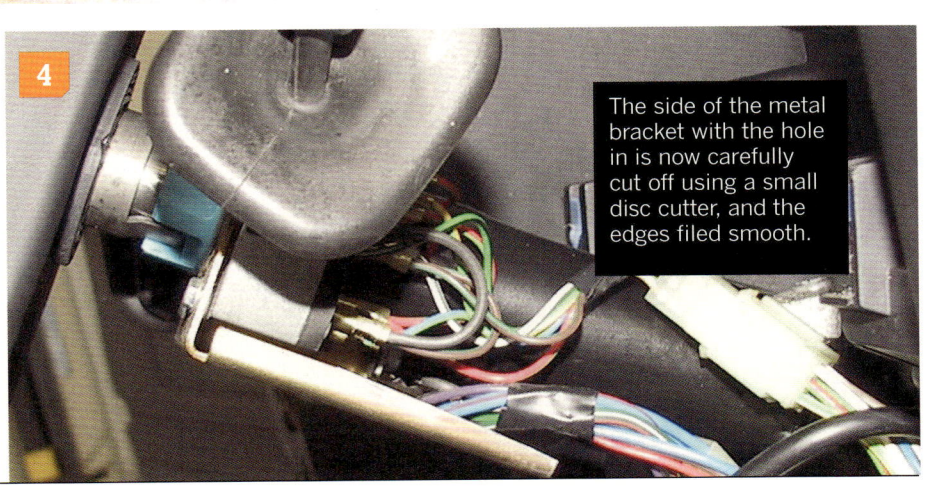

4 The side of the metal bracket with the hole in is now carefully cut off using a small disc cutter, and the edges filed smooth.

Fit Cruise Control

5 The switch harness is fed through the hole and the nut and washers fitted over it, before routing the cables to the speaker aperture.

6 While tightening the nut, the switch can be angled (thanks to its offset ferrule) to ensure it is clearly visible from the driving position.

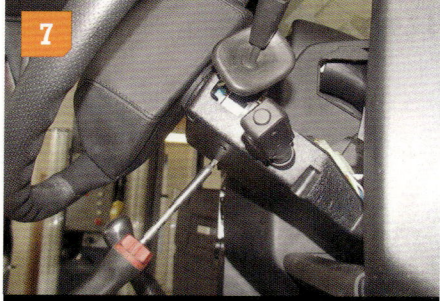

7 With the nut tightened from inside to secure the switch, the two halves of the steering column trim are refitted, securing the switch.

Connecting & commissioning the controller

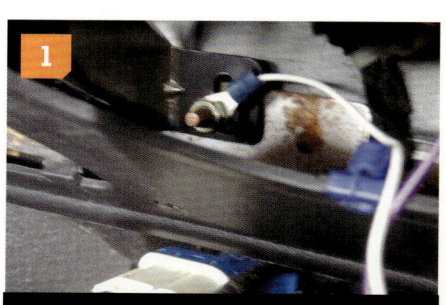

1 An eyelet is fitted to the white earth lead from the control unit and fixed to this facia/bulkhead stud and nut inside the speaker hole.

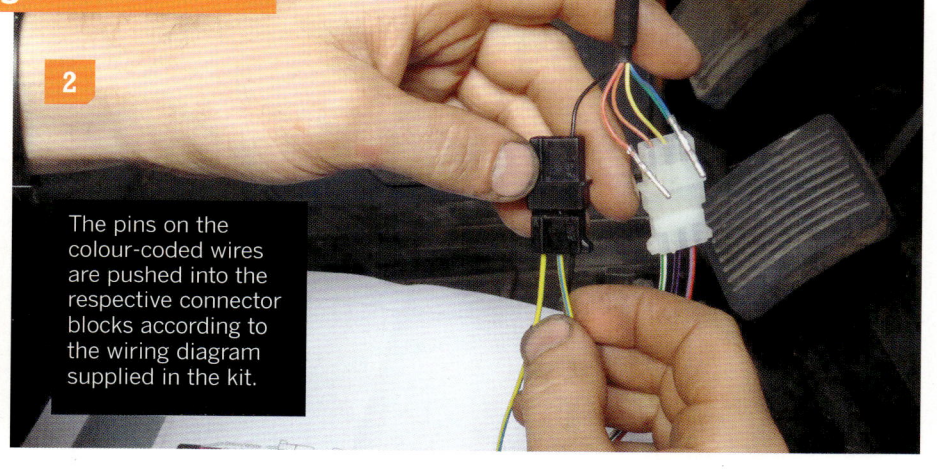

2 The pins on the colour-coded wires are pushed into the respective connector blocks according to the wiring diagram supplied in the kit.

3 The connectors are plugged into the control unit and excess cables are grouped and cable tied ready to go inside the facia.

4 The controller is initiated by operating the column switch in a simple sequence, confirmed by the LED on the back of the control unit.

5 Finally, the controller and cables are hidden in the speaker aperture, and the speaker and instrument panel refitted. Job done.

Transform your garage!

Create a beautifully organised workspace or leisure room within your own home

Dura's award-winning range of modular cabinets are used by professional workshops worldwide and provide the perfect solution for organising your tools safely and securely. Combined with Dura's flexible 'clip-on' wall hook system, interlocking PVC floor tiles and lighting systems, you can create a stunning room to be proud of.

- **Modular storage cabinets**
- **Wall-mounted storage**
- **Interlocking floor tiles**
- **Design and installation**

Products to organise your tools and maximise space

Award-winning cabinets as used by the professionals

Call now for a FREE Design Survey and see how your garage could look!

DURA® Fitted Garages

Europe's leading garage interior company

www.duragarages.com

reddot design award winner | THE QUEEN'S AWARDS FOR ENTERPRISE INTERNATIONAL TRADE 2012 | MADE IN BRITAIN | 5 Year Guarantee

For a FREE brochure call
0845 371 0042
or request via our website

Alternatively, return this slip in an envelope (no stamp required) to:
Freepost RSLX-YXCA-GUTJ, Dura Ltd, St James Road, Brackley NN13 7XY

Name
Address
Tel
Email

DEF/AUT17

TDCi service

The 2.4 TDCi Defenders have been forced to give a nod to modern technology and electronics, but they're still DIY serviceable, as Ed Evans explains

SERVICE GUIDE

DURING ITS LONG evolution, Defender underwent only subtle development, with the most significant changes being the introduction of the Ford-derived (Puma) engine in 2007 and its accompanying six-speed gearbox.

From a servicing aspect, the 2.4TDCi Defender has similar requirements to the early models, and especially to the relatively-advanced Td5 version whose service needs were covered in detail in the previous (August) issue of LRM Technical. That service guide therefore, also provides the basis for servicing the 2.4TDCi models so, in this feature, we look at the late models' special requirements in respect of the Puma engine and its fuel system, and that six-speed gearbox.

Engine variations
From 2007, the new 2.4-litre engine was a significant improvement over the Td5 in some ways. It was refined by Defender standards, whereas the outgoing Td5 did sound like a big diesel and imparted a certain beefy character to the truck. But w the Td5 engine was a tad reluctant to do precisely what we wanted at low revs on difficult terrain, whereas the new TDCi engine management (with assistance from a lower first gear in the new transmission) enjoyed delicate control.

A niggle for traditionalists was that the new engine was basically a Ford unit. The Td5 appeared to be the last home-spun Land Rover diesel engine. It had been upgraded once during its production life to Euro 3 emission standards, but was incapable of meeting the next stage of Euro 4 and, understandably, Land Rover was unlikely to design a new engine for a model that was due for wholesale replacement. Of course, we now know the Td5 won't be the last Land Rover diesel. When the company's new engine plant comes on stream next year, Land Rovers will again receive in-house engines, but they'll be nothing like the big blustering rackety diesels of the past.

We're not covering the 2012 Defender in this service guide simply because these models are still under Land Rover warranty and owner-servicing is therefore out of the question.

The fact that the engine capacity of the 2012 model fell from 2.4- to 2.2-litres was no detriment to Defender, rather it illustrated the general industry trend towards smaller capacity, more efficient engines that better satisfy emissions rules. In this case the new engine met the latest EU5 regulations, helped a diesel particulate filter mounted immediately downstream of the catalytic convertor, while its performance remained similar to that of the outgoing 2.4 engine.

ED EVANS

TOOLS REQUIRED:
Socket spanners, rings and open-enders. Trolley jack, axle stands, wheel chocks.

TIME:
Allow half a day

COST:
up to £100 for fluids, filters and consumables

DIFFICULTY RATING:
2/5

CONTACT:
THANKS to Steve Buck of James French 4x4 (jamesfrench.com) for advice, and to Steve Grant and Britpart for providing the vehicle and facilities.

IN ASSOCIATION WITH
FOLEY SPECIALIST VEHICLES

1 The oil filter cover is easily reached from under the engine bay at the left side of the sump (looking forward). Clean dirt away before unscrewing.

2 Engine oil drain plug is handily placed at the back end of the sump. It's recommended to renew the plug at each oil change.

3 The fuel filter is in the same position as earlier models, on the chassis just forward of the right rear wheel. Twist, then pull down to release.

4 On 2.4 models, fill the fuel filter to the brim with fresh fuel before fitting carefully. The fuel system should not then need priming.

5 To prime the 2.4 the official way, remove the bolt (8mm spanner) from the bracket (yellow) to access the fuel pipe (white) to the injector pump.

2.4 TDCi service notes

AS IN THE Td5 service covered last month, it's important to buy a workshop manual and work to the Land Rover servicing schedules using the specified fluids and lubrication intervals. The following notes are specific to the TDCi Defenders' differences in the engine and transmission systems.

Engine oil filter

The TDCi has one engine oil filter that can be reached from underneath the engine bay. The filter cover has a hexagon on the base to accept a socket spanner, and it's best to place a collecting dish underneath before unscrewing it a couple of turns, then allowing the oil to drain from the filter cover. When fully removed, take out the cartridge and clean the inside of the cover, its screw thread and the mating faces on the engine housing. Install the new O-seal (supplied with the filter) with a smear of new engine oil, then fit the new filter cartridge and screw the cover back on, tightening to 35 Nm torque.

Fuel filter 2.4-litre

Unlike the Td5, the 2.4TDCi does not have an in-tank fuel pump. So when the fuel filter is changed, which inevitably allows air into the fuel system, the circuit needs

TDCi service

6 Disconnect the fuel pipe from the injector pump connector stub by pressing the blue button on the quick-release fitting and pulling back.

to be primed by drawing fuel up the line using a hand pump worked from the engine compartment. To install the pump, the fuel line is split in the engine compartment and the pump's hoses connected into the line. The pump is then worked by hand to draw fuel up the line.

Although the pump is basically a fairly common squeezy-type hand bulb, the pipe fittings are specific to the Defender fuel lines and are difficult to find. The Land Rover unit is expensive, though secondhand items can be found on eBay.

But there is a way to avoid the need to prime, or bleed, the fuel system. Most of the air that enters the fuel line is from the new empty fuel filter so, before fitting the new fuel filter, slowly fill it with fresh diesel fuel until it is brimmed to the top, thus excluding any air. Then, carefully screw the filter into position on the housing. The engine will then start up fine. There is likely to still be a slight amount of air in the line, and you may hear the engine miss a beat after a few seconds as any remaining air passes through. So that's the fuel system primed and running again quite easily.

Fuel filter 2.2-litre
The 2.2-litre model reverted to an in-tank fuel lift pump. Filter replacement is similar to the early TDCi but the system bleeding is carried out using a bleed valve on the fuel line in the engine bay. However, these models are still under warranty, so any servicing needs to be carried out by an authorised garage.

Transmission
The six-speed gearbox oil change for the 2.4TDCi is extended to 120,000 miles or ten years, with the transfer box at 48,000 or four years with a check on the level every 12,000 miles or 12 months. Axle oil is changed at 48,000 miles or four years.

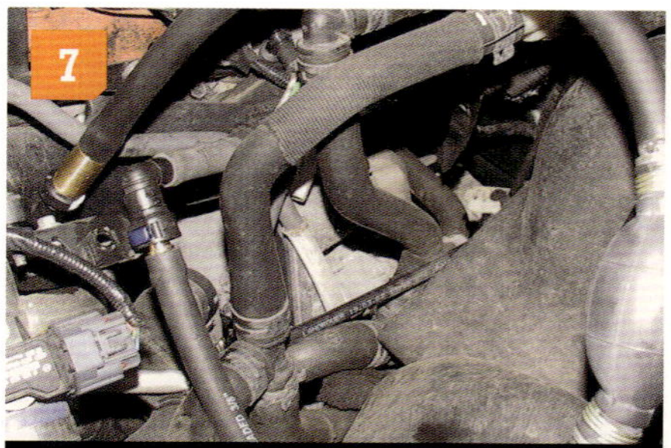

7 Connect the pump hoses between the fuel pipes, and squeeze the bulb until it feels hard, then remove it and reconnect the pipes and bracket.

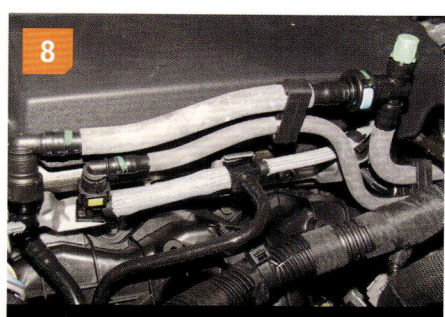

8 The 2.2-litre model has a bleed valve (green at right of pic) in the fuel line in the engine bay. DIY servicing is not appropriate while under warranty.

WORK SAFELY:
When working underneath, try to do the maximum number of jobs while the vehicle is on its wheels. Engage gear and handbrake, and use wheel chocks.

Work on one wheelarch at a time so that when the wheel is off, the vehicle stands on the remaining three.

If working with a helper to check steering joints, ensure you can hear each other clearly to avoid actions that might trap fingers.

Beware of hot oils when draining, and allow the cooling system to fully cool before opening or draining.

Dispose of old oils at a recognised recycling facility.

Wear eye protection when working with fluids and under the vehicle, and protect skin from contamination with oils.

Avoid inhaling brake dust – use brake cleaning fluid, and wear a particle mask.

Get OffRoad.com
LAND ROVER PARTS SPECIALIST

Like and follow us on social media
Facebook: @getoffroad **Twitter:** @getoffroadparts
Instagram: @getoffroadcom

DEFENDER PUMA DASH

SEE US AT THE LRO SHOW PETERBOROUGH SEPTEMBER 2017

NO BULKHEAD CHANGE REQUIRED | NO LOOM CHANGE NECESSARY
FITS DEFENDERS PRE 2007 | CHOICE OF COLOURS AVAILABLE

For more information call us on: 0333 555 0004
or email us at enquiries@getoffroad.com

---

masai

One life... see it!
+44 (0)1543 254507

www.masai4x4.com

Sliding Panoramic Tinted Windows

NEW Headlining / Roof Lining Kits

"Fire and Ice" Tubular Side Steps

NEW Sport Scooped Bonnet with Grill

NEW 3 Piece Winch Bumper

Windows - Roof racks - Lights - Spare wheel carriers - Chequer plates - Snorkels - Bumpers - Bonnets - Tree sliders - Steps

masai We design and manufacture an exclusive range of high-quality Land Rover accessories/parts

Secondhand Td5 engine

SECONDHAND TD5 ENGINE

Choosing a good used engine and hoping it will last, can be a gamble. But Ed Evans finds the solution...

STORY SO FAR:
Our Td5 Defender was bought with a known warped cylinder head, and the aim was to fit a new head and drive away. But not everything goes to plan. After removing the head and confirming its terminal warp, we discovered that the engine block, too, had been damaged by the vehicle being driven in this condition by its previous owner. The complete engine had been reduced to scrap, and all because overheating signs caused by a failed coolant pump had been ignored.

That means that now it's time to bite the bullet and source a complete replacement engine...

CONTACT:
SKAN 4X4 Much Wenlock, Shropshire, TF13 6DD
Tel: 01952 727298 skan4x4.com

IT'S EASY TO FIND a replacement Td5 engine because the models that used them are so common. Few Defenders are scrapped for spares, but many Discovery 2s are now reaching the ends of their economical lives.

Because the Td5 can be a long-lasting engine, as our recent exploration of the engine and head showed, there's a fair choice for sale.

Used Td5 engines are available from breakers' yards and internet sites, or by buying a Discovery 2 with a rusted chassis but decent running gear. In that case, it's possible to hear the engine running or even drive the vehicle to confirm the engine's performance under load and at full working temperature, especially if you buy the complete vehicle.

Buying a stand-alone engine that can't be heard running is risky unless you know the seller and/or the engine's history. Scrapyards usually offer some guarantee, even if it's simply based on the breaker maintaining a reputation. But even then, no-one wants to fit an engine and then find it has problems, only to remove it and return to the seller to argue the case.

The safest route, and the one that I took, is to buy from a known established business that not only gives a guarantee, but also provides traceability, confirming the engine's origin. We know Defenders are occasionally stolen and immediately broken down for their parts, so even inadvertently buying a stolen engine could lead to it having to be removed and handed back to its rightful owner.

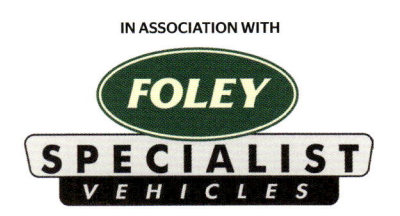

Selecting and preparing the engine

WE CONTACTED SKAN 4x4 which breaks Discovery 2 models. SKAN had a selection of engines, palleted up and on the shelf, and I bought an 89,000-miler for £1200 with a 60-day warranty.

This was a complete engine with ancillaries, so I'd be left with a few useful spares, such as the alternator and turbocharger, from my old engine. SKAN checks the engine's ECU for fault codes, confirming mine was clear and, as we said earlier, they confirm the engine's origin so the buyer knows it is legitimate. In fact, the Discovery that my engine had come from was still in the yard, marked up with its SKAN coding that corresponded with the paperwork. I was reassured to see the vehicle had suffered accident damage to the front quarter, sufficient to write off an elderly Discovery 2, though not sufficient to have caused damage to the engine. I was filled with enough confidence to shell out the £1200 for an engine I hadn't seen running, and it was loaded into the trailer.

Back at the workshop, the Defender's original engine had, of course, already been removed (that story is in the March to May issues of *LRM*), but before fitting the replacement, there were a few significant extra jobs to complete. There's no point going to the trouble of fitting a good engine if there's the slightest chance of any other component failing that might subsequently damage it. And, while we're at this stage, it makes sense to replace any parts whose later failure might mean having to remove the engine again, or the transmission.

Remember, this Defender has covered 150,000 miles, and it's not worth taking chances with old and critical parts.

While the engine was out, and not wanting to risk any future replacements, we fitted a new dual mass flywheel and clutch, plus a new clutch release bearing and fork. The Td5's dual mass flywheel can be thought of as two flywheels which move relative to each other to damp out engine vibrations. When the assembly wears and loosens, it becomes less effective at isolating the vibrations from the rest of the drivetrain. And while the flywheel was off, it was a no-brainer to renew the low-cost spigot bearing in the flywheel that squeals on a cold morning when its lubrication dries up.

To ensure the engine gave good service for a long time to come, it was worth replacing all the coolant hoses and, of course, checking the condition of the vital coolant pump drive. During our previous checks around the Defender's engine bay we'd found a small leak in the radiator, so that will be renewed. The intercooler was damaged too, and will be replaced by a larger EU3-type from a later Defender. On top of that, the engine would receive a fresh oil change with a new full flow oil filter and a centrifuge filter.

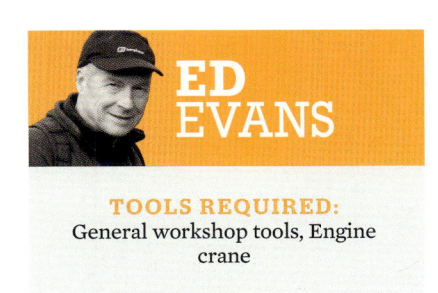

ED EVANS

TOOLS REQUIRED:
General workshop tools, Engine crane

TIME:
one day

COST:
£1800 approx

DIFFICULTY RATING:
3/5

1

SKAN 4x4 had a selection of Td5 engines on the shelf, ready to go. This one will do nicely – and it comes complete with all ancillaries.

Secondhand Td5 engine

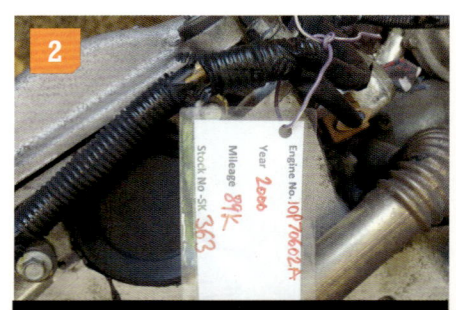

2 The engine has been cleaned and is tagged up with serial number, donor vehicle reference, mileage and the year of registration.

3 The details matched the donor vehicle still in the yard. The VIN number from the body shell will be useful if ordering engine parts in the future.

4 The original clutch and dual mass flywheel are removed and this new pre-lubricated spigot bush is drifted into the crankshaft flange.

5 A new dual mass flywheel is bolted on, followed by a clutch assembly using an old gearbox shaft to centralise the clutch plate.

6 Fuel connector block looks okay, but we fitted the original which was shown - by its regulator (arrowed) - not to be leaking.

7 We renew the ancillary drive belt and its automatic tensioner pulley to be sure of good drive and no belt squeal in the future.

Installing the engine

BEFORE FITTING the engine, the front underside of the gearbox bellhousing is jacked up to its max height in readiness for coupling the engine.

The engine is tilted to match the angle of the gearbox shaft in the bellhousing to help the two slide together. We take our time, continually checking the alignment, and edging the engine back carefully to mate with the bellhousing. Steve has screwed two of his guide pins into the back of the engine so that, as the engine is moved back, the pins would pass through the bellhousing flange holes to help guide the two assemblies together in full alignment.

The guide pins have a screwdriver slot in the end so they can be removed after the engine is bolted in position, and replaced with the normal bolts.

TOOLS REQUIRED:
Use correctly rated and maintained lifting equipment for raising and fitting the engine.

When lifting, ensure helpers know exactly what's going to happen. before the lift starts.

1 The Td5 engine is a fairly uncomplicated lift-and-fit into the Defender, with plenty of working space, even with the body front panel in place.

The engine is tilted down at the rear to mate with the transmission as we carefully edge it back and down to line up.

3 As the engine (left) moves toward the bellhousing (right), the flywheel slides in. Temporary guide pin (arrowed) will enter bellhousing bolt hole.

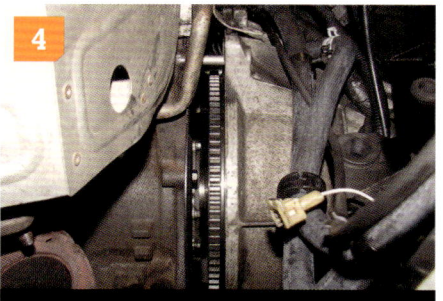

4 As the flywheel moves into the bellhousing, the guide pins have entered the bellhousing flange holes, helping maintain accurate alignment.

5 A new exhaust downpipe flange gasket had been positioned before lifting the engine in, to avoid placing fingers under the suspended weight.

6 With the engine/gearbox bolted up, and the jack removed, the engine is lowered on to its mountings as the turbo studs engage the exhaust flange.

Systems re-connect

WE STARTED re-connecting the engine systems by working gradually forward from the bulkhead. When refitting the power assisted steering pump, we rotated the coolant pump drive dogs to the 12 and six-o-clock position and set the corresponding drive on the steering pump at 90 degrees to them, ensuring they would engage when fitting the pump. We took no chances with the coolant system and used the opportunity to fit new hoses all round. A new radiator was installed, replacing the original leaky unit, and the original damaged intercooler was replaced with a secondhand unit from a later EU3 Td5 Defender. Fresh coolant, engine oil and filters finished the job off.

Before running the engine, we needed to take the cam/rocker cover off to read the code numbers on the injectors and enter them into the engine's ECU. That's when we noticed the injector wiring harness was an aftermarket version. It was probably fine, but knowing the problems these harnesses can cause on the Td5, we replaced it with a genuine harness. The codes were written down for each cylinder in order, and an Autologic diagnostic system used to enter the details into the ECU.

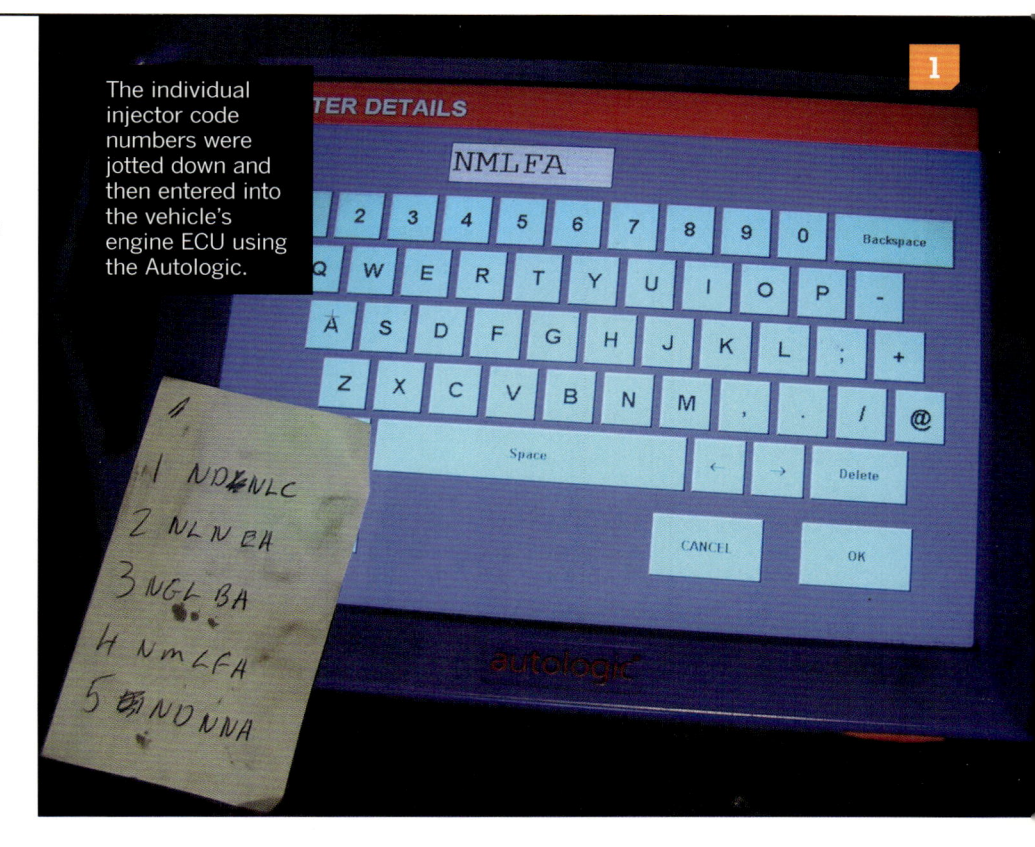

The individual injector code numbers were jotted down and then entered into the vehicle's engine ECU using the Autologic.

179

Secondhand Td5 engine

2

While working on the engine top, we replaced the injector wiring harness and plug with a Britpart Genuine unit, then re-sealed the cam cover.

3 The old distorted intercooler is swapped for a larger EU3 cooler, and a new radiator installed with a complete set of new hoses.

4 With the engine covers refitted, the Defender's engine bay is looking like new. The plan is that it should run that way for a long time to come.

5 Back home after the first 200 miles with only a weeping coolant hose to nip up, attention now turns to the next job on the list. It's a long one.

Budget still intact – almost

AS A WORST case scenario I imagined buying a new cylinder head and associated parts to get this Defender reliably back on the road. While dismantling the engine and finding its true state, that plan was blown out of the water. But at £1200, the complete secondhand engine wasn't much different from the cost of a new head assembly, and even adding the cost of extra parts to make the vehicle totally dependable, I reckon the overall cost of the vehicle is still a tad below market value. Of course, had this not been a DIY job, the garage labour costs would have sunk the ship.

Our strip and inspection has shown that even after 150,000 miles, a Td5 mill can have minimal wear and deterioration – and that a well-maintained and properly-used Td5 should cope with a quarter of a million miles.

WORK SAFELY:
Wear steel toe-capped non-slip boots.

Be aware that the engine may swing on a crane.

Never reach under a suspended engine, and ensure hands cannot be trapped if the load moves unexpectedly.

Ensure the vehicle is securely supported and held in position.

Polybush®

Fit and Forget – Excellent longevity

Great noise damping

Prolonged tyre life

Controlled Suspension Movement

Reduced MOT costs

The **number one choice** in suspension bushes.

- Controlled suspension movement
- Improved turn-in and stability
- Confident Ride
- Excellent Longevity
- Easy to fit without additional tools
- Unaffected by oil, petrol and road contaminants

British Made

From Defender to Freelander, we continue to improve your ride and enhance your driving experience.

Polybush Vs rubber after 9 months! Polybush outlasts rubber, no replacements needed.

Polybush offer a smoother, trouble free ride and last 4/5 times longer than OE, a true long term improvement.

Towing, winching, roads or lanes Polybush have the right grade for you, we'll be there, wherever you go.

Polybush, Clywedog Road South, Wrexham Industrial Estate, Wrexham LL13 9XS
Tel: +44 (0) 1978 664316   Fax: +44 (0) 1978 661190
Website: **www.polybush.co.uk**   Email: **sales@polybush.co.uk**

Seatbelt mounts

Aluminium bodywork corrodes dramatically around seatbelt mounts, but Trevor Cuthbert finds an effective repair kit

SEATBELT MOUNT REPAIR

TREVOR CUTHBERT

TOOLS REQUIRED:
General Workshop Tools

TIME:
1 day

COST:
£118.80

DIFFICULTY RATING:
5/5

WORK SAFELY
Wear protective gloves

Take great care when working under a raised vehicle

Ensure the chassis and components are stable and secured before working

Always wear eye protection when drilling or working overhead

ELECTROLYTIC CORROSION can do a lot of damage to your Land Rover. One common area to rot is around the seat belt mounting points at the front of the rear body tub in commercial Defender 90s and 110s. The brackets are made of steel and bolted through the body to the chassis, so the aluminium structure of the body is sandwiched between the steel chassis and seatbelt mounting brackets. Add moisture, and you have perfect conditions for electrolytic corrosion. In a nutshell, electrolytic corrosion occurs when two dissimilar metals are in electrical contact, in the presence of an electrolyte. One of the metals corrodes in preference to the other – in our case the aluminium corrodes, while the steel is largely unharmed.

Assessing the damage

THE FIRST signs of a problem in this area are often where the rear body tub is bolted to the chassis' tubular outrigger (in a 90) or to the four body brackets (in a 110). It's here where the aluminium of the body is sandwiched between the outrigger and the seat belt mounting bracket, that corrosion festers. We will see in this example, just how far the corrosion can spread in a Defender or earlier Ninety/One Ten.

1 The aluminium around the right side outer seat belt bracket has mostly corroded away, leaving little for the chassis outrigger to bolt to.

2 Looking from the rear aspect, it can be seen that only the steel seatbelt bracket remained bolted to the chassis; the body had become detached.

3 On the left side, it appears that there is more aluminium bodywork remaining around the chassis attachment point when looking from the rear.

4 Looking up at the left side bracket, it can be seen that the floor has completely corroded through – the seat belt reel could be pulled through.

5 The inner seat belt brackets have plenty of surface rust, but the bodywork behind the brackets is still in good uncorroded condition.

6 The battery box (left) and sills on this Land Rover are also heavily rusted and will be repaired before the body is fitted to the new chassis.

7 The seat belt inertia reel and the steel seat belt bracket were loose enough to pull right through the floor in one piece on the left side.

8 Having pulled the seat belt with bracket out of the floor, a large unsightly hole is left which is going to need considerable strengthening.

9 Towards the middle, the inner seat belt points are in good condition on the inside of the cabin, although the mounting bolts are fairly seized.

Preparing for repairs

ALL THE work was carried out on a Defender rear body tub that had been lifted off the chassis to carry out a chassis replacement. Removing the body certainly helps with the access, and with the clarity of the photographs, but the job is still very achievable with the body still attached to the chassis.

Clearly, the chassis mounting bolts would need to be removed but, otherwise, preparation is mainly about removing all of the seat belt mounts, and dealing with the excess flaky aluminium.

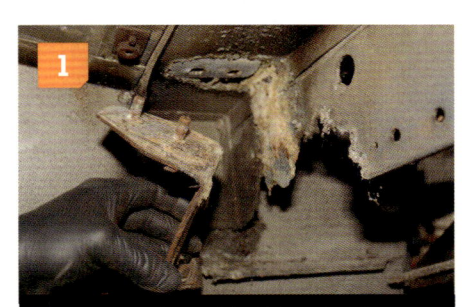

1 The right side seat belt bracket is removed from under the body, after the seat belt inertia reel has been unbolted on the inside of the cabin.

2 Clamped in the vice, the left side inertia reel is unbolted from the seat belt bracket, using a 13 mm spanner on the M8 nuts.

3 This is the remains of the corroded aluminium that had been sandwiched between the steel seat belt bracket and the steel inertia reel mount.

4 Remaining powdery deposits are scraped off the undersidey, along with other dirt, to leave the surfaces as smooth and clean as possible.

183

Seatbelt mounts

5 The two inner seat belt brackets need to be removed, by unbolting the remaining M8 bolt on each and unbolting of the seat belt fitting inside.

6 With the inner brackets removed, further dirt and powdery deposits are cleaned off in preparation for the new repair metal being introduced.

7 These repair panels from YRM Metal Solutions are made from galvanised steel. They incorporate both inner and outer seat belt mounting points.

8 For the inside, these aluminium panels will repair and seal the unsightly corroded holes in the floor section of the body.

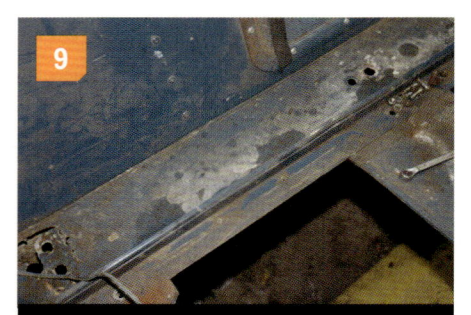

9 The bolts fixing the seat box to the front of the tub are removed and the whole area swept clean of excess dust and dirt.

Fitting repair panels

THE REPAIRS panels (underside seat belt mounting panels and inside tub repair sections) bolt to the front of the body tub, with the original remaining aluminium sandwiched in between. Galvanised steel does not react with aluminium as raw steel does – so the electrolytic corrosion effect will not take place with the lower seat belt mounting panels.

The only tricky part of this job is to ensure that the inner aluminium repair panels are drilled accurately, to allow seat belt mounting bolts and studs to go through in the right place.

1 The shaped inside repair section slots inside the lip at the front of the tub, so has to be carefully manoeuvred in place and slid to one side.

2 When the repair section is located correctly, it is drilled with a 6 mm drill bit to allow the original seat box bolts to be refitted.

3 Underneath, the new repair section is drilled through to allow the new seat belt bracket studs to pass up into the cabin from below.

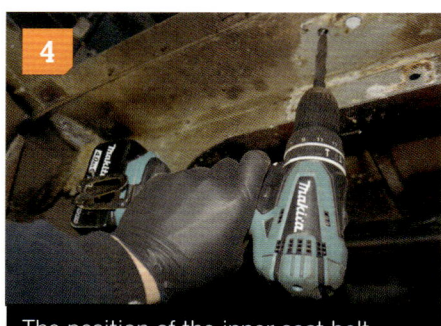

4 The position of the inner seat belt mount holes also need to be drilled through the repair panel from below. Repair panels have captive nuts.

5 The new underside repair panel is offered up from below and will be a nicely engineered snug fit under the front of the body tub.

6 When the galvanised repair section is in place, two bolts are fitted to hold it accurately in place, while umpteen additional holes are drilled.

7 The repair section is bolted to the tub and through to the inner repair section by approximately 24 x M8 bolts on Aeach side.

8 Where the old aluminium has been corroded away, there is now galvanised steel, beefing up the body tub structure and the chassis mountings.

9 Toward the centre are two holes left unbolted (arrowed) where the inner seat belt to chassis brackets will be fixed, when the new chassis is fitted.

10 Inside, the many bolt heads and penny washers will eventually be largely hidden when the seats are refitted, along with the centre cubby box.

11 The seat belt inertia reel is fixed to the new studs with a pair of M8 flange nuts with penny washers and it is all stronger than ever.

12 The inner repair sections not only add to the increased strength in the body tub and seat belt mounts, but the appearance is improved too.

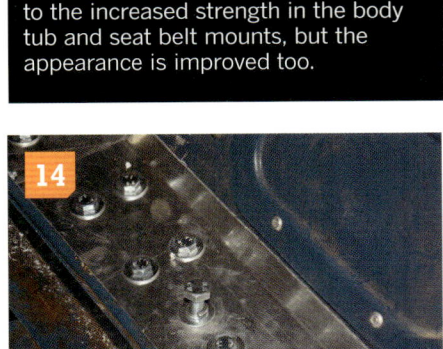

13 Looking up under the seatbox, YRM Metal Solutions' repair sections are well engineered and represent a simple way of strengthening the Land Rover tub.

14 The inner seat belt fixing will be attached to these inner bolts, through captive nuts in the lower galvanised repair section.

Battery box replacement

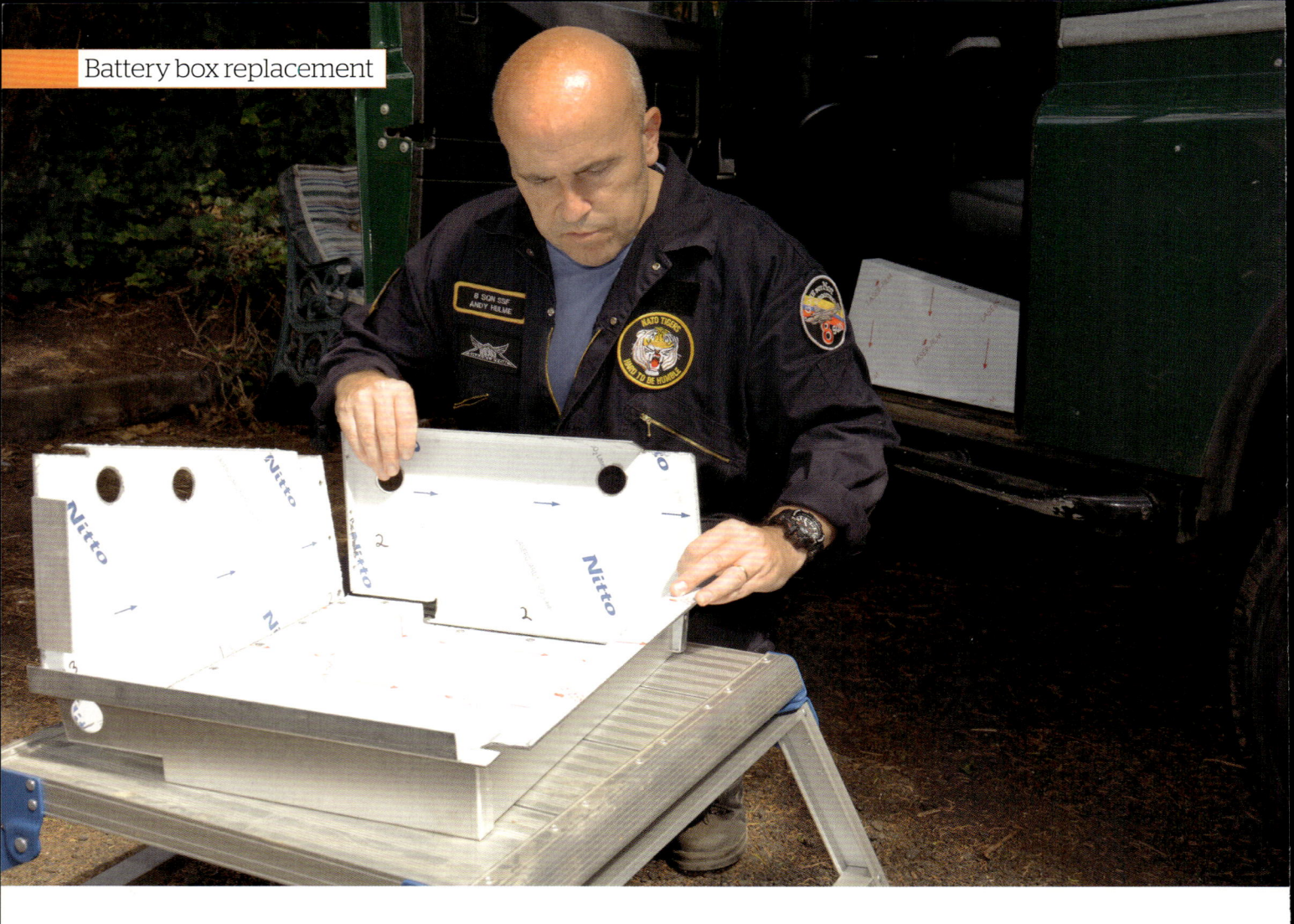

HOW TO REPLACE A RUSTED BATTERY BOX

Corroded battery compartments are common place on Defenders but are simple to replace

TREVOR CUTHBERT

TOOLS REQUIRED:
General workshop tools, riviting tool

TIME:
4 hours

COST:
£92

DIFFICULTY RATING:
2/5

THE UNDER seat battery compartment – or battery box, as it is often referred to – is one of those exposed steel parts of a Land Rover that can become seriously rusty over the years to the point of being unsafe. Holes can form in the structure so that the battery can be seen from underneath, and corrosion around the clamp location can mean battery clamp becomes ineffective without good steel to hold onto.

When this happens, remedial action needs to be taken to keep the battery safe and secure, or there is a risk of spilling dangerous battery acid or creating an electrical short and possible fire. Battery containment and secure fixing is also a common MoT test fail point.

I have seen many attempts at repairing the existing battery compartment. Some of these are professional looking welded patches. Others are more temporary measures, such as riveted on pieces of metal to hold the thing together until a major rebuild of the Land Rover is planned. However, a far more permanent and effective solution is to replace the battery compartment completely with a new (as we're doing here) or a refurbished component.

One good solution is to fit a battery box that has been properly repaired and then galvanised, ensuring that it will not rust again. This involves completely removing the seat box from the Land Rover, which takes a lot of time, particularly when many of the bolts to the sills, floor panels and door jambs are going to be badly rusted too.

A neat alternative repair option, produced by YRM Metal Solutions, is an aluminium kit of parts that allows you to rebuild the battery compartment into the Land Rover without removing the seat box. The left side seat box end needs to be removed, but this is a much easier task than having to remove the seats, plus any covering, and then the seat box itself.

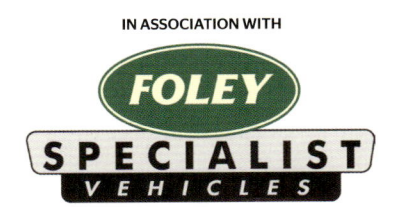

Removing the old battery box

1. The battery box is actually holed underneath, and rust has also crept up the sides towards the rear, making the whole thing weak and far from safe.

2. The seat box end needs to be removed completely. The bolts at the door pillar often need to be drilled out, due to the inner captive nut turning.

3. The bolts along the sill are usually easy enough to remove, because access to the nut underneath is good to get a spanner on.

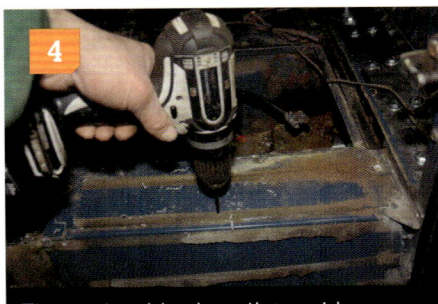

4. The spot welds along the seat box need to be identified and drilled out with a spot weld drill or a conventional 5 mm drill bit.

5. Remaining bits of spot weld can be broken using a suitable flat implement, such as this scraper. A sharp tap with a hammer might be required.

6. This lip of aluminium over the forward edge of the seatbox end needs to be levered clear. Here a pair of pliers is used to complete the job.

7. Now that all of the bolts and spot welds have been removed, the seat box end can be pulled free and discarded; it will be replaced with a new panel.

8. With seat box end removed and the battery lifted out, the compartment looks very weak and shabby; it is definitely in need of remedial action.

9. The structure of the battery compartment is held to the seat box by rows of rivets along its edges. These are all drilled out with a 5 mm drill bit.

IN ASSOCIATION WITH
FOLEY SPECIALIST VEHICLES

187

Battery box replacement

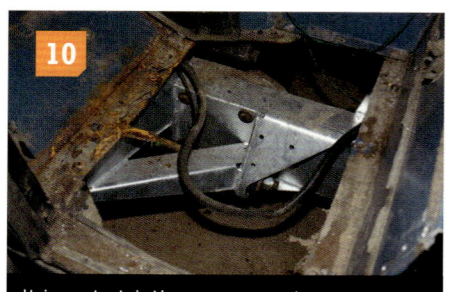

10 It is not strictly necessary to remove the passenger floor panel, but I found it helps with access when removing and replacing the battery compartment.

WORK SAFELY
Always wear protective gloves when handling dirty or rusty parts and those with cut metal edges, and when using an angle grinder
If working underneath the vehicle, ensure it is stable – transmission brake and gear engaged and wheels chocked on a level surface. If raised, ensure it is safely supported
Wear eye protection and protective gloves when cutting metal, drilling, wire brushing, and when using an angle grinder

11 The floor of the battery compartment is supported by the sill. Here it is levered up with a screw driver to unstick it from the sealant.

12 The rear wall of the battery box has been cut with an angle grinder to allow some bending of the box, to help manoeuvre it from the seat box.

13 The short front edge also needs to be cut to allow the box to be bent slightly out of shape. It will now be possible to extract it fully.

14 These old battery compartments can be repaired and then galvanised, but this one is probably too far gone to be worth the effort.

Fitting the new battery compartment

1 The new aluminium battery compartment is a four-part kit from YRM Metal Solutions and is supplied with rivets to assemble it in seat box.

2 If preferred, the white plastic coating on the aluminium sections can be peeled off, and the surface then treated with etch primer before painting.

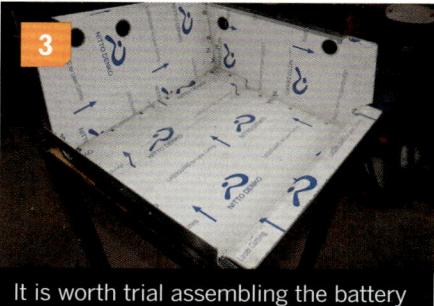

3 It is worth trial assembling the battery compartment in order to become familiar with how it goes together, although it is fitted one piece at a time.

4 Rear section of the new compartment is set in place under the seat box. The sections are very helpfully labelled to help with assembly.

5 The side wall and front section of the battery compartment are fitted in place, according to the 'behind' and/or 'under' labelled instructions.

6 The floor section is then eased into position, where it rests on top of the lipped edges of the other three sections, after a little jiggling.

7 All sections pre-drilled for the fixing rivets door jambs, so if the holes are properly aligned, everything should be in the correct place.

8 Most of the rivets can be secured using the 'lazy tong' cantilever type rivet gun, albeit the space is confined. M5 bolts can also be used in tight spots.

9 The battery compartment is fully built before fixing it to the seat box. Here, the small riveting tool is used at one of the more confined areas.

10 After the battery compartment is assembled together within the seat box, it is fully riveted to the seat box, through the original rivet holes.

11 A replacement seat box end is not expensive and is much better than trying to refit the old corroded and bent original one.

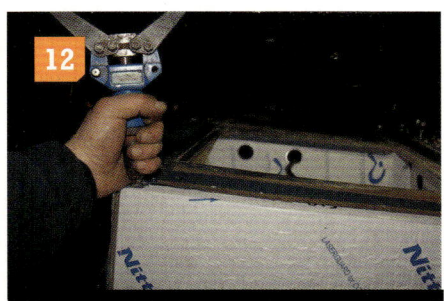

12 The old spot welds were purposely drilled out with a 5 mm drill bit – the perfect size for the new blind rivets that will be used.

13 As most of us don't have access to a spot welder, the next best option is to rivet the seat box end in place. The rivet heads will probably be hidden ultimately.

14 Completed battery compartment comes together neatly and is a strong job. It is a very well designed kit that's simple to fit in place.

CONCLUSION

The job of fitting the new battery compartment from YRM Metal Solutions is definitely easier and less time consuming than full removal of the seat box. It is also less disruptive to the Land Rover. The kit of parts takes away the need to have a steel battery compartment shot blasted, repaired and then galvanised, so it saved even more time in this regards.

All in all a very innovative and effective solution for ridding your Land Rover of one more rust problem.

Transmission renewal

PART 1
REMOVING THE TRANSMISSION

Even the latest Defenders can be improved. Remember the ex-farm truck Defender you first met on page 14? Well here is how we improved the transmission...

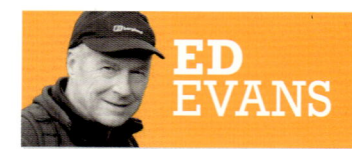

ED EVANS

TOOLS REQUIRED:
Tools: general workshop tools, vehicle lift, transmission jack, circlip pliers, trim clip removal tool, special tools as mentioned in the captions.

TIME:
1 day

COST:
Time only

DIFFICULTY RATING:
5/5

REMOVAL OF THE Defender TDCi transmission assembly on the earlier 2.4-litre TDCi is a fairly straightforward job, with only the complication of the wiring for a few more sensors to deal with.

In fact, the TDCi's six-speed gearbox is slimmer than the previous five-speed unit fitted to the Td5 Defender, helping making its removal a simpler job than on the earlier vehicle.

But that isn't the case on this later 2.2-litre TDCi.

Sure, we're still dealing with the same six-speed gearbox and transfer box casing, and the engine, chassis and engine bay is physically similar, but on this engine we also have the combined catalytic convertor and diesel particulate filter (cat/DPF) to remove from the rear right side of the engine.

Removing that unit demands a bit of time, patience and care, as we'll see later.

Transmission removal on the TDCi is a job for the garage, requiring a vehicle lift and a transmission jack to do the job relatively comfortably and safely.

But we show what's involved in the job, including a few tips and techniques that might be of help to anyone tackling the transmission removal and refit.

A cause of difficulty on these later Defenders is the amount of emissions-related equipment that is packed into an engine bay that was originally designed to accommodate simpler engines with relatively basic emission equipment.

Accessing bolts, electrical connectors, pipes and linkages increases the time taken, and fastener threads that appear to have been assembled dry, can slow the job down by being difficult to release and sometimes needing remedial work on the threads before reassembly.

We're covering this job at the Britpart workshop on Paul Myers' 61 plate Defender (see story so far on the adjacent page, top right), with Britpart's development mechanic, Steve Grant, removing the transmission.

IN ASSOCIATION WITH

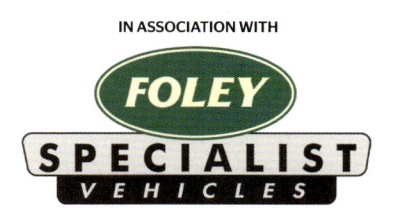

FOLEY SPECIALIST VEHICLES

THE STORY SO FAR

The transformation of this truck from Farm Truck to County Station Wagon is featured on pages 14 to 31, showing how the battered truck cab, bought by Britpart's Paul Myers, was converted into a pristine and bespoke station wagon. Paul has since used the Defender as his daily driver and has had no issues to date other than a door rattle which is probably due to a loose window channel. Paul says: "It gets comments most days, and I've been asked if it's an Autobiography."
Yes, it really is that good – and by working on the transmission we are now making it even better.

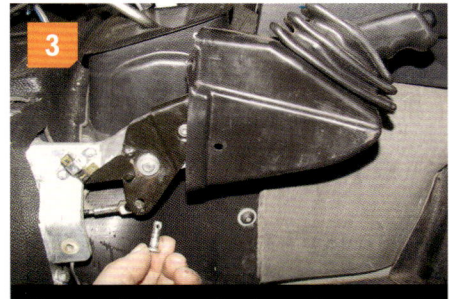

Interior work

1 Start by removing the seats, and disconnecting the battery earth lead (first cycling the ignition on/off and waiting two seconds to avoid alarm.

2 One-piece rubber floor/transmission cover is extracted by lifting the passenger side, and feeding the centre bit around the handbrake to withdraw it.

3 The handbrake gaiter is unclipped and slid forward to disconnect the cable, which is pulled back into the seatbox. Switch cable is also detached.

4 After releasing the two bolts, the handbrake lever is detached, carefully feeding the switch cable through its grommet to tuck safely in the seatbox.

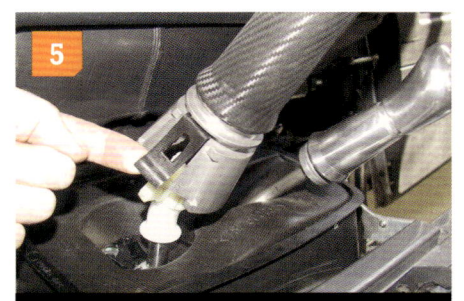

5 The gear levers' gaiter is prised off, and the gear lever removed by pulling the two tabs outward to clear the white plastic pegs.

6 This thick sponge rubber grommet is carefully worked out from its retaining box on the transmission cover, and lifted off over the levers.

7 The seatbox matting is lifted off and the seatbox centre top panel unscrewed, before removing this transmission cover using a long-reach Torx 30 spanner.

Transmission renewal

Underside jobs

1. The front and rear propshafts are unbolted and removed from the diffs and transfer box.

2. The transmission crossmember is unbolted from the chassis rails. There are two upper bolts (shown) and two lower bolts, at each side.

3. A hydraulic body jack, placed between the two chassis rails, pushes them outward slightly to allow the crossmember to be slid out.

Catalytic convertor and Diff

REMOVAL OF the combined catalytic convertor and diesel particulate filter (cat/DPF) is carried out from in the engine bay and from underneath. This unit is bolted at the top to the exhaust outlet of the turbocharger, which is itself covered by a heat shield. At its lower end, the cat/DPF is mounted via a bracket to the rear right side of the engine block just above the sump, the bolts for which are accessed from underneath the vehicle. There are four sensors to remove, and also two pipe connections which are difficult to access.

WORK SAFELY
Due to the weight and size of the transmission, we recommend that it only be removed using a transmission jack equipped with a mounting jig, and with the vehicle supported on a lift.

Fit chocks to each of the vehicle's wheels to prevent rolling on the lift.

Wear eye protection when working below the vehicle.

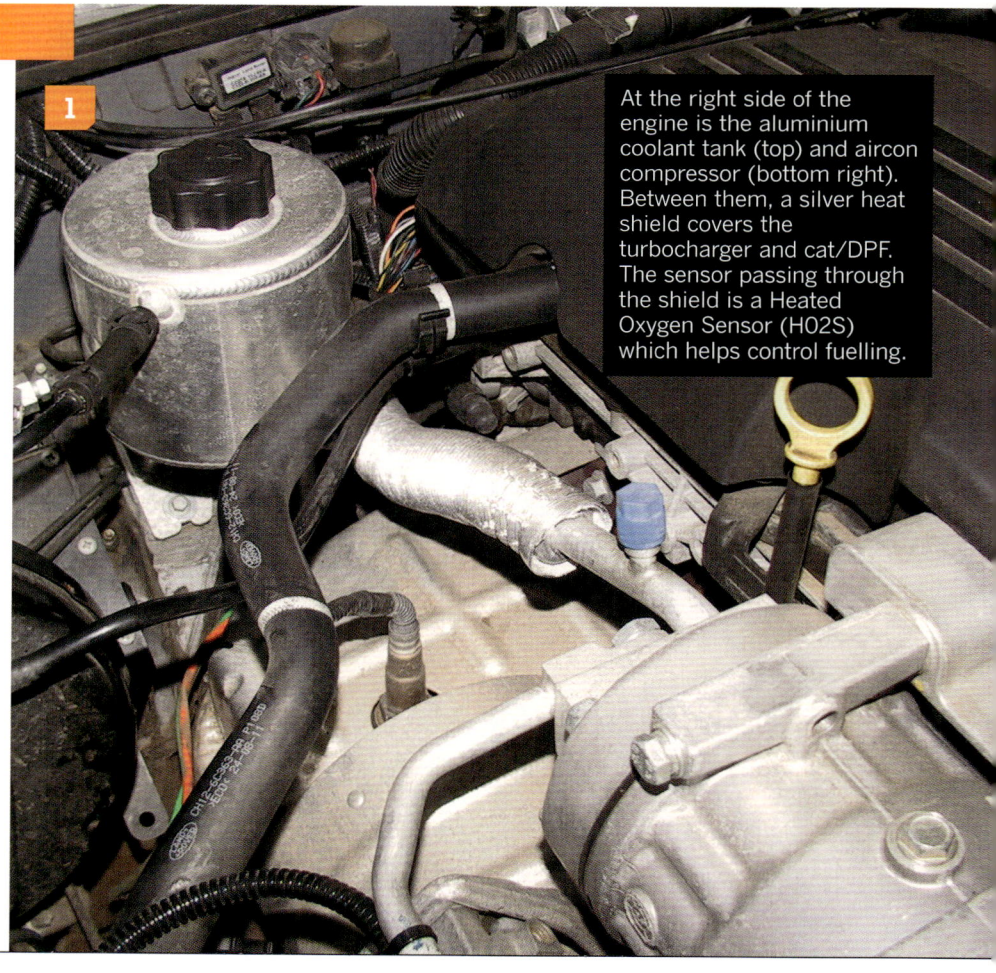

1. At the right side of the engine is the aluminium coolant tank (top) and aircon compressor (bottom right). Between them, a silver heat shield covers the turbocharger and cat/DPF. The sensor passing through the shield is a Heated Oxygen Sensor (HO2S) which helps control fuelling.

192

2 The HO2S lead is unplugged from its harness connector near the wing edge. Engine breather and servo hose are disconnected, and coolant tank moved.

3 The HO2S is removed using this cranked socket. Normally, the shield can lifted over the HO2S, but our aftermarket aircon pipe prevented this.

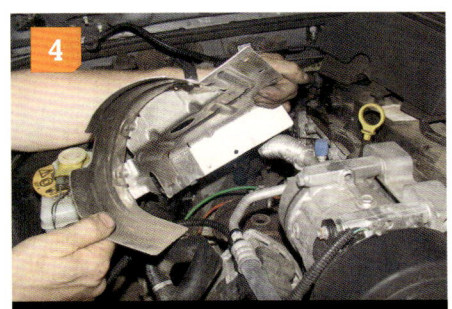

4 The heat shield is lifted off after first unclipping the green and orange temp sensor cables and removing the four bolts (one at rear).

5 We now see the cat/DPF with hole for HO2S (turbocharger at right). The pre-cat temperature sensor (bottom of pic) is unscrewed from the cat/DPF.

6 Lower down, the post-cat temp sensor (green cable) is unscrewed and removed. This was almost seized in, most connections being fiercely tight.

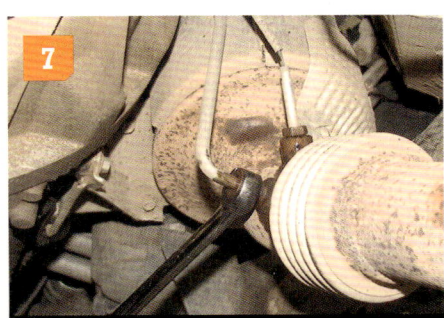

7 Underneath, at the cat/DPF outlet, the post-DPF temperature sensor is seized in, but the post-DPF pressure pipe (spanner on) releases with a struggle.

8 With two of the three temp sensors removed, Steve disconnects their three multiplugs above the transfer box (seized sensor will stay with DPF).

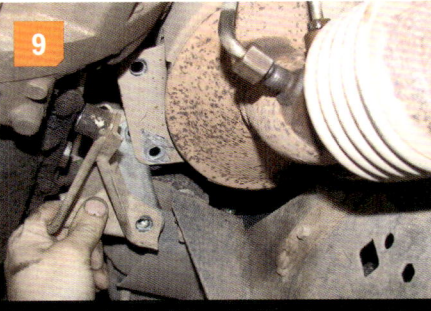

9 The bracket holding the the lower part of the Cat/DPF to the engine is unbolted, and the exhaust outlet pipe is unbolted from the rear silencer.

10 Looking up between the cat/DPF and engine, this pre-DPF pressure pipe needs releasing, but can't be reached – Steve leaves it for now.

11 Up top, after removing this clamp ring to the turbo, the cat/DPF is free, but there's no space between the engine and chassis to remove it.

12 We lift the engine, so the front cover is removed to check the fan/radiator clearance. Also watch clearance between vacuum pump and ECU.

13 The engine mounting nuts are removed. This right hand mount is reached from underneath. Left mount is not visible so is done blind, by feel.

193

Transmission renewal

14 The back of the engine is jacked up (pivoting on its mountings) until there's space to release the pre-DPF pressure pipe that was left earlier.

15 Both of the DPF pressure pipes connect to hoses leading to this sensor unit on the bulkhead. The sensor is detached from the bulkhead…

16 … allowing the two pipes, hoses and sensor unit to be withdrawn down between the cat/DPF to be stored safely out of the way.

17 The engine is jacked further, increasing space to finally jiggle the cat/DPF unit with its exhaust pipe out from between the engine and chassis.

18 But we're not finished with the cat/DPF yet. Those pressure pipe unions were so tight that the surface of the threads tore when undoing the nuts.

19 Here is the worst thread. Damaging one of these beyond repair would be an expensive because the complete unit would need to be replaced.

20 Fortunately, in this case, mechanic Steve is able to cut and reform the distorted threads by running a thread die

Removing the Transmission

1 We now lower the engine back onto its mountings and refit the nuts so its rear can be tipped downward to remove the transmission.

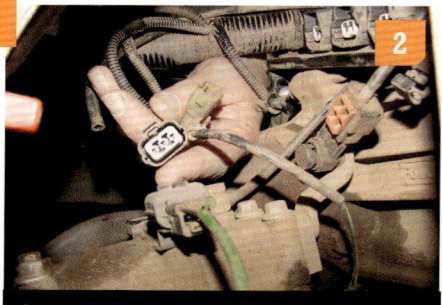

2 On top of the transfer box, the handbrake's link lead and hi/lo and diff lock cables are unplugged, and the main harness is unclipped.

3 Breather pipe (white arrow) is detached from transfer box (refitting bolt and washers). Detach ratio-change link by pressing black button (yellow).

4 Lower down, this nut is removed to release the diff-lock link from the transfer box. Next, the gear lever housing is removed to give clearance.

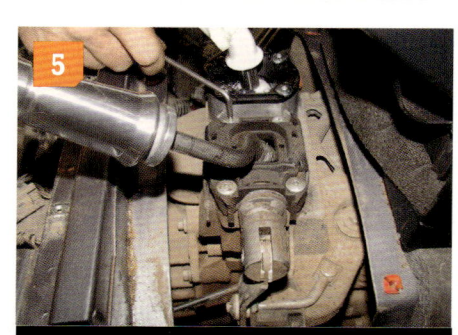

5 We remove the transfer lever mounting by extracting the four Torx25 screws and lifting off, leaving the difflock strut (foreground in slot) behind.

6 The gear lever housing is lifted off after removing four bolts: one in the transfer lever housing and three in the housing's outer mounting flange.

7 Main earth lead is unbolted from left of transfer box, and another from right side. Exhaust silencer is unclipped and hung over axle for space.

8 The clutch hose is clamped and the pipe bracket unbolted from the gearbox. Battery positive cable (also held by bolt) is moved aside.

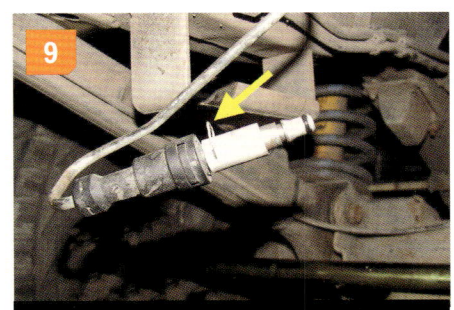

9 Further up the steel clutch pipe, this slave cylinder adaptor is released from the gearbox by pulling out the wire spring clip (arrowed).

10 Steve bolts his purpose-made jig to the underside of the transmission. It can be angled during lowering, and is essential for transmission removal.

11 With the transmission raised 20 mm by the jig and transmission jack, the transfer box mountings and brackets are unbolted and jiggled out.

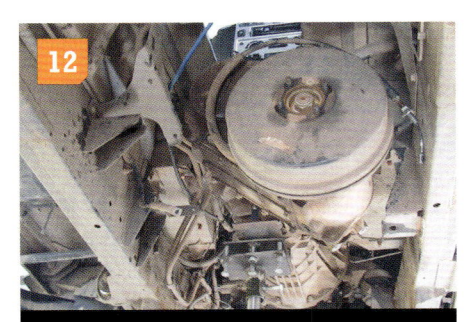

12 With the transmission lowered back down again, the bellhousing bolts are all slackened and the jig and jack adjusted for best angle and height.

13 After checking the wheeled transmission jack is stable, the bellhousing bolts are now all removed (heat shield removed at right side).

14 As transmission is carefully pulled back, the jig's angle is adjusted to maintain an equal gap between the bellhousing and engine flanges.

15 When the gearbox input shaft has fully exited the clutch assembly on the engine, the transmission is lowered to a safer height.

16 With the transmission removed, the front of the engine is chocked with a wood block to preserve the engine's angle for refitting the gearbox later.

Transmission renewal

PART 2
FITTING A HEAVY DUTY CLUTCH

If your TDCi Defender has a power tune, or if it's used for towing, a heavy-duty clutch will help ensure long-term power delivery

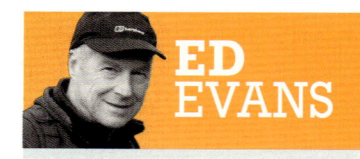

ED EVANS

TOOLS REQUIRED:
General workshop tools, special tools as mentioned in captions

TIME:
1 hour

COST:
£223.80

DIFFICULTY RATING:
2/5

THE DEFENDER heavy-duty clutch is actually standard Land Rover equipment, but it's only fitted to the top spec Autobiography Defender with the uprated 148hp TDCi engine. Hence, the HD clutch is a straight swap onto any other TDCi Defender. The heavy-duty clutch friction plate has different specification springs that contribute to its increased ability to handle higher torque loads but, because the clutch cover (or pressure plate) is similar to the standard version, the assembly does not affect the amount of push needed on the clutch pedal. It is a worthwhile fitment on standard TDCi models where the engine has been tuned or where heavy towing is involved. The clutch can be fitted to any TDCi model.

Compared with last month's job of removing the transmission, changing the clutch assembly is simple and quick, once the transmission is out. We're continuing the work in Britpart's workshop with development mechanic Steve Grant carrying out the modifications.

THE STORY SO FAR:
THE TRANSFORMATION of this farm truck to a bespoke station wagon was featured earlier in this issue (full story starts on page 14). In Part 1 we removed the transmission from the vehicle, ready to install clutch modifications that will make this an even more competent truck.

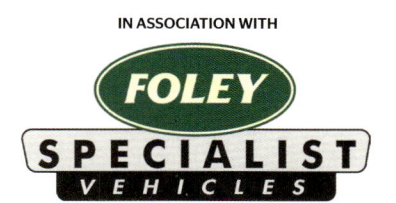

Removing the clutch

In Part 1 we showed how the transmission assembly was removed. Here, it is fully disconnected, ready to be lowered from the chassis.

We can now see the clutch pressure plate bolted to the flywheel. The DPF/cat, removed last month, was bolted to the turbo exhaust (top right).

The bolts holding the clutch cover to the flywheel are released gradually and evenly. To prevent the flywheel turning, Steve screws a dowel into a bellhousing bolt hole in the engine backplate. This provides a rest for a pry bar inserted between the flywheel ring gear teeth to stop the flywheel turning.

The clutch cover and friction plate inside are lifted off, revealing the flywheel. The flywheel face that contacts the clutch friction disc is clean and serviceable.

WORK SAFELY:
This job assumes the transmission is already removed. Ensure the vehicle is firmly supported and cannot roll during the clutch change, applying handbrake and wheel chocks.

Wear eye protection and a bump cap, when working under the vehicle.

Steel-capped work boots are standard wear for any Land Rover job, but especially when lifting components up under the vehicle.

IN ASSOCIATION WITH
FOLEY SPECIALIST VEHICLES

197

Transmission renewal

Inspecting the parts

The springs in the original friction plate (left) are intact, the fracture issue of earlier models is long resolved. Note, new standard plate on right, for comparison.

Compared with new standard friction disc (right), the grooves on the old plate (left) which help eject dust, are worn away – it's serviceable, but not for long.

Close inspection of the friction plate springs shows some polishing where they have contacted the steel support plate, but this is not a concern.

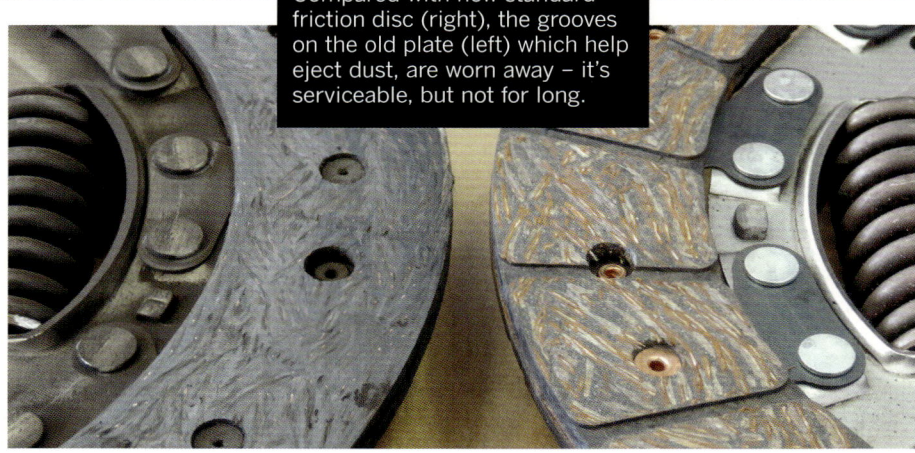

Before fitting the new clutch, the surface of the flywheel (which the clutch friction plate works against) is cleaned and checked for imperfections.

The spigot roller bearing in the flywheel centre lasts well on the TDCi. Ours is smooth, quiet and correctly greased, so no need to change it.

PARTS AND PRICES:
We fitted Britpart's heavy-duty clutch plate and cover kit, which has part number LR 072972, and typically costs £223.80 from Britpart stockists. That's a massive saving over the genuine Land Rover heavy-duty clutch plate and cover kit that is priced at around £1566.

Fitting the HD clutch

We're fitting Britpart's heavy-duty clutch kit comprising a new clutch cover and pressure plate assembly, and the new uprated friction disc.

The new clutch friction disc is centralised to the flywheel using an alignment shaft inserted through into the flywheel's spigot bearing.

Although new, the working face of the pressure plate is wiped clean. Sometimes a preservative fluid has been applied and should be removed.

NEXT TIME: In Part 3, we show you another important modification for the clutch system that will make the Defender easier to drive. We will also advise you on a few worthwhile checks you should carry out on the transmission while it is out of the vehicle, before explaining how to refit it into the Defender.

The clutch cover and pressure plate is passed over the alignment shaft, engaged on the flywheel locating studs, and the bolts fitted lightly.

The shaft is wobbled to ensure all is centralised before tightening the bolts evenly. Shaft clearance is re-checked before torqueing the bolts and removing the shaft.

199

Transmission renewal

LIGHTER CLUTCH & TRANSMISSION REFIT

PART 3

ED EVANS

TOOLS REQUIRED:
General workshop tools, special tools as mentioned in captions

TIME:
1 hour

COST:
£223.80

DIFFICULTY RATING:
2/5

A heavy clutch pedal on this Defender was easily cured while the transmission was out...

THIS EARLY 2.2-litre (2012) TDCi Defender has a notably heavy clutch pedal which, to some extent, spoils the driving experience. Here at Britpart, there is a fleet of all types of Land Rovers which are used to test and develop the company's aftermarket parts, so it was a simple matter to compare the clutch pedal effort with other TDCi Defenders. When we checked one of the earliest 2.4-litre TDCi models we noticed it had a much lighter clutch pedal than our 2012 model. Then, on checking a 2014 TDCi, we found the clutch pedal even lighter than the old 2.4 version.

Clutch parts have been re-designed during the life of the Defender TDCi, but the friction and pressure plates remained the same from the late 2.4 model to the final 2.2-litre version. The clutch release system however, has been updated since our 2012 model was built, so the plan is to fit this later system to achieve a light clutch pedal that would match the ease of the 2014 model.

All TDCi Defenders use a concentric slave cylinder bolted centrally onto the inside of the bell housing, with the gearbox input shaft passing through it. The slave cylinder and clutch release bearing are one assembly, and the hydraulic fluid is supplied via a rigid adaptor pipe that passes through the bellhousing casing to connect with the release assembly inside. Where the adaptor pipe protrudes outside the bellhousing, it is connected to the master cylinder by a hydraulic pipe and hose, via an in-line peak torque limiter. This torque limiter reduces the shock load to the transmission in the event of the driver's foot slipping off the pedal during a gear change. There is also a bleed nipple on the end of the adaptor pipe.

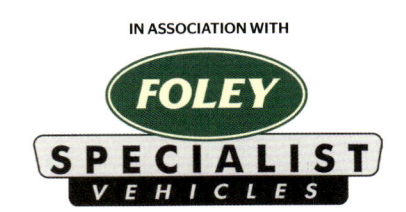

IN ASSOCIATION WITH
FOLEY SPECIALIST VEHICLES

The later adaptor pipe and clutch release assembly are a matching set, so they have to be fitted together, and are not individually interchangeable with earlier components. Unlike these clutch release components, the peak torque limiter has not been superseded so we will retain the original part.

The transmission needs to be removed to fit the new clutch release components, so it's worth also considering having a look at the clutch and replacing this if it is at all suspect. A clutch should last well over 100,000 miles, given normal road driving but, if you're working the vehicle off-road or using it for regular or heavy towing it's worth considering a replacement clutch for the relatively small additional expense. Under such arduous conditions it's also worth considering the heavy-duty clutch which we covered in Part 2.

We start this job with the transmission already removed from the Defender. The transmission removal was covered in Part 1, with Britpart's development mechanic, Steve Grant. Here, Steve assembles the clutch release system, refits the transmission and then reconnects the clutch hydraulics. Finally, we retest the pedal force to see if it's now as light and easy to use as the later 2014 model.

THE STORY SO FAR:
THE TRANSFORMATION of this farm truck to a bespoke station wagon is featured elsewhere in this issue (starting on page 14). We are now concentrating on the tarnsmission. In Part 1 we removed the transmission and, in Part 2, we fitted a heavy-duty clutch. Now we're completing a further upgrade to the clutch system before finally refitting the transmission.

Testing pedal force

BEFORE REPLACING the clutch release components, we measured the force needed to move the clutch pedal down by placing an electronic weighing scale on the clutch pedal, and pushing down to depress the pedal. Our 2012 TDCi that we're working on here recorded an effort of 11.4 kg to push the pedal. When we tested the later 2014 model for comparison, the effort was only 7.0 kg.

We will re-test the pedal force later, after fitting the new clutch release components, to see if our TDCi has achieved the lightweight clutch pedal of the later model.

The scales recorded a hefty push of 11.4 kg to depress the clutch pedal of the 2012 TDCi Defender featured here. That's quite some effort.

When checked against a later 2014 TDCi Defender for comparison, the effort to press the clutch pedal was only 7.0 kg.

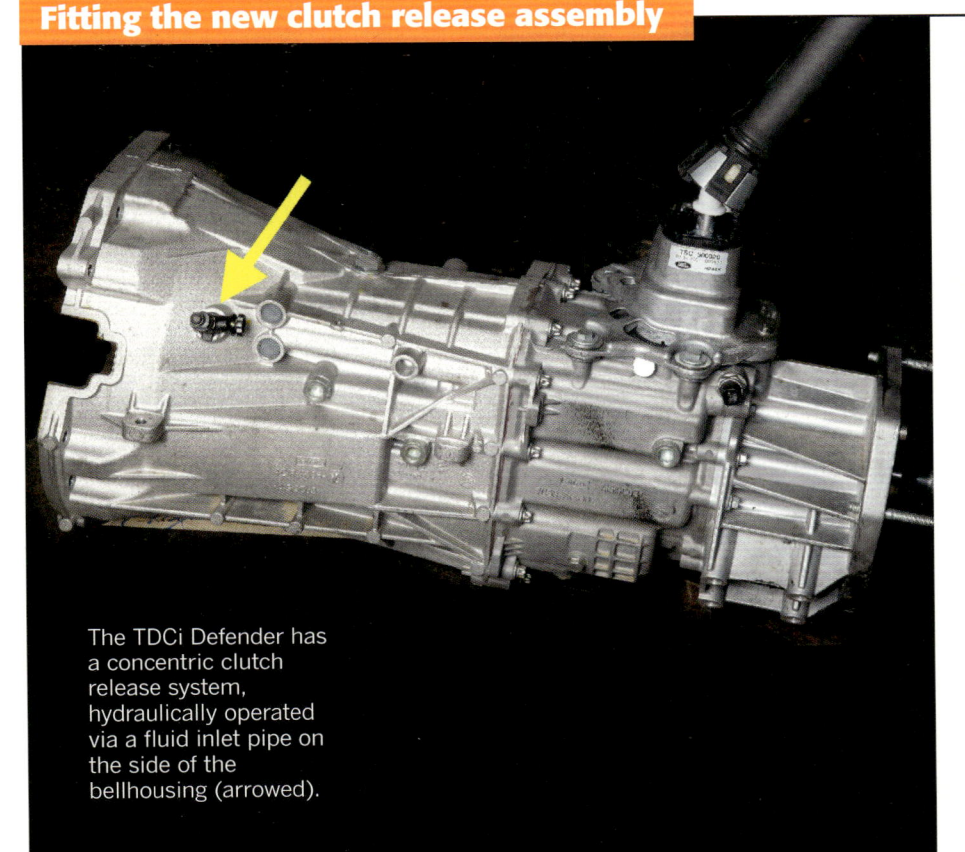

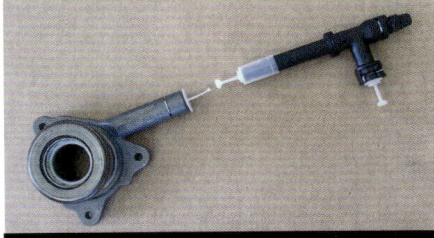

Fitting the new clutch release assembly

The TDCi Defender has a concentric clutch release system, hydraulically operated via a fluid inlet pipe on the side of the bellhousing (arrowed).

These are the parts inside the bellhousing: left is the combined release bearing/slave cylinder; right is the pipe adaptor with bleed nipple.

Inside the bellhousing, we detach the old adaptor pipe from the release bearing housing by pulling this spring clip partly out.

201

Transmission renewal

The old adaptor pipe is then simply withdrawn through the outside of the hole in the bellhousing as you can see.

The five Torx-head screws which hold the release bearing to the back of the bell housing are removed using a ratchet and extension bar.

The combined release bearing and concentric slave cylinder can then be lifted off. It really is as easy as that.

After cleaning the mounting faces, the new slave cylinder/release bearing is bolted into position, and the new adaptor pipe inserted.

The adaptor pipe is tapped into the release assembly until the spring clip locates. The protective external cap is left on until the transmission is fitted.

WORK SAFELY:
Due to the weight and size of the transmission, we recommend that it only be fitted using a transmission jack equipped with a mounting jig, and with the vehicle supported on a lift.

Fit chocks to each of the vehicle's wheels to prevent rolling on the lift.

Wear eye protection when working below the vehicle and when working with spring clips.

Refitting the transmission

RE-INSTALLING THE transmission is a straightforward reversal of the removal procedure described in December 2016 issue. Last month, we showed the clutch friction and cover plates being fitted using an alignment tool, and this is essential to confirm the two plates are accurately positioned and concentric with the spigot bearing seen in the flywheel.

With these components aligned, the transmission is offered up to the engine at the exact angle needed for the gearbox input shaft to slide through the clutch and locate in the spigot bearing as the gearbox bellhousing is moved forward to mate with the back of the engine. To assist with this, Steve temporarily fits two screwed pins into the engine backplate's bellhousing bolt holes, and these are used to guide the transmission accurately to mate with the engine.

Once it was correctly aligned, the transmission pushed in easily to mate with the engine, then all the bellhousing bolts were fitted and gradually tightened while ensuring the gap between the bellhousing flange and engine backplate stayed equal all around until it was fully bolted up. The upper three bellhousing bolts are best tackled from inside the cab.

The transmission is raised using a hydraulic transmission jack to take the weight, while a purpose-made jig holds the unit at the required angle.

Two dowels, screwed into the engine backplate, guide the transmission in as the bellhousing bolt holes slide over them.

With the transmission mated to the engine, the dowels are removed as the bellhousing bolts are fitted (one holds the starter's heat shield).

The bolts are tightened gradually and evenly, keeping the mating flanges parallel. Upper bolts, here, need extension bar to reach under bulkhead.

The transmission's rear mounts are refitted between the transfer box and chassis on each side, thus securing the transmission safely in place.

The transmission jack and the jig can now be removed, and the systems re-connected in reverse order to removal.

Connecting and testing the clutch

BEFORE WE removed the transmission, the clutch pipe with its peak torque limiter was freed from the adaptor pipe at the bellhousing. With the transmission replaced, this was reconnected to the new adaptor pipe. The clutch hydraulic system was then filled with fluid and bled.

With the Defender fully assembled and back on the ground, we tested the clutch pedal force needed and recorded just 7.0 kg, which is the same as the later 2014 TDCi which we tested earlier, and was our target figure. Changing gear is now a more relaxed operation.

The pipe from the master cylinder is clipped on to the new adaptor pipe which leads out of the bellhousing.

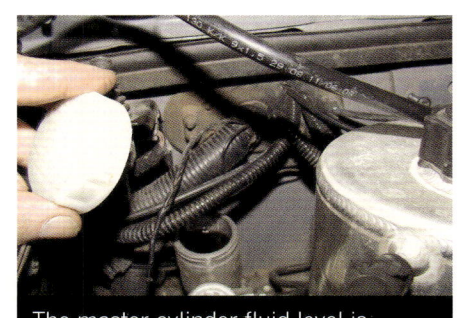

The master cylinder fluid level is checked and topped up as necessary during the clutch bleeding.

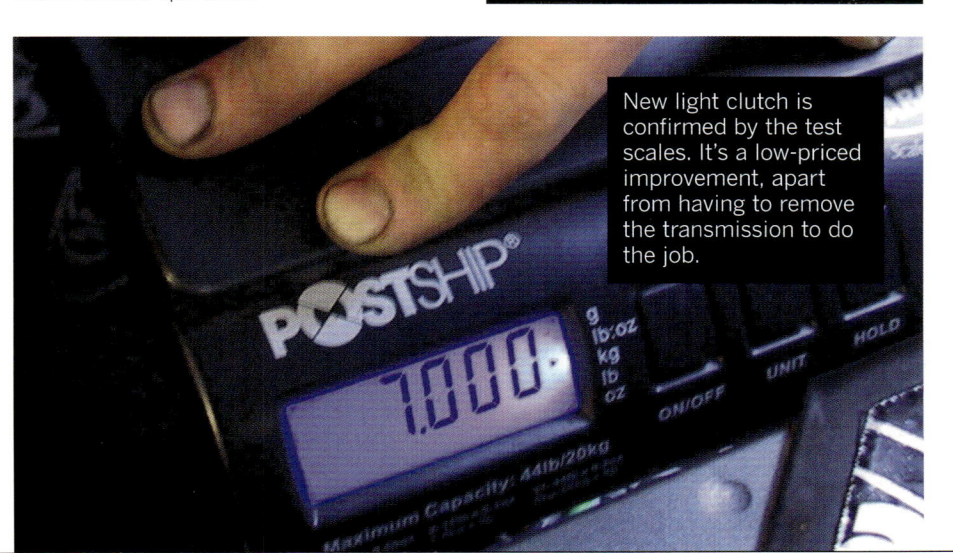

New light clutch is confirmed by the test scales. It's a low-priced improvement, apart from having to remove the transmission to do the job.

PARTS AND COSTS:
Clutch slave (combined with release bearing), Britpart LR 068979G, priced around £55.
Adaptor, Britpart LR 068981, around £30

Rocket cover gasket

TD5 ROCKER COVER GASKET REPLACEMENT

Changing the rocker cover gasket on a Td5 is a simple job. Alisdair Cusick shows what else to do, while you're there

ALISDAIR CUSICK

TOOLS REQUIRED:
Tools: 8 mm socket, 13 mm socket and ratchet, hose pliers, brake cleaner, sealant

TIME:
30 mins

COST:
£32

DIFFICULTY RATING:
1/5

IN MY VIEW, the Td5 is the nicest diesel engine fitted to a Defender. Torquey, quiet and, with a lovely characterful tickover beat, it is a super match to the vehicle. Rather than the odd number of cylinders, the Td5's real showpiece is the injection system. Instead of the then popular common rail system, where fuel is fed to all injectors at a constant high pressure along the whole fuel rail, the Td5 injectors contain their own pump plunger to pressurise the fuel in each injector unit separately. The Defender was the first passenger vehicle to use the technology, until then it had been common in truck engines. The benefit is a lower pressure along the fuel system right up the injector, but then the injector plunger does its job and much greater injection pressure is created before injection into the cylinder. High pressure helps combustion - and is one of the reasons for the superb power and torque outputs of the Td5.

So why the history lesson? Well, these injectors partly dictate the large flat shape to the top of the engine. Compared to long and thin rocker covers of previous in-line diesels which have the injectors or the common rail mounted down the side of the engine, the Td5 design housed the injectors actually under the rocker cover (or valve cover), alongside the rockers (which operate the injector plungers) and the injector harness.

There's a lot going on under there, so it should come as no surprise that the rocker area can be the source of a number of Td5 problems. One the simplest to cure is the gasket sealing the rocker cover to the cylinder head, which can start to leak. But it's an easy job to sort on a Td5, and usefully provides a chance to check the condition of a number of other components whilst doing the job.

Typical symptoms of a gasket leak will usually be a small oil stain under the vehicle. Looking above will usually show oil dripping the bottom of the bellhousing, suggesting a crank seal has failed, or sometimes the pressure regulator block's gasket. However, chasing the oil trail up further will likely reveal it is actually starting above the bellhousing, to the rear of the rocker cover-to-head joint. The oil usually leaks from the half moon shaped cut out on the rocker seal and, with enough oil escaping, it leaves an oil trail all the way to the floor. So this job is a useful one to hone the diagnosis skills on, as well as to get the spanners on.

Here, we are following the job through with James Holmes, Land Rover specialist based in Bedworth.

IN ASSOCIATION WITH
FOLEY SPECIALIST VEHICLES

1 The leak can typically be traced to the rear of the rocker cover. A mirror and headtorch is useful to look all around the rear of the engine.

2 James starts by removing the plastic acoustic cover from the engine – one bolt on the right hand side, two on the left.

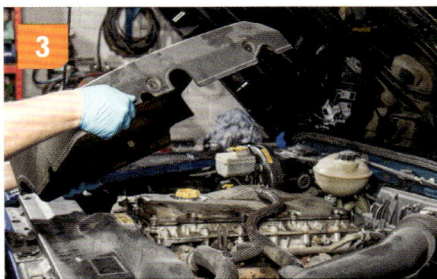

3 Lifting it off reveals the top of the engine, in particular the large flat aluminium valve/rocker cover which we'll be removing.

4 Remove the emissions breather hose and tuck it out of the way. Dedicated hose pliers are best, as James uses, but pliers or grips will do.

5 With an 8 mm socket, undo the bolts around the cover edge. Note the front left one here also holds the clip for the injector loom.

6 Carefully remove the rocker cover bolt ferrules and their seals. You can leave them in, but removing prevents them falling out as you refit the cover.

7 Simply lift off the cover. The old gasket should come away with it, unless too much RTV sealant has been used when the last one was fitted.

205

Rocker cover gasket

8 The top of the rocker area is revealed. Note black injector loom casing along the left, a line of injectors, and the rockers on the right.

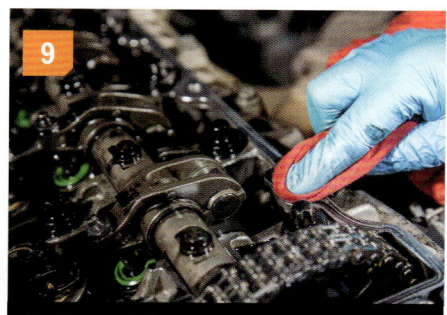

9 Next, carefully clean the rocker face, using just a little brake cleaner on a rag and a cloth, ensuring the face is smooth.

10 This is the half moon seal on the rear. Clean out any residual sealant, or oil which may prevent new sealant curing, resulting in a leak.

11 Remove the old gasket from the cover. Note this one has gone hard with age and repeated heat cycles, compared to the pliable new one.

12 Clean the rocker cover using brake cleaner, paying particular attention to the gasket locating groove, at which the jet is being aimed here.

13 This is what you're aiming for; a spotlessly clean gasket face for the new gasket to seal against, with all sealant, oil and dirt removed.

14 Fit the new gasket into the rocker cover. You can use some sparse dabs of RTV sealant to hold it in place, but no more than a smear.

15 There are two types of gasket; so check your VIN number. The difference is the size of the half moon. Ours is a later, smaller cut out engine.

16 To help seal the gasket's half moon insert, James prefers to use sump sealer, which he applies with a thumb to the recess on the rocker.

5 MINUTE HEALTH CHECK

The injector unit. If you have a leaking injector seal, best practice is to change the seals on all five injectors.

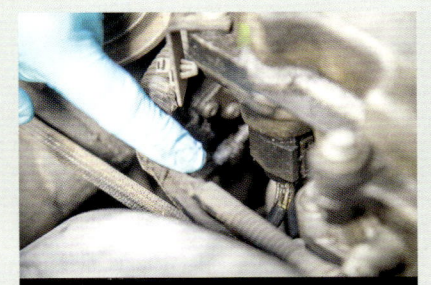

This is the connector on the front left, that's situated just below the rocker cover.

Dimple between James' hands shows breather has started rubbing. For what it takes, swapping it is best practice.

- Whilst you've got the rocker off, it make sense to check a number of other components for condition. Other common problems centre around those injectors. The most complex of all are injector seals failing. Curing this involves removing each injector, and replacing the small copper tip washer, and the rubber seal half way down each injector body. Symptoms of those failing would be more cranking needed of a morning, noticeable black smoke, or evidence of diesel in the engine oil. In extremis, you may notice the oil level rise in the sump over time. With the rocker off, just have a look for any evidence of diesel fuel.
- Another Td5 Achilles is the injector loom. It's mounted on the right hand side of the rocker area, leading to a connector where it passes out through the front corner of the engine to connect with the engine harness leading to the ECU. Oil can seep into the harness, eventually making its way to the ECU. This could show as oil inside the red multiplug at the ECU. If left, it can cause misfiring and/or rough running.
- Lastly, a simple one. The rocker cover emissions breather hose can leak, or begin to chafe against the corner of the rocker cover, causing oil vapour to escape. To check this, whilst you're disconnecting this breather hose, just have a good look around it. Check too it hasn't gone hard, or brittle. If so, replace it.

17 To refit the rocker cover, ensure any bolts are secure. Line it up front to back, then rotate it down, avoiding dropping the gasket off.

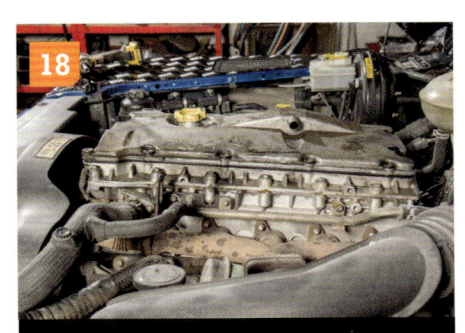

18 Check all around that the gasket is seated well, and not pinched or folded in any way, preventing a good seal.

19 Refit each of the bolt ferrules and seals (after cleaning them) then refit all the bolts, but only take them to barely finger tight for now.

20 Don't forget to fit the front clip for the injector loom, under this bolt, and replace the cable tie (if needed) securing the wiring loom.

21 Then, working from the middle outwards, tighten down the rocker cover bolts. Torque only to 7 Nm, don't overtighten them.

22 Finally, reconnect the rocker cover breather hose and replace the acoustic cover, ensuring it is correctly seated, and tighten the bolts.

Buying Guide: Introduction

IT SOMETIMES SEEMS as though everybody wants a Defender. What was once seen by the general motoring public as a rather agricultural workhorse is now in huge demand.

Defender's transformation fromo niche vehicle to must-have fashion accessory began less than a decade ago and intensified as production of the iconic model neared its end in early 2016.

But the huge demand has seen values rise, with even battle-scarred veterans of 20 or 30 years old fetching surprisingly high prices.

This has certainly seen a shift in attitudes among Land Rover fans. Is it our imagination or are there fewer Defenders out there on the off-road courses and rough tracks? It seems some folk are less inclined to abuse their Defenders and are keeping them for "best" while using a cheaper secondhand Discovery from the same era for mud-plugging – a remarkable reversal of fortunes for both models.

But don't get the impression that all Defenders are expensive and out of the price range of ordinary Land Rover fans. There are plenty of bargains out there to be had, as long as you know what to look for – and that is what this special BuyingGuide is about.

Read on as we reveal the idiosyncracies of all Defender models, including what to pay, what can go wrong and what to expect from living with one.

Defender ownership is your passport to adventure and driving pleasure.

HOW TO BUY A DEFENDER

There were a bewildering array of Defenders produced between 1984 and 2016. To guide you through the maze of what's available, what to look for and what to avoid, here is LRM's Ultimate Defender Buying Guide

IN ASSOCIATION WITH

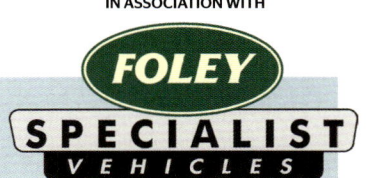

FOLEY SPECIALIST VEHICLES

NINETY/ONE TEN

SPECIFICATIONS
1983-1985: Engines as Series III/Stage One V8. LT77 five-speed fitted to four-cylinder models. **1985-1990:** 2.5-litre petrol, 80 bhp,
129 lb-ft torque; 2.5 diesel, 68 bhp, 113 lb-ft; 3.5 V8 petrol, 113 bhp,
185 lb-ft, 134 bhp from **1986**. LT85 five-speed fitted to V8 models.

PRICE GUIDE
Poor: £2000 – £2900
Average: £2900 – £4500
Good: £4500 – £6500
Excellent: £6500 – £13,000

DEFENDER Tdi

SPECIFICATIONS
2.5-litre turbo-charged, direct-injection diesel. 107 bhp, 195 lb-ft torque. LT77S five-speed transmission.

PRICE GUIDE
Poor: £2700 – £3800
Average: £3800 – £6000
Good: £6000 – £11,900
Excellent: £11,900 – £35,000

DEFENDER Td5

SPECIFICATIONS
2.5-litre five-cylinder turbo diesel, 122 bhp, 221 lb-ft torque. R380 five-speed transmission, permanent four-wheel drive.

PRICE GUIDE
Poor: £3800 – £5300
Average: £5300 – £7300
Good: £7300 – £12,000
Excellent: £12,000 – £20,000

DEFENDER TDCi

SPECIFICATIONS
2007-2012: 2.4-litre four-cylinder turbo diesel, 122 bhp,
221 lb-ft torque. **2012-on:** 2.2-litre four-cylinder turbo diesel, 122 bhp, 265 lb-ft torque. Six-speed MT85 gearbox, permanent four-wheel drive.

PRICE GUIDE
Poor: £6200 – £8200
Average: £8200 – £12,800
Good: £12,800 – £18,500
Excellent: £18,500 – £60,000

Buying Guide: Ninety & One Ten (1984-90)

Ninetys and One Tens are as popular today as when they were when introduced in the early 1980s. Dave Phillips explains how to find a good 30-year-old workhorse

DEFENDERS IN ALL BUT NAME

IF YOU NEED A reminder of just how long the Defender has been around, you need to go back to 1984 when the One Ten was unveiled to the world. That, and the short wheelbase Ninety that was introduced a few months later, changed Land Rovers for ever. Out went the leaf springs that had been the trademark of Land Rovers since 1948 and in came coils. The Ninety and One Ten models were a quantum leap forward for Solihull. Although some would argue they were merely an updating of the 88 and 109-inch Series III models, the changes made paved the way for the Defender models to follow for the next 30 years.

In fact they are Defenders, in all but name. The Defender model-name was introduced in 1990 to save confusion with the newly-introduced Land Rover Discovery.

The One Ten came first, launched at the Geneva Motor Show in March 1984, just weeks before the 35th anniversary of the 1948 launch of the original Land Rover. Although it shared the same engines as the Series III – 2.25-litre four-cylinder petrol and diesel variants, plus the much more powerful 3.5-litre V8 petrol – as well as some body panels, it was built on a new chassis supported by coil springs all round. It also had disc brakes at the front, a flat front end inspired by the Series III Stage One V8, and a one-piece windscreen.

At first the Series III models continued in production, but with a marginal price difference, few were sold – especially from June 1984 when the Ninety was launched. With it came a new 2.5-litre diesel engine, that was also fitted in the One Ten.

This 12J engine, created by lengthening the stroke of the venerable 2.25 diesel, produced a modest 67bhp at 4000rpm and 114 lb-ft maximum torque at 1800rpm, but like its predecessor it was a rock-solid performer, unrivalled off-road. On-road, it would cruise uncomplainingly all day at 60 mph.

Sadly, the lack of a turbo and fickle motoring fashion saw the downfall of this splendid engine. Japanese 4x4s of the era were nippier on-road. They were nowhere nearly as good off-road, but the public wanted something faster and Solihull obliged by bolting on a turbo. The 19J Diesel Turbo replaced the 12J in 1986. It was faster, but sadly it was a bit too much for the old engine— and wasn't nearly so reliable as it predecessor.

Many owners of Ninetys and One Tens have kept them totally original, while others have opted to update them by installing Tdi engines from later Defenders. When I bought my own 1984 Ninety four years ago, it was still running the original 12J engine and LT77 gearbox, but its performance in modern traffic left a lot to be desired, especially on uphill sections when speed would drop to less than 50mph. So when the gearbox finally expired last year, I took the opportunity to replace engine and box with an ex-Discovery 300Tdi and R380 gearbox. It means I can drive on main roads without queues of traffic building up behind me.

In common most older Land Rovers, it's like Trigger's broom, with all many parts replaced over the years. Originality isn't important to me, so I replaced the rusty doors with Series-style doors, with sliding windows, which I much prefer to wind-up windows. The dark blue paintwork and chequerplate were added by a previous owner.

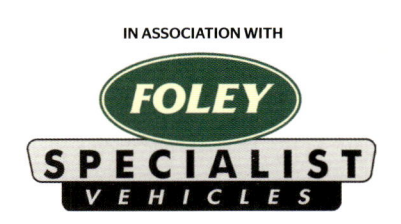

Other owners, like LRM's Steve Miller, who is currently restoring a Ninety of the same vintage, decide to keep them original. It is a matter of choice.

ENGINE
The 12J 2.5-litre naturally-aspirated four-cylinder engine is pretty bulletproof. For drivers used to modern diesels that start instantly from cold, it takes some getting used to waiting 20 seconds for the glow plugs to heat up before turning the starter to fire it up. But once it's going it just keeps on going.

It's also a lot more rattly then modern diesels. Older diesels like this have a rotary injection pump which pumps fuel directly to each injector, whereas modern common rail diesels have computers to determine exactly when and how much diesel to deliver to each injector. It is perfectly timed, and quieter, but not nearly so simple.

You can trace the 12J back to the earliest Land Rover diesel engines. They simply evolved over the years. The 19J Diesel Turbo, 200Tdi and 300Tdi engines were further developments of this same basic diesel engine.

A lot of people describe these engines as "agricultural", but that's not a bad thing. It means they are simpler to fix and that you can get repairs done by local mechanics in the middle of Africa, or wherever.

They are also incredibly reliable. My good friend and Defender specialist, Terry Hayward, told me that it is very rarely he gets asked to fix a 2.5 naturally-aspirated, unlike the troublesome later 19J Turbo Diesel, which was basically the same engine with a turbo bolted on, and wasn't one of Land Rover's better ideas. The engine wasn't designed for a turbo and the extra stress caused many to fail.

Rocker cover gaskets on both engines are prone to failure. It's not at all serious, but the leaking oil will make a mess. They are easy to replace – just remove the rocker cover, scrape off the old one and renew.

Compared to more modern, compact models, the starter motor is huge and a bit sluggish on very cold mornings. You might want to consider replacing it with a smaller and more powerful one from a Tdi. It is also worth fitting a modern, heavy-duty gel battery rather than the older-style lead-acid one. The standard alternator is plenty powerful enough to keep it fully charged.

Although most Ninetys and One Tens were fitted with diesel engines, some owners opted for four-cylinder petrol models on early models, or the 3.5-litre V8 petrol from the Range Rover and outgoing Series III Stage One. Both are more powerful – the latter much more so – than the diesel options, but neither can

This One Ten was restored and given a soft top by LRM writer Steve Miller.

GEARBOX
The Ninety and One Ten inherited the LT77 gearbox from the Rover SD1 saloon car – and it wasn't a bad legacy. It has earned the same "agricultural" reputation as the engine it's attached to, but again that's nothing to be ashamed of. They're simple, sturdy and don't go wrong very often.
In fact the LT77 outlived the engine, as it was later teamed up with the 200Tdi engine before finally being replaced with the slightly more sophisticated R380 box with the advent of the 300Tdi, in 1994. The LT77 is not quite as nice to drive as the later R380, but it just keeps on going for ever. It also takes a bit of getting used to finding reverse at the top left of the gate.
Incidentally, if you find the clutch a bit stiff – a common complaint from drivers new to Ninety and One Ten ownership – replace the pedal with one from a 300Tdi, which is spring-assisted and much easier on the calf muscles.

HEATER
Now let's talk about the heater – or should I say lack of heater? There's no escaping the fact that the heater on a Ninety or One Ten is feeble. A light waft of lukewarm air is the best you're going to get. Owners of naturally-aspirated Ninetys and One Tens tend to dress up warmly in winter.
Just like their Series predecessors, the Ninetys and One Tens were fitted with cold-running engines. This was deliberate, to prevent them overheating in hot climates. A lot of Land Rovers were exported and Solihull didn't want them boiling up in the middle of deserts and jungles. It is possible to improve the heating output by fitting the heater from a 200Tdi Defender, but the cheapest and simplest solutions are to either replace the viscous fan with an electric fan, or fit a radiator muff.

Buying Guide

expect the same longevity of the oil-burners which, when properly service, should be good for 200,000-plus miles.

Change oil and filter at the recommended intervals. No need for fancy synthetic or diesel oils. Ordinary mineral oils are fine for this non-demanding engine.

Very early models had an external bonnet catch, but many had a later bonnet and internal catch fitted retrospectively. Incidentally, if you find the bonnet catch pull lever a bit stiff, and you don't boast biceps like Popeye, you can easily swap it for the improved version fitted on the Defender Td5.

LEAKS
Puddles of water in the footwells is something many owners accept as standard fare if you own a utility Land Rover, but it doesn't have to be that way. Contrary to popular belief, it is possible to keep the elements out.

On an older vehicle like a Ninety or One Ten, unless the original rubber seals have been replaced they are sure to have deteriorated badly – especially those around the doors, ventilation flaps and windscreen. They are not difficult to replace – in fact they are straightforward DIY jobs. Even the windscreen seal is something you can do at home in a morning, but do it carefully and make sure you get one or two friends to give you a helping hand.

Badly-fitting doors also cause leaks (and do little to help keep the interior warm in cold weather). They are easy to adjust and can be done at the same time as you replace the worn seals.

BRAKES
Ninetys and One Tens were fitted with disc brakes at the front and ten-inch drum brakes at the rear. This is seen by some as a weakness, but in fact it is a better system than discs all round like you get on later Defenders.

Why? Because if you're a farmer, an off-roader or anyone else who uses your Land Rover for what it was intended – namely driving in mud – your rear brake discs and pads will wear out quickly, especially in parts of the country where the soil is very sandy and the fine particles act like grinding paste. That doesn't happen with drum brakes, because the drums keep out the mud,

> "Contrary to popular belief you can keep the elements out"

and the shoes inside enjoy a long working life. Some owners don't like the transmission handbrake, complaining that it is unreliable and tends to seize, but that's only because they neglect them. If you service them regularly and keep them properly adjusted, you won't have any problems.

WHEELS AND TYRES
Land Rovers are easy to modify. It's something we all like to do. But sometimes we should accept that Land Rover's engineers got it right in the first place and the changes we make in some areas will actually detract from the performance of our Land Rovers. A case in point can be wheels and tyres.

The 16-inch wheels fitted as standard on Ninetys and One Tens have the effect of keeping the gearing down and providing livelier acceleration than you'd get by replacing them with bigger wheels. Yes, big alloys can look the part – but they won't do such a good job on vehicles powered by non-turbo diesel engines.

BODYWORK
The good news for owners of Ninetys and One Tens is that your chassis are likely to be as good as, if not better than, the much newer Defender Td5. They might be a couple of decades older, but there's no doubt that the steel used on the chassis of the 1980s was of better quality than that of the late 1990s.

That's not to say that a 30-year-old chassis is going to be pristine. Outriggers will usually have been replaced and the rear crossmember is also vulnerable, but these are relatively cheap and easy to replace. I have replaced the rear chassis on my own Ninety with a Britpart pattern part that fitted perfectly.

Bulkheads are also generally longer-lived on these early vehicles, but they are thinner steel than chassis and you will get rot, especially in the upper bulkhead around the vents. Beware of vehicles that have had these areas patched with filler, which seals in the rust, and which will in turn continue to spread under the filler.

The only way to deal with rust in the bulkhead is to cut it out and have new metal welded in. If you're uncertain whether your vehicle's upper bulkhead is packed with filler, try a simple magnet test. If the magnet isn't attracted to the bodywork in this area, it means there's plastic under the paintwork rather than

SEATS

After more than a quarter of century of hard use, seat material wears out – especially if the material is the shiny vinyl found on many early Ninetys and One Tens (cloth trim was an option). You have the choice of retrimming, fitting seats covers or replacing with later Defender seats.

A common complaint from Defender owners is lack of legroom, as well as the standard seating position being too close to the doors. This is caused by the provision of a third, middle seat (often replaced by a cubby box).

Bearing in mind that few use the middle seat, it makes sense to get rid of it and move the two remaining seats further inboard. But I have kept mine in place because my dog loves to sit there, beside me (wearing a doggy seat harness, of course).

If you are desperate for more legroom, there are solutions. Terry Hayward has fitted special rails that move the seats up an inch or so, giving him slightly more legroom, and an inch or so across, to increase elbow room. It means he can have neither middle seat nor cubby box, but it transforms the comfort. The other option is to cut out the bulkhead behind the seats, but this isn't for the faint-hearted, as you will need to fabricate new braces to maintain the structural integrity of the vehicle. Unless you know what you're doing, entrust this task to a specialist engineer.

212

COOLING SYSTEM

It's a sad truth that as Land Rovers get older, they're more likely to be owned by somebody who tries to cut corners and save a bit of money by neglecting servicing or proper repairs. This includes neglecting to put antifreeze in the cooling system.

Like most corner-cutting exercises, this is a false economy. You need antifreeze in your cooling system at all times – not just in winter – to prevent internal corrosion of your engine and radiator.

If you're not too sure of its past, drain the coolant, flush the system through and start again with fresh coolant with the correct mix of antifreeze. I did that immediately after I bought my Ninety and was staggered to find that not only was the cooling system full of rust-coloured water with no antifreeze, but there was no thermostat in the housing either. The moral is to never underestimate the bodges and corner-cutting carried out by some owners.

STEERING AND HANDLING

Vague steering and disconcerting bumps and wobbles are all too often accepted as par for the course when it comes to older Land Rover ownership. But it doesn't have to be that way. The steering on Ninetys and One Tens should be just as taut and positive as a modern Defender. If not, check the system for signs of wear – universal joints are prime culprits that can either wear or work loose – and tighten up the steering box to take up any play.

Power steering was an option on early models. It is easy to retrofit if necessary.

But I found the biggest cause of poor handling on my Ninety was caused by worn rubber bushes, which were responsible for some undesirable handling characteristics. I was amazed at the transformation I got by swapping them with Polybush replacements. Again, it will feel like you're driving a brand-new vehicle.

FINAL VERDICT

Ninetys and One Tens are brilliant vehicles. They paved the way for the Defenders and the fact that there are so many of them still around after three decades of hard work proves what brilliant Land Rovers they are. Service them regularly, keep them clean and Waxoyled, and don't neglect those little jobs that need doing. You'll be rewarded with a vehicle that's good for another 30 years of active service.

Rust at the top of the bulkhead is a real problem. This rotten section on Dave's Ninety was cut out and repaired by Nigel Hammond.

metal. That was the case on my own Ninety and I got my good mate and master welder Nigel Hammond to cut out the old rusty stuff on the offside and replace it with new metal – which he did, perfectly. In the next year or two the same operation will probably need to be carried out on the nearside.

Another area prone to corrosion is the doors, which comprise aluminium alloy skins on steel frames. The reaction between the two different metals accelerates the rate of corrosion, with the result that most Ninetys and One Tens have had their original doors replaced by later Defender ones, although as I mentioned earlier I went for the retro look and Series doors with sliding windows, working on the assumption that anything with less moving parts is simpler and therefore better.

As always, prevention is better than cure. Use a pressure washer to blast away the mud and salt trapped in the crevices under your Land Rover and get it Waxoyled – including inside the doors – regularly.

ENGINE SWAPS

Some owners love the 12J naturally-aspirated diesel engine. It's an uncomplaining workhorse that's happy all day as long as you don't want to take it higher than 60mph. But today's roads are different places to what they were 30-odd years ago and the 12J is not powerful enough for some, who look for ways of getting a bit more oomph out of their 2.5 lumps. There aren't any performance tweaks that will make a real difference, so the only viable alternative is an engine transplant.

Avoid the 19J Diesel Turbo, which is unreliable. The much better 200Tdi is the obvious swap, as it mates up with the same LT77 gearbox and even the engine mounts are in the same place. Until fairly recently there was a ready source of secondhand 200Tdi engines from scrapped Discoverys that had succumbed to terminal corrosion. They're rarer now, although there are currently plenty of later 300Tdis from the same source. However, the 300Tdi isn't a straight swap and will need new engine mounts, among other modifications, to make it fit. When I went down the 300Tdi/R380 route last year, I enlisted my mate Nigel to help me and he made a great job of the conversion.

LIGHTS AND VISIBILITY

Standard lights on a Ninety or One Ten are adequate, but can be improved by modern lighting that has been developed in recent years. For example, halogen is an easy upgrade, as are LED side and tail lights. Neither are expensive.

Ninetys and One Tens didn't come with rear wipers/washers as standard, but they can be fitted and will certainly improve your rear view in hard top and station wagon models.

As for front wipers, some owners – myself included – don't realise they are self-parking. I had assumed it wasn't fitted, but in fact the park switch that was attached to the wiper motor had broken. It was simple to fit a Britpart replacement – it plugs into the wiper motor.

Buying Guide: 200Tdi & 300Tdi (1990-98)

THE CLASSIC TDiS

The 200Tdi and 300Tdi Defenders are as popular today as ever. They're holding their values but you can still find a bargain, says Dave Phillips

YOU WON'T HEAR anybody slagging off the Tdi Defenders. The 200Tdi and 300Tdi models transformed Defender ownership and even today they are hugely popular – not least because they are as tough as they come.

It all started with the 200Tdi, which was a landmark model when it was introduced in 1990. The new turbodiesel was by far the most potent oil-burner ever to put in an appearance in a Land Rover utility. In fact it was the first purpose-built turbodiesel, because the earlier 19J Turbo Diesel essentially consisted of a turbocharger bolted on to the existing 2.5 naturally-aspirated diesel.

The new engine soon developed a justified reputation for being robust and a solid, reliable performer. For many years it was the power-plant of choice among serious off-roaders, for example. But it wasn't in production for long: just four years later it was replaced by the more refined 300Tdi, which had the same power and torque but was slightly more free-revving.

Mated to the 200Tdi was the LT77 gearbox, which many say was the best ever made. It had been around a long time and had proven itself to be a solid performer – very strong and it didn't suffer synchromesh problems.

The exciting new engine-gearbox combination was, of course, a welcome by-product of the development of the original Discovery 1, launched at the end of 1989. It was an exercise Solihull would repeat until 2003, with both the 300Tdi and Td5 engines powering first Discovery and then Defender models.

These days, of course, Defenders famously share their engines with Ford Transit vans. Is that why so many enthusiasts look back on the vehicles from the first half of the 1990s with nostalgia? They certainly snap up 200Tdi Defender 90s, which fetch surprisingly high prices for 20-year-old models. In fact the popularity of the 200Tdis grows every year.

In recent years all Defenders have become more desirable, but especially those timeless 1990s classics, the Tdis. Norfolk specialist Terry Hayward tells me: "To be honest, it's hard to keep up with demand for 200Tdi and 300Tdi Defender 90s. The prices of good ones get higher and higher all the time and will only get higher still. They are a lifestyle statement

214

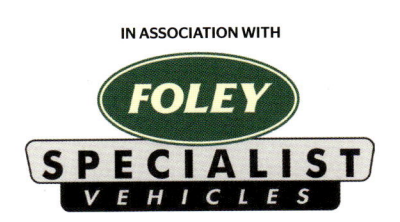

"The Tdi models have become timeless classics"

The light and elevated driving position of the Tdi cabin. Most middle seats have since been replaced by cubby boxes, though

and have become very fashionable outside the enthusiast market."

Terry says Tdi Defenders are particularly popular because they are relatively simple vehicles and claims they were better built than the later Td5 models.

"Corrosion is the biggest problem area for all Defenders, with the chassis and bulkhead the most prone to rust," he says. "But as the years pass it is becoming increasingly obvious that Td5 Defenders rot a lot quicker than the earlier models, including the 200Tdi and 300Tdi. It seems that the quality of metal used by Land Rover from about 1998, when the Td5 was launched, was of lower quality."

It's a controversial view, but one shared by many owners and buyers. Even though they are now two decades old, well looked-after Tdi Defenders are snapped up at high prices. But just because a Defender has a £6000 price ticket on the windscreen doesn't guarantee it's a good one.

Would-be buyers should keep a close eye on bulkheads, especially, paying particular attention to the footwells, where rust can get in between the two layers of sandwiched steel. The front bulkhead outrigger can also be a big problem area.

The best rust remedy is preventative. Once you've bought your Tdi Defender, get it Waxoyled immediately - and repeat regularly. Some experts say as often as every two years, especially if you live near the coast, where onshore winds are laced with damaging salt - and make sure the pressure washer is used regularly to dislodge mud from all the hidden nooks and crannies, especially if you take it off-road.

Mud also accumulates in the radiator fins, where it can bake hard and cause overheating, but don't blast this with a powerful jet washer or you could damage the rad. You need to go gently here, with an ordinary low-pressure hosepipe.

But what about the mechanical bits? Is it true that the 200Tdi will go on for ever? And, if so, how can you make sure yours eventually gets a telegram from the Queen? Like all Land Rovers, it's down to servicing. That means every 6000 miles or six months, whichever comes first. When you're buying a Tdi (or any Land Rover, come to that) ask to see its service history. It's unlikely that a 20-year-old Defender will boast a full service history, as it is likely to have had several owners in that time, but the more paper evidence of caring ownership the better.

When you do get it serviced, don't waste your money on synthetic or semi-synthetic oils. The 200Tdi engine was designed in the 1980s for the high-quality mineral oils that were prevalent in that era and the 300Tdi that followed in 1994 is similarly undemanding.

Compared to modern diesels, the Tdi engines are relatively crude, which means the engine oil soon goes black, especially on older engines. Don't worry, but do make sure you use the very best oil and fuel filters you can afford if you want your Tdi to rattle on beyond 200,000 miles. The air filter is less critical, but do change it more often if you are regularly working in a dirty or dusty environment. For that same reason, a snorkel (aka raised air intake) is a bonus.

The otherwise bulletproof LT77 gearbox does have an annoying trait – one that's particularly alarming to fellow motorists – and that's the ease in which reverse, located to the top left of the gate, is easily engaged instead of first, by mistake. This can be entertaining in queues of traffic when the reversing lights of the 200Tdi Defender in front suddenly illuminate as its driver fumbles to locate first gear to pull away. The terror in the eyes of the driver behind is a sight to behold. This only happens in older LT77s. The most likely cause is a seized spring and plunger on the side of the selector housing, which is easily cured.

The later R380, which was introduced at the same time as the 300Tdi, does not have the same problem, with reverse at bottom right. It is a slicker gearbox but isn't quite so tough as its predecessor, with less robust synchromesh and bearings more prone to wear.

Having said that, most 300Tdi Defenders still have their original gearboxes, so it's pretty tough.

So what else do we need to keep an eye

Buying Guide

Tdi Defenders were a mainstay of the gruelling Camel Trophy off-road events for many years

on? Well, we all know that fluid leaks are part and parcel of Land Rover ownership - at least on older vehicles - but it was an issue Lode Lane was already addressing by the time the Tdi engines were designed. That means leaks should be minimal, although slight oil leaks from the timing cover, for example, are nothing to get too worried about. Diesel leaks, however, are another matter - fuel contamination of the timing belts can cause damage. Timing belt failure, of course, is usually terminal - requiring either an expensive rebuild or, more likely, a donor engine transplanted from a Discovery 1 that has corroded beyond economical repair. Remember, however, that the older 200Tdi ex-Disco engines are now less easy to find than the later 300Tdis.

Another place where you could find leaks are the clutch slave and master cylinders, where the seals are prone to seepage. If you find you have to keep pumping the clutch pedal, check the levels and the seals, and if you are going to change the clutch, always fit a heavy-duty clutch arm.

All Defenders have disc brakes at the front, but your 200Tdi Defender could be fitted with either drum brakes or discs on the rear wheels. Land Rover switched to discs all round in 1993. Late 200Tdis and all 300Tdis have discs all round. Some owners of early models have converted their rear axles to discs, but as we saw with the pre-Defender Ninetys and One Tens, rear drums are a better bet if you do a lot of off-road driving, as the abrasive action of mud quickly wears discs and pads.

The other thing to look out for on disc brakes is seized callipers. If your Defender is pulling to one side under braking, check them out. When replacing brake components, always use either Land Rover parts or brands you can trust. Many owners wouldn't risk cheap components in an area where safety is so important.

The handbrake drum on the transmission tends to collect mud and should be cleaned regularly. To prevent this chore, you can upgrade to a disc handbrake conversion, which is straightforward to fit.

If you are getting play in your steering, check out the UJs and ball joints for wear. Sometimes the drop arms on the steering column come loose. If they do, they just

> "A decent Tdi is the perfect expression of Defender ownership"

need tightening. If your Tdi Defender has never had its bushes replaced, the odds are it is time to do so. Again, Polybush is a safe bet.

Modifications are a matter of taste. Some owners like to upgrade springs and shock absorbers to increase ride height, while others prefer to maintain the sort of suspension set-up designed by Land Rover. After all, Land Rover spent millions of pounds and thousands of man hours in testing to get it right. But one modification many Tdi owners make is swapping the transfer box for one from a Discovery. The ratios will give you up to an extra 10 mph and improve fuel economy, but remember that you may need to recalibrate your speedometer.

Water leaks are the bane of all Defender owners, but there are simple cures. The vent seals on the flaps between the bonnet and the windscreen need replacing from time to time. Door seals can be easily renewed, but add a bead of silicone inside to prevent water running down, within.

Windscreen rubbers will also split and allow water ingress in time - and can also be replaced at home. Refitting them is straightforward, but requires a little patience. Use genuine Land Rover replacement rubber, as it is less prone to splits. The same applies to sunroof seals.

Compared to the light output of modern vehicles, the headlights on Tdi Defenders are puny. Replacing the originals with modern clear crystal lights will make a big difference. Likewise the rear lights - especially the fog and reverse lights, which collect water and corrode. Consider fitting larger and better-sealed NAS-style lights.

Weekly checks: engine oil and coolant levels, plus tyre pressures. The gearbox level should be checked at every service. Grease door hinges and lubricate handle mechanism. It stops the pins from seizing.

Land Rover didn't offer an automatic gearbox option on Defenders, but it is possible to transplant both engine and gearbox from a 300Tdi Discovery, which drops in neatly (with a few modifications). But this is not a job for the average home mechanic.

Rattling front seats? Most likely caused by failure of the brackets on the seat boxes, to which they're fitted. They are only pressed together and easily separate. Reunite them with a blob of weld, which will cure the rattle instantly. Grease the seat runners to prevent them seizing.

Twenty years of slamming doors shut will probably have cracked the panels behind the door strikers. They should be replaced - easy but a bit fiddly. Also keep an eye on the seat belt mounts, where the meeting of aluminium and steel can cause a corrosive reaction.

If your Tdi Defender is seldom used off-road, it will most likely end up with seized diff-lock linkages, which can be cured with lubrication.

At the end of the day, a decent Tdi Defender is the perfect expression of Land Rover ownership. It won't be cheap, but it won't lose value quickly, either. We can't see Defender prices continuing to rise at the current rate indefinitely, but we don't expect the bubble to burst suddenly, either. Some see Tdi Defenders as investments for the future, but at LRM we like to see them as tough and versatile workhorses, as good today as they were back in the 1990s.

The Raptor Defender Dash Console
....designed by enthusiasts for enthusiasts

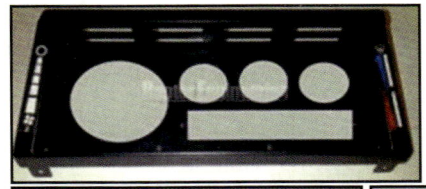

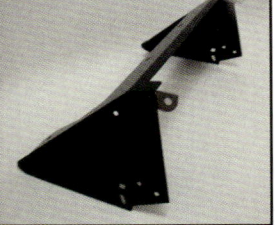

Our famous Dash Console has become a massive success amongst enthusiasts who for years have faced the heartache of where to mount their additional equipment. Our Console is made from steel and aircraft grade aluminium with removable, interchangeable pre-cut panels along with a unique bespoke service offering custom cut panels. Suitable for pre 2000 (prior to TD5 Facelift) Defender & SIII. To complement your Raptor Console please see our website to view the full range of our products available including Steel Binnacle and Binnacle Mounts, Extended Fuse Box Cover, Trim Panels, Pods, Glove Box, Cubby Box, Switches & Sockets.

We also produce Puma Glove Boxes/Pods & Discovery Consoles

To place your order please visit
www.raptor-engineering.co.uk

AUTO SPARKS
CLASSIC BRITISH QUALITY
WIRING HARNESSES
Made In Britain

WE HAVE A HUGE RANGE OF WIRING HARNESSES FOR DEFENDERS OR SERIES LAND ROVERS

www.autosparks.co.uk
+44 (0) 115 949 7211
sales@autosparks.co.uk

REMANUFACTURED
- Gearboxes
- Transfer boxes
- Differentials
- Steering boxes
- Engines (to order)
- 18 months / 2 year warranty

NEW PARTS
- Over 20,000 part numbers

Derventio Autocentre LLP

01332 340019

info@derventio-autocentre.co.uk
www.derventio-autocentre.co.uk

8 Dunton Close, West Meadows Ind. Est.,
Derby, DE21 6XB

Buying Guide: Td5 (1998-2007)

DEFENDER TAKES FIVE

EC emissions rules spelled the end of the Tdi engine. In its place, Land Rover introduced the all-new Td5. Is it worth a punt today? Dave Phillips has the answers...

I WELL REMEMBER my first sight and sound of a Td5 Defender. The changes on the outside were minor - three small vents each side of the front panel, between the sidelights and indicators - but the sound was very different. Noticeable by its absence was the familiar clatter of the 300Tdi engine.

The Td5 is an altogether more sophisticated beast. Has the workhorse suddenly become a thoroughbred? And, more important, what should you look for if you are thinking of buying one?

Although it offered more power and torque for the same 2.5-litre displacement, the five-cylinder Td5 was not universally welcomed. The legendary 300Tdi was a popular engine and would always be a hard act to follow. And us Land Rover enthusiasts are a notoriously conservative lot. By and large we don't like change

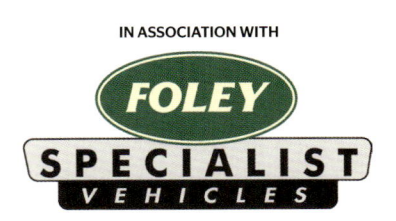

"The Defender Td5 is a reliable, trouble-free Land Rover"

unless it's absolutely necessary. And it seemed an awful shame to replace an engine as magnificent as the 300Tdi.

But the change was necessary. This was the era when EC silliness was starting to make itself felt and the 300Tdi didn't meet the forthcoming Euro 3 emissions criteria devised by some bureaucrats in Brussels. That's why Land Rover had designed the Td5 - a refined new diesel engine for the future with electronic engine management, replacing the mechanical injection systems of its Tdi predecessors. In fact the Td5 was part of the Storm project embarked upon by the Rover company in the early 1990s to produce a whole new generation of four, five and six-cylinder engines for the company's cars and trucks. But then BMW bought the company and the project was scrapped - with the Td5 the only survivor of the German cull.

The first Land Rover to get the new Td5 engine was the Discovery 2, earlier in 1998. It was no surprise that the Defender followed suit. After all, the Defender had also got the 200Tdi and 300Tdi engines soon after they were introduced in the Discovery 1. The Td5 actually enjoyed a longer life in the Defender than it did in the Discovery. When Discovery 3 was launched in 2003, the Td5 was replaced by the TDV6. But Defender kept the Td5 until 2007.

That nine-year production spell means there are lots of Td5- powered Defenders around. But are they worth buying?

The Defender Td5 is a reliable, trouble-free Land Rover - as long as you look after it. It marked the end of an era when engines were simple and cheap to repair or replace. The days when Land Rovers could be abused, neglected and still keep running, were gone. If you don't regularly service your Td5 you're asking for trouble.

Mechanics who work regularly with Defenders will tell you that the electronics associated with the Td5 can prove to be problematical, especially if you regularly take your it off-road. For reasons best known to themselves, the vehicle's designers decided a really good place to put the vital ECU and relays was under the driver's seat. Unfortunately, Defenders - all Defenders, that is, right up to the end of production in 2016 - are notorious for allowing water into the cockpit. Leaking seals around the doors, windscreen and vents allow it to pour in - and if it gets into that box under the seat, it causes havoc.

For that reason, off-roaders, overlanders and anyone else who drives through water a lot, often move their vital electrics to somewhere higher, and drier. And if you are thinking of buying one and taking it

Just as the Tdi Defenders dominated the old Camel Trophy in the 1990s, Td5 Defenders took on the gruelling G4 Challenge in 2003 and 2006

Buying Guide

"Consider a raised air intake to keep water out of the engine"

Td5 Defenders are as tough as any of the models that went before, despite their relatively sophisticated new engine

off-road, we'd recommend you do just that. There are plenty of aftermarket conversion kits available that make it easy for you. And while you're at it, consider a raised air intake, too, to ensure that water does not get into that precious engine.

One of the most common problems associated with the Td5 engine is oil getting into the injector wiring harness on top of the engine.

The first sign of oil seeping into the electrics is a misfire, which will get worse as the problem develops. It's essential to get this fixed as soon as possible, as it can eventually spread to the ECU, so check it out when you're inspecting your would-be purchase.

Another typical Td5 ailment is diesel leaking into the sump, via worn injector seals. The first sign of this is the oil level rising on the dipstick. The engine can literally fill with diesel and cause serious damage, so it's important to physically check the seals at every service. If they've gone soft, they will need replacing.

Leaking seals will also pull air into the engine, which will usually mean poor starting. These problems on Td5s seem to happen around the 80-100,000 miles mark.

Service intervals on the Td5 are 12,000 miles. There are two oil filters to replace. Refill with semi-synthetic oil. The R380 gearbox is the same as on 300Tdi Defenders.

Like all Defenders, the Td5 is easy to personalise. Popular modifications include the suspension, with uprated bushes, springs and shocks. The extra power of the Td5 also means improved brakes are popular, with drilled and grooved discs and stainless steel brake hoses.

Because the Td5 is electronic, it can be tuned by remapping the ECU. You can get more power that way, but our advice is not to go over the top. Speed is all very well in a straight line, but top-heavy Defenders aren't the best cars in the world for taking corners! Also, some Td5 Defenders don't have ABS brakes and run on tyres that weren't designed for high-speed driving.

The original rear lights, including fog and reversing lights, are a bit inadequate, so consider fitting larger NAS-spec or LED lights (if the previous owner hasn't already done so).

For creature comforts you could also install a DIY heated seat kit. Like heated front windscreens, they are popular and easy to fit. The Britpart heated screen works well and is much cheaper than the one made by Land Rover.

Electric windows came as standard on later Td5s but are easy to fit on early models, too.

Like all Land Rovers the Td5 Defenders are great vehicles if you look after them, but they do have their weak points…

Chassis: My good friend Terry Hayward says the steel used on Defenders in the late 1990s was poor quality. Rear crossmembers rust particularly badly.

Doors: Early doors soon fall to bits, but later ones were moulded and greatly improved.

Viscous fan: Prone to seize or even fly off and damage radiator.

EGR: Exhaust gas recycling system can get gunked up and cause power loss. Bypass it with a blanking kit.

Fuel pressure regulator: Prone to leaking.

FINAL VERDICT

Enthusiasts worried in 1998 whether the sophisticated new Td5 would be as tough as its predecessors. Nearly 20 years on, the answer is a resounding yes. As always, ask for its service history and check out the issues we've highlighted in this feature.

The popularity of Td5 Defenders means you won't find any cheap ones unless they are thrashed and neglected old heaps (which you shouldn't touch). But if you buy a good one you can expect long and faithful service.

GOODWINCH LIMITED
East Foldhay, Zeal Monachorum, Crediton,
Devon, EX17 6DH, England
Tel: 01363 82666   Fax: 01363 82782
E: sales@goodwinch.com   W: www.goodwinch.com

TDS GOLDFISH Waterproof Winches for OFF ROAD VEHICLES

TDS GOLDFISH WINCHES - *The Best!*

TDS-9.5c Goldfish complete with wire rope, roller fairleads, and a heavy duty swingaway pulley block. 9,500 lbs. Tremendous value at
£499 + VAT.
Upgrade to 10mm x 100' (30.5m) Dyneema® Bowrope and aluminium hawse in lieu of wire rope
£149 + VAT

GOODWINCH commercial TDS-12 Goldfish Waterproof medium speed 254:1 ratio winches for vehicle recovery trucks, trailers and other heavy duty uses

Also available as a Commercial TDS-12.0c Goldfish complete with wire rope, roller fairleads, and a heavy duty swingaway pulley block. 12,000 lbs. Super value at
£529 + VAT.
Upgrade to 11mm x 90' (27.5m) Dyneema® Bowrope and aluminium hawse in lieu of wire rope
£149 + VAT

Bowmotor replacement winch motors. Large brushes in brass holders, copper welded commutators, superb quality. In three sizes,
Bowmotor '1' 5.6 hp @ 4000 rpm and the longer
Bowmotor '2' 6.8 hp @ 5000 rpm.
Bow '2 Plus' 8.0 hp @ 6000 rpm.
As used extensively in the winch challenge field
Bowmotor '1' 175mm long 12v or 24v £169 + VAT
Bowmotor '2' 196mm long 12v or 24v £199 + VAT
Bow '2 Plus' 220mm long 12v only   £229 + VAT

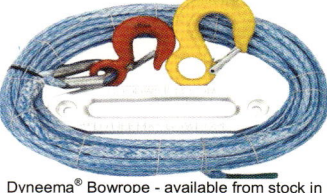

Dyneema® Bowrope - available from stock in 5, 6, 8,10, 11,12 & 14 mm. Ready made ropes are complete with red safety hook or larger yellow competition hook and tubed thimble
10mm x 100' (30.5m) **£189 + VAT**
11mm x 100' (30.5m) **£199 + VAT**
Also available in Green Budget Bowrope
10mm x 100' (30.5m) **£129 + VAT**
11mm x 90' (27.5m) **£129 + VAT**

TDS-9.5i Bridge Model Goldfish complete with wire rope, roller fairleads, and a heavy duty swingaway pulley block. 9,500 lbs.
£509 + VAT
Upgrade to 10mm x 100' (30.5m) Dyneema® Bowrope and aluminium hawse in lieu of wire rope
£149 + VAT

Goodwinch Bow '2' Powered High Speed Commissioned TDS-9.5c Challenge winch upgraded by David Bowyer
£699 + VAT
11mm x 90' (27.5m) Dyneema® Bowrope with an aluminium hawse as an optional extra for only
£149 + VAT

Land Rover Defender Bumper for TDS / EP9 winches
Non Air Con Special Price **£189 + VAT**
Air Con Special Price **£199 + VAT**
For other bumpers and fitting kits please see website

GOODWINCH Turbo Power Controller for the serious competition enthusiast. Instant, on the fly, 24 volts to your 12 volt TDS winch, or any other Bowmotor powered winch for high speed 'winch in'. Complete with wiring harnesses and in cab switching panel
£199 + VAT
Also available for 'Twin Motor Winches'
£299 + VAT

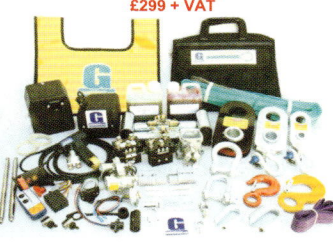

Goodwinch Bow '2' Powered Large Drum High Speed Commissioned TDS-9.5c Challenge winch giving really impressive results.
£899 + VAT
11mm x 125' (38m) Dyneema® Bowrope with an aluminium hawse as an optional extra for only
£199 + VAT

GOODWINCH Air Operated Freespool Kit complete with valve, solenoids, switch, unions & piping. Will fit all TDS winches. (Requires suitable air supply installed on the vehicle.)
£99 + VAT

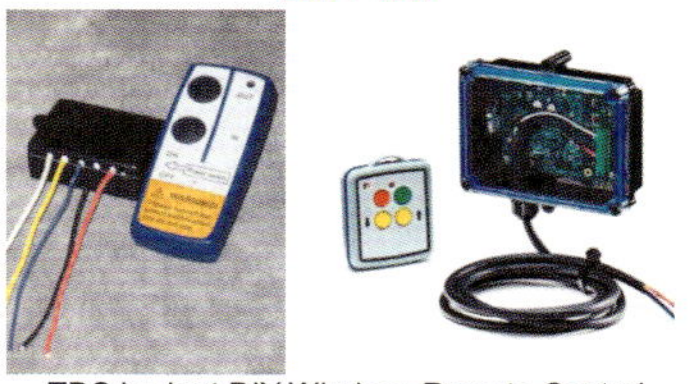

We stock a full range of spares and accessories

All prices shown above are for 12 volt winches. Also available in 24 volt

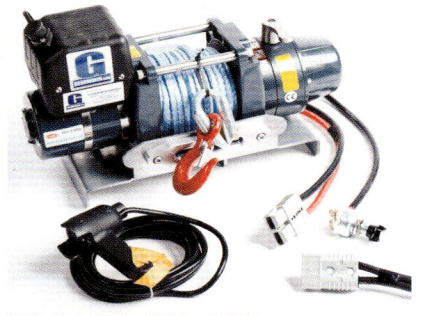

NEW - Short Drum TDS-12.0 Goldfish Winch, available as a bare winch with no rope or hawse, in 12 volts for
£449 + VAT
Or with a 10mm x 75' Dyneema® Bowrope and small Ali hawse for
£599+ VAT
Or as shown in the picture, mounted on a portable Bak Rak kit complete with vehicle harness and Anderson fittings
£699 + VAT
Also available our new receiver hitch mounting kit. See website for details.

TDS budget DIY Wireless Remote Control System for light duty use. 12 volt only.
£39 + VAT
Mini Lodar Wireless Remote Control System. Unbeatable performance. Available in 12 or 24 volt.
£125 + VAT

New G10 Please go to website

New Bull 9.5i **Please go to website**

SPECIAL OFFER WINCH & DEFENDER BUMPER full system Deals
TDS-9.5c or TDS-9.5i bridge model, complete with wire rope, roller fairleads, swingaway pulley block, vehicle wiring kit including cut out switch and battery link, TDS Wireless Radio Remote, a pair of swivel recovery eyes and tested shackles, and a standard Defender non air con Bumper.
All for **£699 plus VAT** (air con plus **£10 plus VAT**) (normally £786 plus VAT)
with Dyneema® Bowrope and Ali Hawse **£848 plus VAT**
We also have special offers for Discovery 1 & 2 and Classic Range Rover

A TDS-Goldfish in Defender Air Con Bumper with optional swivel recovery eyes

A TDS-9.5i Bridge Model with Dyneema® Bowrope and Aluminium Hawse in a Defender Bumper

We have BRB bumpers & fitting kits to suit Land Rover, Discovery 200, 300 & series 2,3 & 4 plus Classic Range Rover and P38

Goodwinch Limited are professional winch engineers in supplying and converting the TDS Goldfish range of high quality winches to suit a variety of special applications.

There are three different ratios, three motor variants and three drum sizes in both 12 volt and 24 volt. All can be Turbo Power Driven to give amazing line speeds.

David Bowyer and his team have a great number of years experience in winch design. David has been teaching the use of winches and using them for nearly 30 years.

He will be pleased to advise you on the most suitable one to have, how to use it through watching his DVD on winching techniques, and any questions you may have.

His Off-Road Training Centre and school facility is now fully open again, and invites you to go to the website www.goodwinch.com and click on 'courses' for more information.

Come and see us at
LRO Peterborough Show
The Showground.
Peterborough
September Sat/Sun 16/17th
&
Newbury 4x4 Vintage Spares Day
Newbury Showground
October Sun 1st.

David Bowyer's Off Road Centre

Importers, Exporters, Wholesale Distributors & Retailers of Winches & Accessories

AS MOST OF OUR BUSINESS IS UK & EUROPEAN 4x4 DEALERS AND OVERSEAS SALES, ALL PRICES ARE PLUS CARRIAGE AND VAT   (e&oe)   Dyneema® is a registered trademark of Royal DSM N.V.

Buying Guide: TDCi (2007-2016)

BY THE TURN of the century, ever-tighter European emissions rules had made the Td5 engine obsolete and a newer, cleaner power unit was required for the evergreen Defender. So Land Rover's owners Ford stuck their own diesel lump under the bonnet.

That was in 2007 and it coincided with a series of changes made to the Defender that year. A much-improved heater and new dashboard layout were welcome, although the loss of the front ventilation flaps below the windscreen to accommodate the new features was painful for diehards like me. Those flaps had been with us for more than half a century and losing them was like losing a close friend.

New safety legislation outlawed the old inward-facing rear seats, so forward-facing rear seats in the station wagons reduced the 90 to a four-seater and the 110 to a seven-seater. At least they were more comfortable. But sharing an engine with the Ford Transit van was not so popular.

Yet why is that? After all, the 2.4 Puma engine had more than proved itself in the popular commercial, enjoying a long and mainly trouble-free life under the bonnet of a van that was every bit as much a workhorse as Land Rover's own utility.

But it was never going to be the fans' favourite, because it marked a turning point in Defender history. Since its launch in the 1980s as the One Ten and Ninety, it had been powered by diesel engines built at Solihull. From the early naturally-aspirated 12J and 19J oil-burners through the Diesel Turbo, 200Tdi, 300Tdi and Td5, they had all been designed and built for vehicles bearing the green oval, by men who sounded like Jasper Carrot.

The new engine was built in Dagenham, by Londoners. And it was part of a big family of engines co-designed by Ford and Peugeot to occupy the bonnet space of a staggering variety of vehicles that included assorted Fords, Peugeots, Volvos, Citroens and even Mazdas.

To underline that the engine hadn't been designed for the Defender, they even had to change the shape of the bonnet to accommodate the taller unit. Hence the distinctive "power bulge" of the TDCi models.

Had the quirky exclusivity of Defender ownership gone for good? You'd be forgiven for thinking so if you listened to what the purists were saying. But that wasn't reflected in disappointing sales for the new model. Far from it. In its twilight years until the end of production in early 2016, Defender was selling in record numbers and became a truly iconic vehicle – not least because that controversial TDCi engine had proved every bit as bulletproof in Defender as it had been in the Transit.

Defender sales were also helped by the fact that the model had suddenly become fashionable. Once the end of production was announced, it was as

IN ASSOCIATION WITH

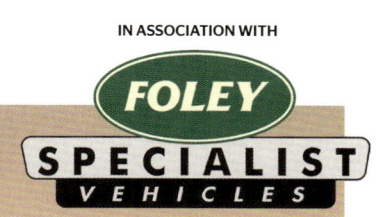

FOLEY SPECIALIST VEHICLES

LAST OF THE LINE

Defender's final incarnation shared its Duratorq engine with White Van Man (among others). But is it value for money? Dave Phillips finds out

Buying Guide: TDCi (2007-2016)

"The engine is not identical to the one in the Transit"

though the motoring public suddenly realised that something they had taken for granted for decades was about to disappear… and they invested in Defender ownership before it was too late. Specialists producing bespoke, luxurious models, like Khan's Chelsea Tractor Company, seemed to spring up everywhere to cash in on the boom. Defender diehards weren't so keen on all hype, of course. If anything, it made them even more suspicious of the TDCi.

So let's have a closer look at that engine. In truth, the 2.4-litre four cylinder is not identical to the one used in the Transit. For Defender application, the lubrication and sealing specification was improved to ensure consistent performance off-road and at extreme angles. At 122 bhp, power output was identical to the outgoing 2.5 five-cylinder Td5, but torque increased from 221 lb-ft to a whopping 265 lb-ft, thanks to the variable geometry of the new model's turbocharger. This yielded a wider torque band, which nicely matched the new six-speed gearbox.

First gear was extra low, for precise control at low speeds, while the sixth gear was a virtual overdrive that reduced fuel consumption as well as reducing noise and making conversation possible in the cabin at 70 mph.

The notchy six-speed gearbox wasn't to everyone's taste and, surprisingly, Land Rover didn't offer an automatic option.

Perhaps they couldn't find a suitable one in the Ford parts bin? This omission, of course, left an opportunity for the many aftermarket developers – but more of them later.

The lunacy of ever-more-stringent emissions laws from Europe saw even the latest engine technology obsolete, and consequently outlawed, in a very short period of time. Such was the case with original 2.4 TDCi, which lasted just four years before Land Rover (by then owned by Tata Motors) was obliged to replace it with a 2.2-litre variant, the ZSD-422, which met the imminent Euro V emissions standards. It included a diesel particulate filter for the first time on a Defender, but power and torque levels were identical to its predecessor.

Defender has enjoyed a massive renaissance in the last few years. New companies have sprung up specialising in professionally personalising the iconic workhorse and, as demand increases, secondhand prices have reached unexpected levels, with somewhat battered Tdi veterans fetching more than much more recent Discoverys and Range Rovers.

It seems the world can't get enough Defenders and that is due in part to the consistently reliable performance of the TDCi models. Both the 2.4 and the 2.2 have been incredibly consistent in achieving high mileages without going wrong. So maybe the Transit engine is enjoying the last laugh.

Defender tuning expert, Dan Padmore, agrees. He is the gifted engineer responsible for turning ordinary TDCi Defenders into snorting, high-performing Icons for Nene Overland. And he loves the basic vehicle he starts with.

"The TDCi is a really strong engine from which you'll get very high, trouble-free mileages so long as you ensure it is properly serviced," he says. "Forget the Transit jokes, this is a really brilliant engine."

There aren't many things that ever go wrong. In the early days of the 2.4 a few vehicles had the clutch springs go weak and start chattering, but the problem was identified by Land Rover, who sent a technical bulletin to their dealers, who

It may share a similar engine to the Ford Transit but can you imagine White Van Man attempting an off-road challenge like this rock-strewn hill?

fixed it. In the rare event of one slipping through the net, you will need to replace the clutch plate, or risk the springs coming out and rattling around in the bellhousing.

The EGR (exhaust gas recyling) valve has also been known to stick in either the open or closed position. You will know when this happens, as it gets noisy when you switch off the ignition and it goes through its cleaning cycle. You can't block off the EGR like you can on a Tdi or Td5, but you can switch it off electronically on the map. But this is something that has to be left to the experts with access to sophisticated computer software.

As far as that rather agricultural six-speed manual gearbox goes, the only known fault is the tail shaft, which is greased at the factory but can run dry and wear out – although that is very rare.

Incidentally, if you do object to the clunky standard manual box, you can always do what Solihull didn't: namely fit an automatic gearbox. Ashcroft Transmissions produce one, although this isn't something you can do in your own garage, unless you are a bit of a whizz with vehicle electronics. Getting the engine and gearbox to "talk" to each other electronically isn't easy when it involves re-mapping. This is one that's again best left to the experts.

The same applies to engine upgrades. It won't have gone unnoticed by eagle-eyed Land Rover fans that the extended Duratorq family of engines includes some siblings that are a bit bigger than the 2.2 and 2.4 units factory-fitted in Defenders. Nene Overland, for example, uses the 3.2-litre, which is relatively easy to fit under the bonnet of a Defender, but again involves some complicated re-mapping. "It's a straightforward way to get more power, but it's something best left to the professionals," says Dan Padmore.

The simple way to tweak a few more horses is to fit a bigger intercooler. We recommend doing this before you think of re-mapping the ECU, rather than the other way around, because increasing the power by re-mapping makes the engine run hotter, which the ECU will detect and will make it back off. A bigger intercooler prevents that.

Be sceptical of so-called "performance" air filters, which don't allow so much air through as a standard paper filter. Replace air and fuel filters regularly to get the most economical performance.

As far as bodywork goes, the latest Defenders look very much like ones decades older – but looks can deceive. The modern paints used on the panels and chassis are much better than the old ones and do keep rust at bay longer than the earlier Td5, for example. Door panels in particular are a vast improvement, thanks to galvanising these days. But regular Waxoyling is still recommended for ultimate longevity.

One personal touch that bespoke specialists like Nene Overland are often asked for is extra legroom, as even the latest Defenders weare notoriously cramped for tall folk. The answer is to fit seat risers, which allow them to move back further. Remove the bulkhead behind the seats and you get even more legroom, but as always ensure that you know what you are doing to avoid making the vehicle structurally unsound.

All these tweaks of course make the Defender even more desirable. And with values holding hard, you can be sure that the lowlife scum otherwise known as car thieves will also find your TDCi very desirable indeed. Even if they can't drive it away, they will try their best top remove valuable parts, like those galvanised doors, so make security a priority.

Unlike the older models, the TDCis are not the sort of vehicles for the average home spannerman to tinker with, unless you truly understand electronics. But if you're prepared to learn, or leave it to the experts, you can rely upon the latest Defenders to offer no-nonsense, workmanlike reliability.

THE FINAL VERDICT
The tired old Transit jokes are now wearing thin. TDCi Defenders are great vehicles with a level of reliability at least equal to all models that have gone before.

You won't find any cheap ones. You probably won't find any bargains, either, as very late production Defenders are now fetching more secondhand than they cost new. If you can afford a good one, you've got a vehicle for life, if you look after it.

4x4 TYRES.CO.UK

WWW.4X4TYRES.CO.UK

Time to change Tyres? or Wheels?

LARGEST UK 4X4 FITTING NETWORK
CHOOSE FROM OVER 500 LOCATIONS NATIONWIDE

The UK's Leading 4x4 alloy wheel & tyre specialist providing professional advice for all 4x4 enthusiasts.

CALL NOW: 01789 774884

16" VBS ENCORE ALLOY WHEEL
Available in Gloss Black, Anthracite & Silver
from £115 pw

Why shop with 4x4 tyres?
- Price match guarantee
- Money back guarantee
- Finance Available
- Secure Shopping
- Fast & Free Delivery*

Pay 4 Later

Please see Termas and Conditions for more info

EU MADE | TUV PENDING 7x16 ET20 8x18 ET10
Gloss Black
Anthracite

16" & 18" OEM STYLE SAWTOOTH ALLOY WHEEL
7x16 ET20 8x18 ET10 No Spacers Needed!
from £115 pw

BFGoodrich · COOPERTIRES · LAND ROVER · Ministry of Defence · GOODYEAR · KUMHO TIRE

Revotec

THE ULTIMATE **ELECTRIC FAN CONVERSION** FOR YOUR **LAND ROVER**

WHY YOU SHOULD CONVERT USING A REVOTEC ELECTRIC FAN KIT

A Revotec Variable Temperature Fan controller. Variable from 70-120°C, with an instant response & No leaking.

A set of Laser cut, vehicle specific Brackets and all necessary fittings for a professional installation.

A High Power COMEX Fan which is: Waterproof to level IP68, Bearinged, Balanced and rated to operate 24hours.

· INCREASED PERFORMANCE · BETTER MPG ·
FASTER ENGINE WARM-UP · MORE EFFECTIVE
HEATER · QUIETER RUNNING · WATERPROOF FAN ·

Revotec Ltd | Tel: 01491 824424
Fax: 01491 833711 | www.revotec.com